# ONE THOUSAND DAYS

Northern Vermont, 1970s

## BOB VERNEUILLE

## Contents

Maps v

1. LUCAS BROOK REFLECTIONS 1
2. ROCK WALKING 5
3. PATHWAYS 15
4. PHUNEE FARMHOUSE 27
5. BLUE-BIRDERS 33
6. LOST BETWEEN BROOKS 45
7. BRONZE BEACH 55
8. COED COMPANION 63
9. CAMPFIRE TALES 71
10. FAUGHT MILLS 79
11. ARRIVAL—FIRST NIGHT 87
12. FIRE & ICE 97
13. WINTER'S GRIP 107
14. ENOSBURGIANS 117
15. KILGORE TROUT SALOON 127
16. BACK FROM THE BEACH 131
17. WALKING STAFF SAGA 139
18. VISITOR LOG 145
19. IT'S MAY, IS IT SPRING YET 157
20. NORTHWAY INCIDENTS 165
21. ENCOUNTERS & ESCAPADES 173
22. FOR A TIME REUNITED 181
23. YEAR TWO 191
24. VEGETARIAN THANKSGIVING 197
25. BREAD & PUPPET 203
26. MIA'S STORY 211
27. MOUNTAIN MAN MENTOR 215
28. TWO STEPS FORWARD 223
29. SPRING FORTH 231
30. THIRD SUMMER 239

| | |
|---|---|
| 31. SIBLING SURPRISE | 247 |
| 32. HOOLIGANS | 251 |
| 33. MONKS AND THE FALL | 257 |
| 34. ASTRAL & OTHER TRIPS | 263 |
| 35. UNRAVELLED | 269 |
| 36. AND THEN WE WERE NONE | 275 |
| Epilogue | 279 |
| In Case You're Interested . . . | 285 |
| About the Author | 291 |

# Maps

Lucas Brook Valley

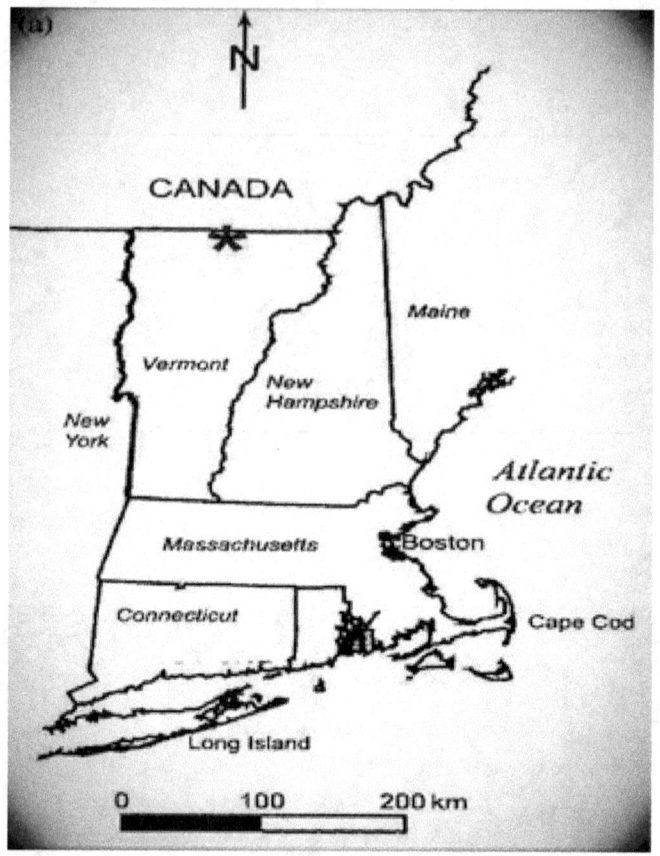

Northeastern USA

## 1

## LUCAS BROOK REFLECTIONS

*What induces you, oh man, to depart from your home in town,
to leave parents and friends, and go to the countryside
over mountains and valleys,
if it is not for the beauty of the world of nature?
~ Leonardo da Vinci*

A gentle breeze cooled the forest air, a relief on a hot summer afternoon. Chasing the origins of a fantasy manifest, Craig and I were "rock walking" on Lucas Brook, drawing upon the energy of the forest, and sharing thoughts of how we came to this magical valley. Lucas Brook Valley is located at the base of North Jay Mountain, which is one of the northernmost Green Mountains of Vermont. The brook became a central figure in the many tales and adventures of our quasi-communal experience, which began in 1974. Our journey was a welcomed break from the daily toil of farm life. We were suburban-raised Long Island transplants trying our hands at farming, living as wannabe hippies in a communal world of peace, love, sex, drugs, and rock and roll with actual survival at stake.

The farmhouse where we lived, the last vestige of civilization in the valley, stood sentry to the encroaching forest. Burnt Mountain and

Owl Ridge envelop the valley, remnants of an ancient glacial cirque that formed a giant natural amphitheater that frames our land. The Lucas wound down North Jay, carving its way through the valley and sculpting the terrain. At the edge of our property, the brook, which can be more than forty feet wide when swollen with spring rain and snowmelt, leveled and merged with the smaller Castleton Brook, a mile or so south of the Canadian border.

"The mountains are calling and I must go." ~ John Muir

It was eighty-five degrees, hot for Vermont. The August air was thick with humidity outside of the forest. Near the water, the forest was cool like natural air conditioning dropping the temperature several welcomed degrees. Brilliant sunbeams broke through the dense canopy, shafts of light exposing a ballet of motes and other things previously unseen, then dappling the forest floor, as splashes of light danced ahead of us on our rock-strewn path. A full growth forest of sugar maple trees mixed with beech, yellow birch, paper birch, and coarse bark ash trees rose over forty feet.

Inspired by our love of the forest, we worked toward our goal of living a self-sufficient life beyond the white-bread suburban world where we grew up. If we couldn't grow it, build it, find it, scrounge it or fix it, we didn't want to need it. Tomes such as *The Whole Earth Catalogue, Living on the Land and The Homesteader's Handbook* helped us further our dream, as they had done for the many back-to-the-landers that preceded us. A wise person once said, "In life it is better to run toward something rather than away from it." We ran toward a dream. That said, we also ran *from* something: the disappointment of social, environmental and political activism.

In some ways, we arrived before we ever left our Long Island home. The path to this mountain Shangri-La unfolded in our preteen Boy Scout years. Later in high school, our route was clarified after reading a book that ignited a spark, beckoning us toward the wild mountain wood. *My Side of the Mountain*, written by Jean Craighead Hugh, is the story of Sam Gribley, a twelve-year-old boy who sought a different kind of life from New York City, far away from other people and material possessions. This short book became my vade mecum, leading me to my own side of the mountain.

We spent much of our teens protesting the Vietnam War, marching for equal rights, helping Native Americans and the disabled—trying to save the world. Dearest to my heart was the environment. It may be true that the ecology movement was started by the CIA to break up the anti-war movement—well, if so, they got me. We were active with land and stream cleanups, elementary school environmental education programs and introduced early village recycling programs. In 1972, a bunch of us seventeen-year-old, long-haired, braless, reefer smoking environmental idealists went to a Village Hall meeting and asked to borrow their town. We closed down Main Street and held an Earth Day parade and festival—a tale for another time perhaps.

Long before we became aware, the hippie scene of San Francisco, New York and other cities dispersed into hundreds of communities somewhere in the backwoods of the United States, such as The Farm in Tennessee which grew into a small town, Drop City in Colorado, featuring Buckminster Fuller inspired geodesic domes and in Vermont, Earth Peoples Park grew large and wild, while others, like the Dreamers, went on to become the foundation of Vermont's future entrepreneurs.

We were ready to follow. Before the communal movement peaked in Vermont, I said to no one in particular, "The world is screwed up and nobody cares (my fractured idealism) so let's pull the covers over our head and go hide in the mountains." I was nineteen; I knew everything. Didn't I? The more successful communes were started by college graduates, many with careers who waded deeply into the capitalist world before seeking the land, and others who were on the fringes of society, but most with some funding behind them. We were high school grads. Craig had two years of college with little money between us. I knew everything except how vulnerable we were to the vagaries of time and manipulation of those with bad intent. Our loose credo, never formalized, was to live off the land in a spiritual, intellectual (pseudo perhaps), non-technical and even mystical lifestyle. In reality, we were privileged, albeit lower middle class, displaced, young Long Island wannabe hippie types pretending to survive on the land. Well, pretending may be a bit harsh because we placed our fate and lives up against a tough and sometimes dangerous natural environment. Had we known what darkness would find us in the coming years, maybe we would have had a more protective manifesto.

We believed in the off-the-beaten-path world we were building. Sincerity fueled our energy which lay like a protective aura over the valley—a blanket wrapping denizens and transients alike with a sense of peace, love and spirituality. Folks came and went, but sometimes they stayed and our numbers grew. Others stayed when they should have left. The winds of change were building and the harbinger of change was time. The outside world beckoned to Craig before I ever heard its whisper. It was my hope on this trip to synchronize our thinking and re-center our goals, but as we traveled upstream, absorbed by the peaceful calm of the valley, we were completely unaware that the serene and idyllic life we knew was destined to explode into violence, sudden death, and murder.

# 2

# ROCK WALKING

*Memory is a net: one that finds it full of fish
when he takes it from the brook,
but a dozen miles of water have run through it without sticking
~ Oliver Wendell Holmes*

Rock walking was our preferred means of traveling through the forest. In the summer and early fall months the water level was low, revealing rocks submerged during the wet season and iced over in winter. The brook was like a highway winding through the forest. Upstream, rocks and boulders made up a multicolored potpourri of geology, strewn throughout the shimmering water rushing towards us. We bounced from rock to rock down the center of the rapidly moving brook. Dazzling sunlight breaching the thick forest canopy refracted through the water, projecting a prismatic rainbow flitting on the underside of the overhanging foliage; the focused beams of light revealed shimmering water sprites dancing within the water's spray.

Along the banks, nourishing sunlight encouraged patches of wildflowers, such as Queen Anne's lace, yellow Yarrow, and wispy stalks of daisy fleabane that we would braid into flea collars for the dogs. An understory of young saplings stretched upward toward the precious sunlight. The sweet scent of the flowers mixed with the musty tones of the forest floor. The surrounding terrain was eerily dark with the exception of these bright kaleidoscopes of sunlight dappling the forest floor. We foraged these areas for edible plants, the heady smell of wild onion drawing us into the light.

"Hey, Craig, we're in luck. These onions look ready; let's pull a few for later."

"Sounds good, I'll get a few, too. Ya know, Bob, it's strange to see chicory growing here. Don't you love those blue flowers?"

"You're right, I usually see them by the road; they like the salt. I wonder if some of the salt washed down from route 105. It's only eighty or so yards up there," I said, pointing south.

"Could be, I guess; there's a lot of chicory here. Hey, let's try to remember where these are. The roots make for a decent coffee alternative."

"Well, it's an alternative anyway. I don't know about decent, Craig. It's like that Queen Anne's lace over there. You can eat them like carrots, but they're more like bitter parsnips."

"It's all Umbelliferae to me."

"That's cute, Craig."

"Anyway, those big flowers are pretty cool. They're like white saucers balancing on sticks."

"Craig, bring your nose over here. Can you smell that?" The scent of licorice wafted in the air from a wild fennel plant, all but its aroma was hidden behind the wispy fronds of ostrich ferns.

Our goal was to reach the base of the Owl Ridge escarpment, where we planned to explore the area before returning overland through the forest to a favorite place on the other side of the valley.

Trekking far beyond the five hundred acres we rented, barefoot and clad in cut-off denim shorts, our light shirts were tied to our waist with a wine sack and few provisions. We learned the geology lay and picked out the best rocks to navigate our sojourn upstream. Sometimes the rocks were mere stepping stones sitting in still waters, and at others the water rushed around huge irregularly shaped boulders worn smooth by countless years of water, racing, swirling and eddying around the mammoth rocks.

We moved at a quick pace, leaping from boulder to rock to stone. Our feet toughened from months of similar travel, allowing us to launch from the perch of a high boulder, jumping across an eight-foot stretch of water landing five feet below. Fleet of foot and mind, we alit on each stone almost floating, before moving to the next. Landing on an unstable rock changed our trajectory or we risked falling into the water or worse against the other rocks. At times a loose flat rock moved forward with our momentum upon which we surfed a short distance before springing to the next—very cool. Noticing a landing point was wet, caused us to resort to contortionist-like twisting, turning in flight before touching on the next dry perch. Some boulders were odd-shaped or slanted, adding a more challenging component, but using this rock highway was often faster than taking the land path that wove through the trees alongside the water.

We were serenaded throughout the walk by the brook's rapid staccato beat into smaller pools below. Small branches, trapped in pools, spun in clockwise spirals against branches along the bank like a muted xylophone, joined the quiet chorus, cascading over soft sedimentary rock, singing a perpetual oratorio, like the disparate tunes of street musicians. A mile from where we entered Lucas Brook, the tenor of the brook's melody began to change. Shielded from view, the waterfall was heard long before seen.

The impromptu notes of nature changed, replaced by a vociferous new song of the rush of water as the terrain steepened. The song of the falls morphed into a crashing, cascading, bubbling cacophony of power like an orchestra in an infinite crescendo. Maybe it's the magic of a waterfall or just the awesome power of nature, but we were drawn to it like a siren's call.

The rock trail zigzagged through the center of the brook up a series of stepped stones, like the teeth of an ancient behemoth. Close enough to feel the powerful spray of the falls, a leap over a wide pool brought us to the gravelly shore. Erosion from decades of rain, snow and ice carved a pathway through the slope, exposing twisted tree roots. The roots served as a crude ladder facilitating the climb to the top of the embankment. Another vertical trail with hand and footholds rose to the top through an enormous boulder split in half framing a natural sluice, narrowing the brook. Frenzied into a raging torrent, the surging water dropped fifteen feet to the pool below.

The pool was carved deep by the cavitation of the brook. Over six feet deep, the narrow pool provided a swimming hole between the upper falls and the cascading water that flowed downstream. A gnarled, weathered tree trunk crested the falls and lay partially submerged, angled sharply where it lodged just below the rim of the falls.

Another large log was trapped at the top of the falls spanning the huge boulders, forming a foot bridge. The slick surface dampened by the spray of the waterfall made for a treacherous crossing. The span is just eight feet, but so dangerous at times that we would be forced to travel further upstream to find a safer spot to cross over to the far side.

Once over the log bridge, we continued upstream where the terrain leveled out, slowing the pace of the brook, exposing a cobble of flat rocks that made it easier to rock-walk. Our pace quickened again as we ran and leapt, almost dance-like, among the colorful mosaic of stones scattered throughout the water ahead. The water quickened as we moved toward the steeper elevation. We soon reached a frothy cascade of water speeding over a small falls into a wide pool. Even with the natural air conditioning, the sun-draped air was warmer here. Fallen trees opened the canopy, showering the pool with sunlight.

There is a certain spirituality to non-sexual nakedness. Last summer, naked young men and women, visitors and denizens, moved rocks from the edges and bottom of the pool. After several forays, the new hole allowed for swimming in addition to bathing. In the warm summer months, despite the distance from the farm house, this became our primary swimming hole and served for routine bathing, using organic soaps like Uncle Tom's. I did say that this summer day was warm, but the temperature of the Lucas never did get much beyond nippy. Invigorating!

The rock-walking trail ended with nothing but the fast-moving swollen brook for a hundred feet or more. Leaping up several rocks positioned like stairs, we hopped off the highest rock and jumped the four feet to the steep bank. Craig jumped first and landed well. I followed but my foot slipped and I started to fall backwards. Craig grabbed onto a root with one hand and my forearm with the other, arresting my fall so I could get my footing.

We continued up the steep embankment, spotting a lone boulder at the cusp, awash in sunlight. We climbed atop the giant boulder, with a large cavity comprising rose quartz. The cavity was a notch cleaved by water seepage. The smooth surface created by the quartz and the shape of the notch made for a comfortable seat. Soaking up the sun, we relaxed high above the brook, watching the water passing by, drinking wine, smoking joints and waxing poetic about the road that brought us to this mountain Eden. Lying back with a good buzz, I gazed up at the kaleidoscope of the forest canopy thinking about how we came to be friends and our love for the mountains. Sitting on the bank of the brook, we shared thoughts of our friendship, our original dream of homesteading or buying land in Oregon or elsewhere in the Northwest, and the experiences that led us to this place and the profound changes within ourselves. The journey to Vermont took quite a circuitous route. Good time to light up a doobie and sip some wine.

## Sixties

I was the oldest in my family of five boys, but Craig was my older brother. We met in Boy Scouts in the mid 1960s. I was eleven, and he, two years older, was my first Patrol Leader. His dad was one of the scoutmasters, knowledgeable and witty with a great sense of humor. He taught me plenty, and Craig much more. Scouting is where I got my first real taste of nature. As a youth, I would build forts in undeveloped wooded lots or in the woods that lined a small local airport. These woods were nestled in the suburban sprawl of the south shore of Long Island. I had never been camping. Scout camping trips taught me a lot about living in the forest. Sleeping in tents, building campfires and cooking over an open flame was a fulfilling learning adventure.

"I was thinking about Camp Baiting Hollow the other day, Craig. There are parts of the trail down to Bronze Beach that reminded me of the trail at the camp."

"I had a similar thought," Craig said. "I really loved it there, great memories. It was the best week of the year: camping, canoeing, campfire sing-along at the big bonfire, the mess hall."

"I'll never forget the *Order of the Arrow Ordeal*. You did it before me, but I sure was proud when I completed it. I really envied you guys with that white sash with the red arrow. I was happy to earn mine. With only bread and water to eat, I learned the hard way what 'arduous' meant and a lot about Native American culture.

"The thing I remember the most was that night sitting in the dark, on the mess hall floor on July 20, 1969. The only light came from an array of small and large black and white television sets, as we watched the lunar landing with several dozen other scouts. We were awestruck youths, transfixed, mouths agape absorbed in a deafening silence, broken by the TV announcers, "The Eagle has landed." We sat there until after three AM, spellbound when Neil Armstrong stepped foot on the moon, followed by Buzz Aldrich twenty minutes later."

"You got that right. That memory is embossed on my mind."

## Melody Mansion

Craig continued, "It's a long way from Baiting Hollow to Melody Mansion to this rock on Lucas Brook. Remember that church Jim and Mindy bought?"

Before heading to Vermont, Craig was living in Rocky Point on the north shore of Long Island. The corner lot at Oak and Nymph was big for Long Island standards, with three dwellings known as "Melody Mansion." It was inhabited by young spiritual and/or intellectual hippie-type people. It was a time of freedom sought and liberation gained. I came of age at this place so foreign to my childhood home. "How could I ever forget? Melody Mansion exposed me to a new way of thinking. You all had that spiritual thing going on, especially Peter's knowledge of Eastern Philosophy. I'll always remember his Tibetan eye chart, though I never got to know him well, at the time. Who would have thought he would make it up here last month."

Craig jumped down from the rock. "Peter is a great guy." He opened doors of thought that led to who I am today."

"I'm glad I got to know him as a peer instead of sitting on a pedestal," I said. "I learned so much that opened my eyes to many worlds. I was drawn by the concept of a nature-based religion. I wonder if I would have pursued it otherwise. My mind was opened. The "Mansion" set me on a path experiencing spirituality beyond the dogmatic Catholicism of my youth. Hard to believe I considered becoming a priest at age twelve like two of my mother's cousins."

"That would have been weird 'Fadda' Bob," Craig said, using the voice of Slip Mahoney from "The Bowery Boys," the 1940's television show.

Ronni and Bruce were living in the dirt-floor basement. Gregg was in one of the outbuildings or living in his car. Jake and Millie lived in another building that was an odd but cool dwelling. They went on to buy and convert a church into a hippie house. It was there that I had a life changing experience with lysergic acid diethylamide, better known as LSD. My first encounter with acid was at Melody Mansion; the lifestyle and music made this a surreal place for an impressionable youth.

During Craig's time at the "Mansion," we worked our plan to buy land and fantasized about everything we would do. We had a lofty plan to save three thousand dollars and buy land. This included learning to fly, buying a plane and putting in an airstrip. What? Is that a non-sequitur? It was 1973, I graduated from high school and we came up with an insane plan to join the Air Force, learn to fly, get educated, get out, and start the homestead. We went to Fort Hamilton, in Brooklyn, New York for a physical and the military intake process. We had yet to sign on the dotted line.

"Bob, I feel like a shit sometimes. I really let you down, backing out when it was time to sign up for the Air Force. I'm really sorry!"

"Craig, are you kidding? It was my choice. You were fortunate enough to get talked out of the silly notion by the enlightened folks at the Mansion. I wish I was that smart. It wasn't all bad. Amazing, that was almost three years ago. I withdrew from college a few weeks into the first semester, signed up and flew to Lackland Air Force base in Texas. Let's suffice it to say that was a bad decision. Twenty-one days later, after packing my USAF-issued duffle bag with my new black spit-shined combat boots, dress shoes, underwear, some socks, sundry other items and sporting a short crew cut, I was on the second flight of my life heading home—Honorable Discharge in hand. I was upgraded to first class, with free drinks—must have been the buzz cut. After negotiating the plane, airport, two buses, a train and a cab, I walked into my family home. Surprise! I never told anyone I was coming home."

Jumping down from the rock, I brushed off some gravel sticking to my sweaty leg. Craig was staring up at the hillside, deep in thought.

"If you joined up with me, it might have been harder to get out. Besides, Craig, if you did, would we have found our way here? The way I see it, when Gregg followed Jason to Vermont, he opened a veritable wormhole, pulling Bruce and Ronni soon after."

"Hey, thanks, Bob, you're right about that. Leigh and I may not have followed those two summers ago. I told you that we took over for Jason and Gregg when they moved into Enosburg Falls."

Craig continued, "I didn't tell you the whole backstory but I think you can relate. Gregg and the folks at the farm were big psychedelic drug fans. LSD, mescaline, peyote buttons and shrooms were all good and as a result, they were of good humor and laughed a lot, causing Gregg to remark, "This is a funny farm." They all burst out laughing, not knowing that forevermore the *funny farm* name would stick."

"You told me some of it, Craig, but I never got the psychedelic reference. I learned the first day I came to visit with Bill that name went local. Remember? Those guys we asked for directions knew nothing of the Mackenzie farm; they only knew it as the funny farm. It was too hard to change the name but I liked the way we changed the spelling and how you lettered the mailbox. We may have confused some people for awhile, but we wore it with pride." Our mailbox read: PHUNEE FARM.

# 3

## PATHWAYS

*As a single footstep will not make a path on the earth,
so a single thought will not make a pathway in the mind.
To make a deep physical path, we walk again and again.
To make a deep mental path, we must think over and over the kind of
thoughts we wish to dominate our lives.
~ Henry David Thoreau*

Craig and I left our farmhouse just before noon, leaving a note: *Gone rock walking then to the cupboard—be back late.* About that same time, a light blue Rambler, heading east on Route 105, stopped to pick up a hitchhiker. Four hours earlier, and two-hundred and seventy miles south, two other hitchhikers held up a sign in front of the toll booths on a northbound onramp to the New York State Thruway.

### East on 105

The lone hitchhiker leaned into the Rambler's passenger side window, then stumbled back away from the car, shrieking. At first, the driver did not recognize the woman on the side of the road. As she pulled over, she leaned toward her passenger and said, "Do you know who that is?" The passenger smiled but shook her head. "You don't remember her from the Phunee Farm?"

"Maybe," the passenger hesitated.

The driver leaned closer to the passenger and whispered conspiratorially. When the hitchhiker approached, they screamed "Skye Blu!" as the driver and passenger made silly faces and acted crazy when the hitchhiker looked in the window. "Holy freak'n shit. Sorry, Fae. I can't believe you're here! I didn't even know you had a car, Tara."

"Yup, she's called Bluebird."

The Bluebird continued east. Fae moved to the back, offering the co-pilot seat to Skye. Tara turned and asked, "So Skye, fancy meeting you here. When did you get to Vermont? Craig's been asking about you." Skye smiled.

## Two at the Tollbooths

Waiting for a ride, standing in the sun on the hot pavement, traffic was sparse. It was only eleven AM and they were getting fried. Their car broke down at the New Paltz campus, but they were determined to go north. They'd been holding up the sign for two hours with no luck, which was nothing for him. Once he got stuck on a ramp in Idaho for two days. He hadn't been back north in over a month and he had big plans. He couldn't wait to show his girlfriend; this was her first trip.

The sign read Plattsburgh, then Albany, and then just NORTH. Minutes after changing the sign, a VW micro bus pulled over. They ran up to the yellow flower painted vehicle, thinking they grabbed the gold ring. Casey Jones was blasting from two big speakers while sweet smoke billowed out of the open door. Two obvious Deadheads sat in the front, their long hair held in place with colorful headbands. The driver's tee shirt read Grateful Dead - Fillmore East—April 71. The passenger said, "We're going north, dudes, hop in. I'm Phil, that's Donny."

"Thanks for stopping, bro. I was at that show," He said, pointing at the shirt, "They jammed until three. This is Fern, I'm Hugh. How far are you going?" He stowed their packs careful not to damage the flute sticking out of the bigger knapsack. He removed the Super 8 camera's lanyard from around his neck, then climbed onto the mattress in the back of the van joining Fern.

"Plattsburgh," Donny said. "So, Hugh, where are you folks going?"

"We're heading to the Phunee Farm, my crib in the mountains near the border in Northern Vermont. After that, we're going to Glover."

## North with Hubert

My first visit to the farm made a big impression on me and I was determined to return. I didn't want to drive up on my own and we wanted to start a commune, so I checked with Andy, one of my more adventurous friends. He could always get backstage or someplace close, at a concert. Once we sat on a couch in an opera box, next to Jack Cassidy's mother at a Hot Tuna show. He was not interested, but suggested I check with Hubert, who I knew as Hugh.

We left Long Island unknown to each other, but you get to know someone on a long, snowy car trip. Hugh, I came to learn, was a soft-spoken, intelligent guy with a heart of gold and nary a mean bone in his body. In time I learned he was fearless of heights, the unknown, strangers and new experiences, but shy with women. He would almost never go anywhere without his flute and Super 8 movie camera. He was one of the freest spirits I ever met. Hugh was of the earth, and with his iconic "smiling trees," he embraced and quickly melded with our dream.

The first leg of the trip wasn't bad. We stayed overnight in the girls' dormitory at Albany University where we knew a couple of girls. No, not like that; platonic. We were two svelte nineteen-year-old, long-haired hippie wannabes. My thin hair had grown back to ponytail length after being shorn a year or so earlier. Hugh's thick long hair and full beard did nothing to hide his welcoming eyes and smiling face.

The tale of our back-to-the-land adventure attracted a small crowd of coeds.

The next day, groggy and somewhat hungover, and determined to get to our destination, we collected a few phone numbers and new rooms to visit on our next trip—less platonic. We said our goodbyes, grabbed some coffee for the road and headed north.

The snow started anew in the middle of the night. Nothing was plowed. So what's a little snow? My 1965 Dodge Dart Supra was heavy with axes, bow saws and several tool boxes. Besides, it had decent snow tires and could handle the snow, but just in case, I also had a shovel. Eight hours after leaving Albany, we found our way into Enosburg Falls, double the normal travel time. It snowed every one of the two hundred miles we traveled. Exhausted and road weary, we crashed at Leigh's apartment for the night.

## Bluebird

Tara, Fae and Skye arrived at the Phunee Farm forty minutes later after stopping for provisions. Skye said, "Looks like they've been busy, the house looks good painted green." When they arrived, they didn't see anyone. Skye called into the house; Tara checked the barn. Fae looked in the orchard, they went inside, sat down at the kitchen table and found our note.

Tara said, "That's not the only change, check out the floors. Shit, the place is clean and organized. After reading the missive, they raided the kitchen adding to the stuff they brought with them. The ladies left for Bronze Beach with a full load, planning to surprise us with a campfire-cooked meal.

They walked toward the head of the valley along an active logging road beyond the barn. Tall thin poplar and birch trees interspersed with wildflowers took root on the hillside lining the road.

"Look at all the pretty flowers," Fae sang as she picked a bouquet of mixed wildflowers and danced down the road.

"Tara, I hope you still remember how to get there? We've been walking a while."

"I think so but I haven't been there since last year. Hold on, I think I recognize something up ahead. Yeah, it's coming up. Look up there, where the logging road turns north, see all that purple. It's hidden behind that clump of fireweed right after the blanket of white flowers."

"Okay, Tara, which ones are the fireweed? I see two kinds of purple flowers. Are they the ones that look like daisies?"

"No, those are coneflowers. The fireweed has the long purple pointy flowers."

"As long as I'm asking, what are those white flowers?"

"They're called pearly everlasting. They make great dried flowers. They're aptly named," Tara quipped. "They last forever."

"Geez," Skye commented, "If you didn't know there was a trail here you'd never find it."

"Fae," Tara said, "can you help us? There's a secret trail somewhere behind those flowers. I heard it was protected by the fairy folk. Wait, I think I just saw a fairy fly by."

Skye picked up on it, "Over there. Look, I just saw two of them fly through the light. Did you see them, Fae? Look into the sunbeams."

Tiny shapes danced in the bright rays reflecting the light. Otherwise invisible dust motes floated in the turbid air.

"I think I see them," Fae said running into the light behind the flowers. Tara followed behind, the trail unfolding ahead of them.

"You found the trail, Fae of the fairy folk, good job! Wow, look down there. Is that where the fairies live?" Tara asked, pointing to a clump of large red-capped mushrooms with white spots. Don't ever touch them, they're dangerous to humans. Well, you found the trail. Lead the way."

## Somewhere on the NYS Northway

Phil asked "Did you say Glover? We're going to Glover next week but we're picking up our ladies in Plattsburgh first. We have family up north near Jay. Peter asked us to come up and train as puppeteers. Have you heard of the Bread and Puppet Circus?"

Hugh could have been a body double for the VW's driver but, unlike the clean-shaven Donny, his long mane merged with his full beard. They were among kindred spirits, drifting on the fringe of society. Hugh and Fern met at New Paltz College. She was studying solid waste management, a prescient field of study for the time. He was out for the ride, taking eclectic classes and sprouting seeds of civil unrest.

A few hours later, the VW Bus took a detour off the Northway and discharged its passengers at Port Kent, New York. Their new friends gave them a couple of doobs then they walked over and bought tickets for the Lake Champlain Ferry to Burlington.

## Vermont State Trooper

Eleven months earlier somewhere south near the New Hampshire Border, a truck stopped to open a camouflaged screen hiding a secret road. The passenger checked to be sure there were no cops in sight. The coast was clear, but they dallied too long before moving the screen. As they drove through, a Vermont State Trooper pulled over a new red Corvette twenty yards from the entrance. Noticing the cop, the driver tried to back the four-wheeler out of sight. It was too late. The Trooper didn't know what to make of it at first. He was paying attention to the Corvette's driver getting out of the car. The loud speakers blared.

"You, in the Corvette, get back in the car and put your hands on the wheel." Hearing the admonition to the Corvette driver and thinking they might still be hidden, the driver continued backing up. The loud speaker rang out again, "You, in the Toyota, stop the vehicle; turn off the engine and throw the keys out the window."

The driver's first reaction was to brace for a fight or at least to speed away back the way they had come. His passenger pleaded, "Please, stay calm. Do what he says."

The speaker barked again, "Put your hands through the window and get out of the car, slowly." The terrified passenger threw her hands out the window. She couldn't believe the driver sat there gripping the wheel, glaring at the trooper.

At this point, the trooper was thinking that he may have stumbled on to a real situation. Unknown to the interlopers, at the Trooper's morning briefing, his sergeant advised them to be alert for drug smugglers operating in the area and that the department's anti-drug plane, known as the narco-plane by the local growers, spotted a large pot field in the area. He recalled his sergeant's warning to watch out for booby traps. The growers were reported to be well-armed with high-powered weapons.

## Bronze Beach

The Bluebird, parked in the driveway at the Phunee Farm, was still warm when the women stepped through the tall flowers following their leader into another world. It was as if a veil was lowered when they passed from the bright sunlight. Eyes dilating in the darkened forest, they continued along a steep narrow path descending across the slope to Carleton Brook, twenty feet below. Traveling with packs on their backs and arms full, in preparation for the surprise cookout, they navigated the steep path. Well, they weren't all women. Fae at four years old was part of the team, her small arms wrapped around a blanket. Smart, precocious with long blond curls she hated to have brushed, was wise beyond her years.

A short distance into the woods, the undergrowth thinned as the canopy thickened and blocked the light. Ostrich and Bracken ferns fared well in the low light, lining the path the rest of the way down.

"Be careful Fae, go slow." Fae giggled as she pushed through ferns tickling her face.

"It's dark in here and very steep. We're almost there, Jelly Bean."

"I'm tired! Can we stop?"

"Your mom's right. Listen, can you hear the brook? We're almost at the bottom," Skye said pointing, "Bronze Beach is over there. Look, can you see the cupboard?"

Bronze Beach - The Cupboard

"Yeehaw, we made it," they cheered, dropping their gear and falling to the ground. They rested a bit, played with Fae splashing in the brook, and then it was dusk. Nearing dinner time, they set off to seek firewood and build a fire.

About the same time I found a walking staff, high up in a tree on the other side of the valley. Hugh and Fern were getting off the Champlain Ferry in Burlington, while Tara and Skye were gathering firewood. Tara said, "It's been picked clean around here; let's wade across the brook for better options."

It took a while to gather enough wood for a cooking fire. "Tara, we'll have to go upstream. We can't get past that huge rock."

"That's okay, those trees are mostly softwoods anyway. That is, except for that little birch tree growing from that crack in the rockface." Ten feet above, atop the massive rock, a stand of fir trees had rooted in the thick soil.

"It's spooky dark over there," Fae said, "but the blue rocks are pretty." Carleton Brook flowed past the blue lichen-smeared rockface creating a narrow cave. Under the shadow of towering evergreens, it was dark even on a sunny day.

"Hey, ladies, over here," Skye said. "We hit the motherlode." Snapping the smaller branches was quick work. Skye went over to a large branch, "If I could break this branch we'll have plenty of wood." A loud snap followed. The branch broke with a resounding crack, then crashed to the ground taking her with it. Landing with her face close to the loamy floor, the musty aroma filled her nostrils. They were all woodsy. Skye was getting up, laughing, and spitting out moss-laden dirt, "I'm okay." Tara and Fae, dropping their haul of wood, came running over.

"Are you sure? You went down hard, you're covered with dirt." After brushing off the soil, still laughing, Skye dragged the whole branch back to the beach while Tara and Fae gathered the piles they had dropped. Fae's pile was a bunch of small twigs. They had enough wood for a great fire. Tara started to build it.

The women set up a camp kitchen. Skye unpacked a camping cook kit: a flashlight, some veggie burgers, cooked brown rice, a few condiments, a bag of weed, a pint bottle of Jack and two quarts of potent home-brewed beer. Tara packed in blankets for when Fae fell asleep, a loaf of fresh-baked whole wheat bread she found in the warming oven and a couple of toys. She also had a small kerosene hurricane lamp. Who knows what else she might have had in there.

## Aflame

Tara and Skye dawdled for a long time before they started building the fire. Then they had trouble getting it started, even with the matches and a lighter they brought for their smokes.

"Tara, did you bring any paper to start the fire?"

"Shit! No, I forgot."

"All of the tinder around here is damp."

After scouring the forest floor with little luck, Tara said, "Hey, Skye, look under some of the branches. I just found some dry tinder under this branch. Use your lighter to dry it a bit more."

"Cool. Tara, we should have enough to get a fire started." They stacked the twigs Fae collected into a pyramid over the dried tinder. Using one of the matches, Tara lit the tinder. The flame flared up, consuming it as the fire licked the twig pyramid, then flared out.

Tara looked at Skye, "Okay. What do we do now?"

It was then that Fae, playing by the cupboard, found a small stub of candle. It was a common white utility candle an inch in diameter and two inches long. She was just four years old yet she paid attention to the women's plight. She picked up the candle and walked it over to Tara and said, "Will this help?" Tara burst out laughing, as did Skye, a laugh that had Fae beaming with pride and laughing right along. Tara took the candle from Fae and, giving her a big hug, said, "I love you, Jelly Bean. You are the best!" After restacking the firewood, they had a roaring fire going at Bronze Beach.

## Earlier on Lucas Brook

Upstream the terrain steepened. Lucas Brook appeared to vanish behind the foot of the mountain. Rock walking transitioned to rock climbing. Reaching the base of the escarpment, we followed the curve of the brook and discovered a tremendous Roman-like arch, a hundred feet long and almost as high, supporting the road far above and serving as an aqueduct for Lucas Brook.

On the far side of the cavern-like space, the brook stepped down twenty feet, dropping over three falls into several pools spilling over a cascade of rocks, then rambled through the culvert, and broke into the sunlight. It felt like we were in the middle of the wilderness. Well yeah, we almost were! The nearest dwelling was our farmhouse over a mile to the northwest. In all other directions, hundreds of thousands of forested acres rose to the surrounding mountaintops. We rested with our feet in the water, cooled by the fine spray rising in the air.

# 4

# PHUNEE FARMHOUSE

*Announced by all the trumpets of the sky—*
*Arrives the snow, and, driving o'er the fields—*
*Seems nowhere to alight: the whited air—*
*Hides hills and woods, the river and the heaven—*
*And veils the farmhouse at the garden's end.*
*~ Ralph Waldo Emerson*

## Farmhouse

A typical two story, L-shaped building, the house sat on a hill at the end of Lucas Valley. Built at the beginning of the twentieth century, the walls of the farmhouse wore every year with pride. The clapboard siding was washed gray and worn weary from exposure to the harsh elements. The trim boards were barren of color but for a trace hint of white shielded from winter's assault. Rusted nails loosed from its seven-decade ordeal were visible on the naked wood. The roof was a patchwork of rusted tin roof panels that showed signs of repair. The farm, abandoned before World War II, was unoccupied for several decades. With no one to care for the house, the harsh winters, spring rains, and short baking summers pounded away at the building.

The tin roof panels clung to the roof for years before they succumbed to the incessant battering of the seasonal winds peeling sections of tin and cast them sailing through the air like flying carpets off to points unknown. Exposure to the sky, unshielded from the torrents, rain and snow, wreaked havoc on the painted plaster walls, accruing significant damage to the interior as the years passed. Thanks to the superior craftsmanship of the builders, the bones of the house escaped serious structural damage.

We made several major structural and cosmetic repairs, including moving the Magee Beacon parlor stove from the cellar. After much bending and lifting and cursing, four guys covered in soot ushered the stove through the house to its new home in the corner of the living room. With her ornate filigree door and embossed frame, "Maggie" became the new centerpiece. What better place for a parlor stove? Influenced by the weight of the Acorn stove in the kitchen, the first floor sagged. The stairs to the second floor canted toward the sag. Moving Maggie, we discovered the reason for the sagging floor; a rotted main beam. In response, we jacked up the house and replaced the beam.

It didn't stop there. We painted the interior then took on the floors, installing a cheap rug in the living room and blue linoleum in the kitchen. The house became ours—more lived in, more suburbanish.

We were ready to take on the outside of the house. Once again, our suburban way of thinking drove our need to paint the outside. The house was thirsty and sucked up paint like a parched man reaching an oasis desert. It was as if every molecule of paint was absorbed by the dry, weathered clapboard. I moved the ladder to the west end of the house to paint the peak and soffit. With the paint bucket in one hand and the brush in the other, I climbed to the top of our makeshift ladder. I painted my way up to the peak, not realizing I painted over a hole that bees were using to access their hive within the eaves.

Moments later my face and head were swarming with angry bumblebees. I was at a disadvantage, clinging to the rickety ladder fifteen feet in the air with both hands occupied. I dropped the brush in the paint can as I swatted at the bees. Big mistake—I was stung on my hand and the top of my head. One flew into my mouth and stung the inside of my cheek. This all happened in a split second as I descended the ladder, trying to save the precious paint, and jumped down the last few feet. I dropped the bucket, which fell upright, spilling a little paint. It was getting into the late afternoon and I decided to tend to my wounds until dark when the bees would settle down. Later that evening, I tied the paintbrush to a long stick and painted the area the bees had protected. Even old Cedric Morse, our farmer neighbor, commented that the house hadn't looked that good in a generation. The house had character and it wore its new face well.

In the kitchen, our prominent Acorn wood cook stove was a popular farmhouse stove when the house was built in the early 1900s. The warming oven door was decorated with an acorn design above six removable plates on the expansive range top. The oven door took up about two thirds of the base with a silver handle, mounted on both sides of a mica viewing window. An embossed cast-iron door opened into a small fire box. It took a long time to learn how to regulate the temperature and duration of the fire in the stove in order to bake bread. We scored buckets of scrap kiln dried ash from a hockey stick factory; it burned hot and was plentiful.

Acorn Wood Cook Stove

The Acorn stove was built with a hot water coil which we connected to a five foot tall cylindrical fifty gallon galvanized tank that we scrounged up. It fit snugly in the space behind the stove across from the bathroom. A real Rube Goldberg hot water system followed. A pipe ran from the tank up to the ceiling and then over to the bathroom and down to the sink and tub. It worked great for awhile. The firebox on the stove was small, which meant a short burn. The fire went out one cold night and the water in the coil froze and burst—no more hot water. The cold water, unfrozen, continued to run as liquid; the Mpemba Effect theorizes that hot water freezes before cold. I learned of this phenomenon from Tom, my plumber friend. He insisted that when on a no-heat call, the hot water often froze before the cold water. To this day there have been contra experiments by many scientists, some acknowledging a narrow set of reproducible facts.

## Barn

A ubiquitous red dairy barn, thirty feet away from the farmhouse, was the last vestige of humankind in the valley. Five stories tall it loomed above the old farmhouse. There were three main sections to the barn: the upper hayloft, the stable area at ground level, and a concrete-lined milking room. The true magnificence of the barn was the high-reaching upper level. The barn stood about fifty feet high at its peak. It's skeletal superstructure was like a work of art. The aged brown colors of the large-scale lumber was so awesome you could visually smell the wood. Giant beams constructed with mortise and tenon joints, joined with wood dowels and huge spiked nails, spanned the upper reaches of the barn in open layers. Daylight shone through many of the gaps in the barn board siding. The hayloft was no longer viable, but once sat high in the upper section of the barn.

Viewed from Lucas Brook

The upper barn doors were at ground level so a vehicle or horse drawn wagon could enter. Just inside the barn, the floor was solid but some of the boards were dry rotted. When we pulled the rotted boards up, the hole in the floor gave us the idea to install a mechanics pit to service our vehicles. This proved to be helpful from changing the oil to changing an engine.

Barn North Side

The lower level had a low ceiling used for a few of our husbandry efforts, but it required the taller folks of our group to duck to avoid the huge joists. Ceilings were low by design to help retain the cow's body heat. Portions of the lower level still revealed whitewashed stalls, now faded with chipping paint. This lower section was accessible through large cross-buck barn doors opening into the driveway. Next to the whitewashed stalls, an access door led to the back pasture, a pigsty for our three pigs, and corral for Lady, a visiting mare.

Another door led to a small room with a concrete floor, walls, and a stepped platform where the milk was pasteurized by the dairy farmer ages before. We used it as a chicken coop. Behind the chicken coop the lower level exposed the dirt of the hill the barn was built on, littered with old machinery, random metal and wood, where an unusual discovery awaited.

## 5

# BLUE-BIRDERS

*Can miles truly separate us from friends?*
*If we want to be with someone we love, aren't we already there?*
*- Richard Bach*

As Craig and I walked through the night-draped forest, their arrival yet unknown to us, we talked about how long it was since we had seen Tara and Skye and the unusual circumstances of how we met the women. It was months since we saw either of them.

### Rock Picking

Hugh got me a sweet job last spring, paying more than twice the minimum wage. It proved to be one of my strangest but best jobs. A twenty-six-year-old dude named Conner inherited a fortune and invested in a farm for tax purposes. Rather than removing rocks from a new cornfield using heavy farm equipment, he hired starved-for-work locals and emigrant hippies to pick rocks.

Fifty people were milling around the field in clusters of three or four. I joined one of the groups and began picking rocks, tossing them into a pile in the middle. When all reachable rocks were picked, we stepped back as other people joined the widening circles. I noticed an attractive blond woman picking rocks across the field in a circle that was spreading toward mine. I steered toward her, but my circle overlapped with someone else first. Tara, a beautiful woman with long, wild dark hair as attractive as the blond. She glowed with effervescence—we hit it off right away. Tara was a local from St. Alban's City in the northeast corner of the state. We continued picking rocks as our circles combined. She introduced me to her friend Jane, the woman I was aiming for; and when we were done for the day, we all headed off to a swimming hole. The next day, Tara and Fae, who was born on my birthday, came to visit. The following day they moved in with me, beginning a new phase of my growth and sexuality.

*Although I started dating in grade school, I was sexually naïve until my sophomore year. My first "date" was in the fourth grade, when I took Luanne to see the "Santa Clause" movie. My dad was one of the managers at the movie theater and I felt so cool holding her little hand and walking into the theater, passing the ticket taker like a celebrity. Despite my naiveté, I had several relationships with girls who were older than me, and then they graduated. Working at a club fundraiser one spring, I met Rachael and was enamored with her. Without thinking, I slipped my hand into hers, which led to my first true love and real sexual experiences. We got pregnant at 16. I thought it was the greatest thing in the world; her father did not. The course of my life changed. I was, at the time, Catholic and had a hard time reconciling an abortion. I wanted to kill myself; a life for a life. I came as close as bringing a pair of scissors to my stomach, but never broke the skin. I was sexually screwed up for a long time thereafter.*

## Tara and Fae

When Tara and Fae moved in with me, it was one of the best times of my life. Tara, zealously oversexed, drew me most of the way out of my sexual morass. Lots of sex, drinking and drugging followed. A couple of things happened. I fell in love with both of them; sharing a birthday with Fae was an omen, she was also about the age of a child never born. Tara had a rough life before meeting me, and I offered calmness and a bent toward the spirituality she craved.

While traveling to Long Island to see my parents, we stopped at Bill's place in Huntington, New York, which was true to his South Bronx roots as we were the sole Caucasian household in a ten-block radius. We planned a party for the night before Father's Day. This is one of two lifetime drinking episodes of which I have but a fragmented memory. Drinking was not my strength; Tara and Bill were skilled. Addiction entered deeper into my life. Bill entered Tara's life.

A month later, I realized I was unable to keep up with Tara's lifestyle. She was still sowing wild oats while I was settling down into a traditional family role. We remained great friends, and both she and Fae became long-term regulars at the farm. While coming together for the occasional sexual foray, Tara took turns living with Hugh and Craig, and in time moved in with Bill on Long Island.

## Hitchhikers

Last summer, Skye, Sally and Tess, all from Connecticut, were hitchhiking along Route 105. They left home for a summer fling two weeks earlier. Skye was the alpha of the group. I was driving east through the Berkshire Flats with Hugh in my trusted 1965 red Dodge Dart Supra. Frustrated, unable to get a ride, the women were resting, anticipating the three-mile hike into Richford.

Hugh, an avid hitchhiker, traversed the country with his thumb, and I did my share of hitching as well. We would have picked them up even if they weren't three beautiful women. Skye cut an intriguing figure as an earthy hippie chick. She wore a loose-fitting blue-green paisley halter top cradling her ample breasts and micro short denim cutoffs. She was leaning against a large backpack. Sally was standing; her shoulder length blondish hair was much shorter than Skye's. With a more athletic body type, she wore a skimpier reddish-brown halter top, tighter than the loose flowing halter Skye was wearing, the taut fabric hinting at her smaller, firmer, rounder breasts. She wore a flowing muslin skirt stopping just above her knees that lifted with the wind exposing lean muscular legs. Tess, the shyest of the three, had long dark hair and a button-down peasant blouse, cut low and square at the neckline exposing a hint of cleavage; her long legs were covered by a full-length skirt with similar material to Sally's, but with a colorful light green and yellow brocade trimming the hem, sleeves and collar. It was hot, they were sweaty. We came through a long lonely winter and a difficult muddy spring and even survived winter's parting shot, a final May snowfall. Pulling over to the side of the road, Hugh rolled down the window and asked, "Need a ride? Where you heading?"

Rising to their feet, grateful for a ride, Skye and Sally remarked, "That depends. Where are you guys going?"

"We're heading to the Phunee Farm, off the road to Newport," Hugh responded. After loading their packs into the trunk, they climbed in. We lit up a joint for the ride, and pointed out landmarks as we drove through Richford. Starting up the mountain, we passed the maple bobbin factory where they made industrial bobbin spools. Folding one finger down, we held up our hands and joked that it was a dangerous job resulting in workers losing a finger to the task. Dark humor, but everyone laughed.

We continued past the monk's house. Two of the monks were working in their garden wearing heavy brown robes; we beeped and waved. They were big men, like Friar Tuck of Robin Hood fame, but with full beards.

Sally asked, "Are they real monks? Do you know what kind they are?"

"I'm not exactly sure, but they are an interesting group. I asked once; they were very cryptic. Despite their dedication to their religion, they loved to party.

Their order bought the land, believing it was touched by God. A long walk into the forest is a stand of virgin maples over a hundred feet tall. Standing beneath those behemoths puts things into perspective; creation—evolution. The forest may have been touched by God, but it remained vulnerable to the assault of the evil of men."

"Maybe the monks were right," Tess said, speaking for the first time.

We talked about life at the Phunee Farm and Lucas Brook waterfalls and swimming holes; and in no time the decision was made to forgo their trip back to Connecticut and spend the night at the farm, which may have been decided before we moved off the Berkshire Flats. A mile or so beyond the monks, we turned north onto Route 105A, meandering along the snaking Missisquoi River. A thousand feet from the East Richford border crossing, we veered right onto the East Richford Slide Road, so named for the steep rise. A tumbledown building at the intersection was managed by an elderly gentleman who ran an antique gas station and operated an ancient hand pump to extract gas from the large tank stored in the vintage shed.

"Hey, girls, coming up soon the border is more than just an imaginary line on a map. Do you see that tall cement monument? The weathered brass medallion marks the US-Canadian Border. Check this out, we are in Canada now. See, the next marker is on the other side. Now the northern side of the road was the border.

Sally said, "That's really cool how the road goes in and out of Canada, now I can say I've been in Canada."

About halfway to the Phunee Farm, the Slide became the West Jay Road along which we pointed out an old abandoned one-room schoolhouse amid encroaching birch and sumac trees. Weather-worn clapboard siding clung to the walls struggling against wind and gravity, as it yawed south toward Lucas Brook; the roof was caved in at one end. The schoolhouse sat alone on the south side of the road surrounded by active pastures and hay fields sloping down to the brook. "Once, when exploring the old building, I found a rusted ramrod from an old musket."

"What's that?" Tess asked.

I responded, "The ramrod was used to pack the wadding and gunpowder needed to push the musket ball out through the barrel when the hammer ignited the powder. I thought it was pretty cool, from colonial times, I imagined.

Skye said, "That sounds cool. I'm a bit of a history buff. I'd love to see your ramrod when we got to the farm."

Our pace was slowed by a rutted road left over from mud season and the summer bane of a dirt road. Dust! It was hot, and conversation turned back to the swimming hole. I could feel Lucas' cooling water. Continuing the drive along the Lucas Flats, we turned left onto the driveway and up the steep hill before leveling out past the turnoff to the old Bell place up on the hill. The house and barn coming into view never gets old. The girls were agog from the scenic route and stared at the house and barn with mouths agape. Hugh and I believed in the magic and the quiet spirituality of the house and surrounding land, so we romanticized a bit. Hotter yet, getting out of the car we were all sweaty and opted for a trek to the swimming hole. I led the parade.

## On Lucas Brook

Bare-chested now, I led the way down to Lucas Brook and taught the girls how to rock walk upstream. We followed the same course that Craig and I took earlier. On that late July day, the temperature found its way into the low eighties; we had a purpose. When we entered the brook, Hugh and I tossed our shirts and shoes onto the bank. I looked up and Skye had just done the same; ample and happy to be free. It took another thirty seconds for Sally saying, "Sounds good to me!" as she pulled her halter over her head. She did indeed have an athletic build, no fat at all, well-proportioned, muscled and firm. Tess was uncomfortable about this. As we rock walked she wrestled with her own insecurities and modesty. She was nervous enough walking into the wilderness with a couple of skinny hippies that she met an hour ago. Sensing our wholesome spiritual vibe, she relaxed. After all, that's who we were. Hard as it may be to believe, neither Hugh nor I had any sexual expectations. Tess unbuttoned the buttons that ran down the front of her shirt, teasing each as she did.

Tess was much more comfortable now. She unbuttoned her shirt but did not remove it. It's ironic how two beautiful women, bare-chested, the white edges of their tan lines evident, breasts moving up and down to the cadence of their rock walking steps, were felt to be free and spiritual, semi-naked to the heavens! Yet Tess, walking with her shirt unbuttoned, her breasts moving freely against the fabric to the same rock walking rhythm, was more sensual. Her shirt, at first held tight to her waist, was blowing back from the breeze, offering tantalizing glimpses of her breasts within—naked versus scantily clad. Hmm.

Hugh was pretty shy himself. He hid it well, but his cheeks reddened when the girls took off their shirts. He wandered ahead to avoid staring. We reached the first waterfalls and stopped for another joint. We considered swimming there but the girls wanted to see the swimming hole upstream. Climbing the root ladder to the top, we were rewarded, finding the log bridge across the falls dry. Shimmying across, the girls were so nervous they moved at a sloth's pace, their breasts pressed tight against the water-smoothed surface of the log. They clung firmly as the spray from the falls dampened their skin. I truly had no sexual expectations.

Upstream, Skye slipped on wet rocks and banged her knee as she fell. I was the closest, so I hopped across a rivulet running between two boulders. Helping her up, her dark erect nipple accidentally brushed across my cheek and then she pressed her breasts tight to my chest, stumbling as she rose. At least I thought it was an accident. We reached the swimming hole a few minutes later. Skye felt fine, but she had soaked her shorts. The water was cold even with the sun shining on the brook. It moved through the light at a quick pace as it spilled over the cascade racing toward the Missisquoi. Standing by the edge of the water I asked, "So, who's going in?"

This time Sally was first. She dropped her skirt to the rock where she was standing followed by her light green panties, revealing toned shaved tanned legs leading up to a manicured blonde triangle of pubic hair. The nipples of her perky breasts were erect from the spray of the cold water. Getting ready to step in myself, I dropped my shorts as Skye held my arm while she peeled off her wet shorts and panties, laying them in the sun to dry. She was well formed for a big woman; she joined me in the frigid water. Unlike Sally, Skye was more like the hippie chicks I knew, with a wild dark patch leading to unshaven legs.

Hugh slipped into the water after he discreetly stripped off his shorts. Tess, standing away from the edge, faced a new dilemma. She had to admit to herself that opening her shirt and letting her bare breasts free was empowering. Demurely, but wanting everyone to notice, she let her shirt drop down to the dry flat rock she was standing on. Tess had a short torso that made her breasts appear larger. Larger than Sally's perky round breasts, Tess's were a little smaller than Skye's, but prominent and firm and erect as were her pink nipples in the cool spray. It's great to be nineteen. Since the water was so cold, neither Hugh nor I would impress them with our manliness.

Tess stood at the edge of the pool, her breasts freed as Hugh and I splashed naked with Skye and Sally, taking a few strokes across the long side of the swimming hole. I had just met her, yet it was evident that she was struggling with getting naked. Was she worried getting naked would turn into a wild sex event splashing in the forest, or was it maybe just a puritanical Catholic school residual? The girls were splashing in the cold water trying to coax Tess into the pool.

"Come on, Tess, the water's cold but refreshing after you're in for a while." They knew that Tess just exposing her breasts to any men, let alone strangers, was a big deal. "You look great, what are you worried about? Lose the skirt and come on in," Sally continued. Standing there appearing relaxed with her breasts exposed, she wriggled out of her skirt. They weren't kidding; she had a svelte lean body, perhaps the best physique of the three. Without removing her light blue panties, she waded in, embracing the cold water.

We didn't stay in the water long. Helping each other climb out, we moved to the nearby sun-washed rocks and sunbathed ourselves dry. We stayed for a while, enjoying our nakedness in the forest in the warming sun, with nothing to hide; we were strangers no more. The sun moved behind the trees, dropping the temperature, so we dressed and returned to the Phunee Farm.

Ronni and Craig were home when we returned to the house. Introductions all around, we showed our guests the house and barn. After dinner, Hugh, Craig, Sally and Tess took a walk while Ronni went out to the garden, harvesting veggies for tomorrow. Skye and I were standing in the kitchen looking at the Acorn wood cookstove when everyone else left for the walk. She suggested we stay behind and clean up.

I realized when Skye took my hand that the day's sensuality had evolved. At that time in my life, I was still harboring some post abortion sexual hang-ups. I had no problems with nakedness, having been part of a Wiccan Pagan group that held rituals "skyclad," which is to say, naked. It was the belief of this nature-based religion that to honor the gods there should be no impediment to complete openness, nothing to hide—the endearment of shared spirituality. But when it came to sex, I carried an almost irrational fear of another pregnancy, even after knowing Tara. So I was serious when I said there was no sexual agenda when splashing naked with the girls. I couldn't speak for the girls though. That was all about to change.

Skye led me upstairs. I thought she was going to my room. Instead, she turned toward Craig's room letting her halter fall to the floor. She had already undone the button on her jeans and she was shimmying out of them as she undid my pants and pulled down the zipper. Our jeans hit the floor at the same time. Stepping out of them, she lay down on Craig's bed pulling me on top. She wanted to look through the skylight during the portending amorous experience. I had sex with many women in one form or another. She was a couple of years older than me and experienced. She guided me through what she wanted; I learned a lot. Downstairs, an hour or so later, we were greeted by the returning hikers. Ronni was already back in the kitchen, cleaning beets and giving me a coy, almost "atta boy" smile as we walked by.

Reunited, time passed from dusk to dark. Everyone agreed that a summer evening bonfire would be fun, and in no time we had a roaring fire going. Sitting around the fire, Craig broke out his guitar and we sang and drank and smoked for hours. At midnight, most of us were tired from the day's events. Our company broke out their sleeping bags and opted to sleep on the porch. Sally decided she would be more comfortable on the couch. I fell asleep in minutes. I am pretty sure that Skye returned to Craig's room, having been enamored by him and his guitar.

Sometime after I fell asleep, dreaming of being caressed by a beautiful woman, I was awakened by a delightfully naked Sally lying next to me, rubbing her body, breasts and hands all over my naked body. I reciprocated until we fell asleep. Guess that chilly water didn't matter after all. When morning broke, Sally was back on the couch. Tess's shyness overcome, she offered great conversation the next morning. Later that day we drove them over the mountains to the interstate just south of Newport. The forty-five-mile drive to Newport also brought us to the nearest traffic signal. We left the girls at the interstate ramp after many hugs and some passionate kisses. Even Tess surprised me with her skill at French kissing; sure you can't stay another night? They promised to return, but I never saw Sally or Tess again. However, sometime later, Skye hitched back to the Phunee Farm and moved in with Craig. She became a regular.

## Undetectable

The campfire crackled, but the women thought they heard something distant. Keening their ears, they were sure they heard a muffled shout. Craig and I were undetectable in the dark. Skye looked in the direction of the sound; got up from the log she was sitting on and moved past the fire. The light of the fire washed over her body. She pointed when she saw a light. As we called to them, our light went out. She reached down by the fire and found a maple stick with one end burning, picked it up and waved it like a semaphore flag; she could have used the flashlight or lantern but this was more dramatic. Then she saw a faint answering light. Tara and Skye both yelled back "Hey! What are you doing up there?" Skye, putting the flaming stick back into the fire, said, "I guess we should put more veggie burgers on the fire."

Earlier, darkness was complete and Tara and Skye worried there was no sign of us. They got hungry waiting so long and Fae needed to eat, so they had prepared the first round of veggie burgers. They were also a good part of the way into a bottle of homebrew and feeling pretty light. Despite protestations, when Fae lay down on the blanket after eating, she fell asleep. That signaled time to light up a joint. Every now and then, they would see a flicker of light and then they lost it again. Tara went about getting the meal ready for Fae.

The sweet smell wafting through the trees reached us. "Did you smell that, Craig?"

# 6

# LOST BETWEEN BROOKS

*Walking with a friend in the dark is better than
walking alone in the light.
~ Helen Keller*

Our original vision had morphed over the last year. Just last week we met some new folks in Richford who came up to the farm. They had a lot to teach; we were hungry to learn. We became enamored, oblivious to signs that in hindsight were obvious. We were aware of the change, we thought it good. "This is what we needed, Bob. Getting into the woods."

"Hard to believe, Craig. It's only been a week since Nick and Mia came up to the farm. Without his help, we wouldn't have had the time to take this cathartic trip."

Changing the subject, I continued, "We didn't do so well with the goats, Guinea hens or earthworms. Do you think we should try our hand at raising rabbits? Kendall gave us a lot to think about." Brooke's words rang through my mind.

"Kendall sure had some tales to tell. Maybe we should hold off till spring; my head has been spinning since meeting Nick. I can't even think about it now, but I am amazed how much he taught us in that one night. Mia was a real sweetheart, she sure can cook. But there is something gnawing at me. I can't put my finger on it," Craig finished.

"Nick did seem a little rough, but think of all the wood we cut. We can learn from this guy."

Our final destination was Bronze Beach, named for Gregg "the Guru" who lived there a few summers back. The brook took a sharp turn where smooth pea gravel washed along the bend, forming the beach. Remnants of a rustic cupboard and a table warped from years of exposure survived several winters and were still usable. The "cupboard," was another name for Bronze Beach.

## Overland

"Let's get moving, Bob. It'll be getting dark in an hour or so. Let's follow this deer run downstream a bit before hitting the rocks again," Craig said, pointing to a small trail which soon crossed the brook where we transitioned to the rock walking express.

The water slow-danced over the rocks, the silence broken only by the muted sounds of water trickling into an old moss-covered stream bed cut through the steep embankment. We stepped onto the soft turf, releasing the familiar damp musty odor from the bright green rock moss. A pungent, earthy scent wafted up as we walked through. "I love that smell," he said.

Pushing through the feathery fronds of ostrich and asparagus fern, we walked through the deep ravine moving into the forest. The sun dropped below the mountain; the half-light of twilight settled upon us. We lingered at the base of the escarpment longer than was wise; it would get dark soon this deep in the forest. Navigating by dead reckoning, we started across the valley, as the light was fading. We knew if we kept the Lucas behind us and the rise of the ridge to our right we would get to Carleton Brook, on the other side of the valley. Easier said than done, it was difficult to walk in a straight line. Obstacles forced us to find another route. Navigating around a huge rock, I was scanning the night sky through breaks in the canopy looking for a better bearing when I spotted it.

## Walking Staff

In the last light of dusk, silhouetted high in the crotch of a dead maple tree, I found my long sought walking staff. Thanks, Gandalf. It took some persuasion but the small tree yielded as we pushed it over. With a loud snap, the trunk broke about three feet from the ground. We were propelled forward by the sudden break, stumbled, but stayed on our feet. The tree came crashing down, twisting and snapping small branches on the way down.

"Look at this, Craig. Can you see it? The right side of the fork, It's the perfect walking staff."

"I see the fork , looks like it could be a good staff, but I'm not seeing what you're seeing."

Stepping on the short side while lifting up on the other I split it in two. Inverting the branch, putting the narrow end on the ground and cutting off the small branches with my Buck knife, I introduced my new staff.

"Can you see it now? See the top? It's splayed out like a cobra where it was joined at the fork. When I get back, I'm gonna carve my moonbeam symbol there and add some Runes, but I'll use it for the rest of this trek just the way it is."

## Lost

Darkness crept around us. It was getting harder to see our way through the forest. Moving slowly, still barefoot and watchful for safe footfalls, we picked our way along. We were familiar with the forest terrain, but landmarks were nowhere to be seen. Navigating around the last obstacle, we veered to the east. The ground was rising imperceptibly toward Owl Ridge. With my new staff in hand, Craig and I continued toward what we thought was the direction of Bronze Beach, heading north but veering east. We neglected to bring a flashlight since we planned a day hike; but like most in 1976, we smoked cigarettes. When we couldn't afford pre-rolled, we bought a can of tobacco and rolled our own. Cigarette addiction that it was, it forced us to re-roll the cigarette butts in desperate times. Disgusting!

Lighting a match or flicking the lighter we did our best to find decent footfalls. My new staff led the way. In the dark of the night, the nocturnal creatures begin to roam. We could hear the cracking of branches nearby and the distinctive hoot of an owl high in the trees ready to swoop down for a rodent meal. We always felt safe wandering the woods at night, but we would be wearing hiking boots for a night trek. There were bears, foxes, bobcats and other predatory wildlife that kept clear of us.

We were experienced campers and budding woodsmen trying to emulate the stealthy ways of the Native American Indians. However, we were still suburban youths, noisily walking through the woods. Barefoot in the forest during the daylight was no problem, even when moving at a fast pace, we could assess our footfalls. But the forest dark was murky at best, blocking a clear view of the ground.

Darkness engulfed the forest like a thick blanket; but stars exploded into the moonless sky, visible through random openings in the canopy.

"Craig, did you hear that growling sound? What do think it was?"

Laughing, Craig responded, "That was my stomach."

"I could swear the sound came from over by that bush. I guess your stomach learned how to throw its voice. This rock looks like a good place to sit and take a break. Here, have some cheese."

I took out the last of our "imported" cheese. "So, it looks like we'll need to take a trip up the Sutton road to get more cheese from the cheese lady. I love watching all those goats milling around the barnyard, especially the long-haired white ones. I wonder if she knows we call her the cheese lady."

"Hugh used to take a trip up to Canada every other day. He loved those limburger and onion sandwiches, but I think her cheddar was the best. I'm down for a trip tomorrow. What's your favorite cheese, Bob?"

"Definitely the Tilsit, but I loved them all. I gotta admit I never thought I would like limburger, using goats' milk, no less." We made frequent trips there so that one of the last times I took the ride with Hugh, the border guard joked, "If you boys keep making so many trips for cheese, you will need to get an importing permit." I think he was kidding.

And so we sat on a big rock in the dark for a long while, munching on cheese and sipping wine. Finished, we sat in silence with a dreamlike buzz. We knew we would get there, but it was taking a long time. Pitch black enveloped us.

Walking in the dark, unaware of a surprise waiting at the beach, Craig said, "Did you see that?"

I turned "What?"

Pointing, he said, "I thought I saw a light ahead over there to the left."

"I don't see anything now. Must have been the weed."

"Let's keep moving, but take it slow." As we walked, we had a lot of time to talk about how things were evolving and our plans for the future.

We smelled smoke, that familiar charred wood campfire smell. We looked in the direction of the scent through the naked branches of an old elm. Stars bright in the night sky twinkled behind wisps of gray-white smoke wafting up, reflecting a dim orange hue. The glow brightened and a flickering light flitted in the trees ahead. It became obvious that someone had a campfire going. But it was coming from the opposite direction we were heading.

"I think we are off track, Craig."

"What do you mean? I thought we made that correction a ways back?"

"The fire is behind us. I'm guessing someone is at the beach. But we're heading away from it.

"Holy shit, bro! I think you're right!" Realizing we veered off course, we turned toward the glow. It was further away than anticipated; but we found a homing beacon, a buoy through night wood.

We kept the firelight in sight, happy for the steady light. Getting closer we crept through the darkness, assessing our options. Using my new walking staff like a blind person's probing cane, I waved it back and forth testing the undefined path ahead. Craig had his lighter ready, flicking it on and off from time to time.

The lighter was a classic, unadorned, well worn silver gray Zippo. The kind with a small hinged top and larger bottom. Flipping the top section back on its hinge exposed a friction wheel, flint and wick. We were both pretty good with basic lighter tricks. As we walked along, Craig would snap the lighter between his thumb and index finger and with the same motion open and ignite the flame. A quick scan of the way ahead, then dark again. Walk, flick, darken, repeat.

We triangulated our position with a logging truck heading west coming down the slope from Burnt Mountain, and by the sound, it was unladen, gears singing. With the campfire light and the truck defining the upper rim of the valley, we were on track. Flick of the lighter, ouch, walk, repeat; flick of the lighter, stop! Just as I was about to step forward the light reflected something big and hazy directly in front of us.

"What the hell was that, Craig?" What did that last flick of the lighter reveal? I wasn't arachnophobic, but I was glad we stopped. Craig relit the lighter. "The biggest spider web I ever saw hung like gossamer threads in the night. The leading edge, four inches from my face was attached to the peeling bark of a paper birch, spanning eight feet reaching a nearby young beech. This wasn't just a spider web it was a web condominium. The center of the web was just below eye level, a bull's eye with concentric rings woven in intricate random circles, extending out from the core. Dozens of spokes perpendicular to the hub connected the rings. The web blocked our path. Ahead through the trees, the campfire was getting close, we could smell food cooking. "Craig, flick that light again."

That's when we saw it. Dead center on the web, a woodland spider with a body the size of an avocado pit and eight long hairy legs. The arachnid started to twang the web. Stepping back, we assessed our options. Ahead in the distance, our destination beckoned through the haze of the web blocking our egress. We followed a deer track through thorny brambles before encountering the web. Moonset rendered the forest pitch-black. Starlight did little to light our way, in the darkened forest. Unseen blackberry thorns tore at our skin. We could backtrack and go around the web. Still nursing our wounds, we were hesitant to move back through the thorny gauntlet again.

"Hey, Craig, "Can you Flick that lighter again?"

Once again, a flick of Craig's lighter brought light to the web. It looked like there was just enough room to squeeze past it without veering too deep into the bramble. We abandoned the idea of doubling back. The firelight shone ahead. It was a difficult maneuver as our faces would come within an inch of the web. Our goal was to shimmy past the web, brushing our backs hard against the thorny bramble which without light could be tricky. Keeping the lighter lit long enough would cause the base to get too hot to hold. The spider started to move.

When it moved, it felt like something from a Sci-Fi movie. I didn't think that there were tarantulas in Vermont, but this spider must have had a healthy diet; it was huge. We had stepped into the breach. By the time we reached the middle of the web, the spider was moving rapidly towards us, or so it appeared. Readying my new staff to fend off the attacking beast, I soon relented as the spider ran straight up the web above our heads.

The lighter's light lured several six-inch moths with mottled brown, black and gray colored wings. They were prisoners of the web, wings fluttering to no end. The spider was on the first moth in a snap, paralyzing it before moving on to the next one higher up. As the spider climbed higher up the web, we took the opportunity to move through the narrow passage. I hoped that the light would last; the lighter was getting hot in Craig's hand. Clearing the web, I heard Craig. "Damn, that's hot!" He closed the lighter cradling it with his shirt. The cheese we had eaten earlier was now just a memory as our stomachs panged with the smell of food cooking on the nearing fire. Picking spider webs from our face, hands and arms, we took comfort knowing we were close. The firelight was in clear view.

## Found

Picking up our pace, the underbrush thinned as we moved toward the fire. The ground was rising, but we thought nothing of it as the valley around us rolled up and down. The smell of simmering onions wafted through the air, pulling us forward by our nostrils. Firelight still evident ahead, we continued up the rise coming to a thicket of fir trees growing up to the edge of a ten-foot drop. Our line-of-sight walk had taken us to the top of the cliff downstream from our destination. Getting closer now, we could see the fire and people around it. "Who was there?" we thought to ourselves. They were still a ways off, silhouetted by the firelight. Moving closer to the edge of the drop, we called out to them to let them know we were close.

We hailed them and listened for a response, but they were still far away. High up on the stone promontory, set back from the edge in a thicket of fir trees, we didn't think they could see us either. Craig flicked the lighter, as we moved closer but there was no response. Then we noticed two naked women sitting by the fire.

"Hey, Bob, can you see who's down there?"

"The silhouettes look familiar. I wonder who they are, and for that matter, where they came from."

# 7

# BRONZE BEACH

*There are two kinds of taste, the taste for emotions of surprise and the taste for emotions of recognition."*
*- Henry James*

### Recognition

Craig recognized Skye standing by the fire, white breasts tinged orange in the campfire glow. She was saying something and then we saw her point. She got the other woman's attention and we realized it was Tara. Hails from Bronze Beach reached us in silence, but we knew they saw us. The lighter, running low on fuel, went out.

The ground under the fir trees was soft and spongy, littered with sharp twigs fallen from the sun-starved branches of the tall conifers. Even though our leathery hobbit-like feet could handle rock walking and most of the forest terrain, these sharp sticks along with the dried needles pricked our feet. There was no option to go forward with the sheer drop. We noticed a sturdy-looking young birch tree about five feet down, growing out from a crack in the stone face. Maybe we could have used it to climb down if it were daylight and if we had boots on. Perhaps we would have tried if we were being chased by a bear. We backed up about ten yards and found a place behind the cliff where the ground sloped down. We kept the light of the fire in sight as we descended; the way down steeper than we realized. Slowing my descent, I reached the bottom swinging on a paper birch branch like a Tarzan vine.

"Hey, Craig, don't you love these paper birch trees. Even when growing undisturbed the bark appears to be unwinding off the tree."

Cooking aromas blended with the charred wood smell as we climbed down from the hill. Once down, Craig would flick the lighter every so often, tempting our remaining lighter fluid. The brook was in sight now, but we had drifted a bit upstream due to the lay of the land coming down the slope—the fire always in sight. We could hear voices from the camp.

Tara and Skye shouted, "What took you so long? We were getting worried." The fire flashed, lighting the area; we could see our way clear to the beach. "You can't come over without paying the price of admission."

I looked at Craig and shrugged. "What's the price?" we both yelled back, but we had a pretty good idea.

Laughing they shouted, "Well, you have to get naked before you cross the brook."

"You drive a hard bargain," was our response, taking off our shirts. We dropped our shorts, flipping them into the air and catching them as we stepped into the brook. Fae awoke from a light sleep giggling at our dialog.

"Hey, what's that you're holding?" Tara asked.

"It's my soon-to-be new walking staff."

We crossed the brook and joined the women in warm embrace. I enjoyed the closeness with Tara and then Skye. After Craig embraced them, we all joined in a group hug. You would think that with naked flesh rubbing together, breast against chest, pubic hair tickling torsos, that sexual stimulation would stir the blood. Yet this was not a sexual event; it was an absolute openness shared by friends. Both Craig and I had had sex with each woman, but at different times wandering in out of relationships over the course of several months. Now was a time to enjoy our friendship without the barrier of clothing or sexual distraction. The complete openness always brought us closer together.

We were surprised Skye had returned to Vermont, and more so, learning she was picked up hitchhiking by Tara and Fae. Any time Tara and Skye got together, there was fun to be had. They were quite the pair at our favorite watering hole, Kilgore Trout Saloon, a few miles away in Montgomery.

## Secret Passage

The moment he saw the truck move out of the woods, the morning briefing flashed in the trooper's mind. He felt several emotions at once; "Wow, I think I might have caught a big one." Alone in the middle of nowhere with dangerous people getting out of the Toyota, fear washed over him; what the hell should he do with the Corvette driver who sped past him at one hundred miles per hour? He thought that alone would have made his day. Fear eased, his zeal for a big bust won over. When he first saw the Toyota, he pulled out his service weapon, a Smith and Wesson model 28 revolver chambered for a .357 magnum round, which he held to his side. He appreciated the magnums stopping power—so much more punch than the 38. He approached the sports car. Using it for cover, limited as it was, he yelled to the man and woman in the Toyota, "Put your hands behind your head—step in front of the vehicle—get down on your knees." He radioed dispatch, advising them of his situation before getting out of his car, and advancing said to the Corvette driver, "It's your lucky day, get out of here and slow down, asshole."

As the Corvette pulled away, he stepped over to the tree line, weapon held out, covering the man and woman kneeling on the ground. He was about ten feet from them when he reached a large beech tree. He braced his arm against the smooth gray bark, then, taking a defensive shooter's stance, he waited. It seemed like an eternity to the trooper. The woman started speaking to him. He could hear the sirens, but they were minutes out.

The first car pulled up as expected, and the others, fifteen minutes after that. They called in the big guns. One of the vehicles was a four by four brush jumper, armored with reinforced bumpers, a steel cage around the body and huge shielded tires, a wilderness assault vehicle without the fifty-caliber machine gun.

They were not smugglers, nor were they commercial pot growers. They were a couple of people who were living at the edge of society, one with a nefarious history. In their mind, all they had done was make an illegal exit off the interstate. It must be some obscure law anyway. How often could this happen, the woman thought. Clean cut and without a public blemish, she was terrified, crying and trying to be compliant as she stared directly ahead, seeing only the hollow end of the small round gun barrel that, to her, appeared cavernous.

Getting defensive about his woman and trying to find a way to take control of the situation, the man leered at the trooper with a venomous stare, daring him to come closer. She whispered to him, "Why are you doing this? You said the most we would get is a ticket. Please stop that. We're not doing anything wrong, so what if we get a ticket? Mr. Trooper, there must be some mistake. We're sorry we cut down those bushes, but that's all we did wrong. We own property close to here and we built a log cabin. We used this passage to bring in our supplies. The only other way in is ten miles of dirt roads. All we want to do is live off the land in the cabin we built."

The trooper heard what she was saying but never took his covering weapon off them. He relaxed when the other trooper got out of his car, saying, "Whaddaya got here, Neil?"

### Tara's Story—Ronni and the Bluebird.

We left Leigh's apartment at nine o'clock after partying all afternoon with Craig, Hugh and Bob. I was driving the Bluebird, going out for a night on the town with Leigh and Ronni. We were in a wild mood and up for some serious drinking, dancing and general cutting loose. Fae was at my aunt's house in Morrisville; I was free for the night, and Leigh was free for the weekend. Ronni was having a hard time since she broke up with Biff two weeks before. In fact, Ronni's malaise was the motivation for the outing. Earlier, Leigh took Ronni by the hands, saying "Girls' night out. You ready, Tara? It's only eight-thirty. We can make it to St. Albans in time to hear the band." Ronni was reluctant but relented. The boys went to Tim's house while we gussied up.

After a little coaxing and a bottle of wine, we convinced her to join us for a girls' night out.

Ronni was on life's bumpy road. She moved to Vermont from Long Island with Bruce, her long-time and devoted boyfriend. After a few years in Vermont, their paths drifted apart—then it got complicated. Leigh invited Ronni to stay with her. Soon after, Biff rented the apartment above them. He was in a long-term same-sex relationship with Grayson, a successful and wealthy Playboy cartoonist. They lived well in an amazing house on a small mill pond, in a picturesque dell at the base of a small mountain. The house was decorated with eclectic original artwork, from hundreds of artists, covering every square inch of wall space. Exotic rugs and sculptures covered the floors.

Biff questioned his sexuality and moved out of the house. Their parting words were harsh but open-ended. Is everyone still with me? Biff and Ronni struck up a conversation when providence put them at the same table during a busy breakfast rush at Carney's Restaurant. Ronni stirred something he never felt for a woman and she was intrigued with him—intersecting rebounds. Ronni also stayed with Mitch and Ginny for a while but Biff, a homosexual, was unwelcome in the born-again Christian house. He lived in the barn for a few weeks. Once, while hanging out in the barn, Craig spied a bottle of white wine that had already been cracked. He picked up the bottle, removed the cork, and as he took a sip, he asked Biff, "What kind of wine is this?"

Biff jumped up screaming, "Nooooo! That's my pee bottle!" Craig spit out the fluid and ran to the hose bib and flushed his mouth for a long time. Biff came from wealth and his recent lover was wealthier so he never had to work. You might say he was a kept man. Life seemed good for Biff and Ronni. They got married and moved into the mill house. Maybe it was getting his first real blisters, doing chores, or maybe he missed being able to buy whatever he wanted. Perhaps returning to the mill house reminded him of his life before Ronni. A few months later, he realized he was gay, and moved back with Grayson.

Craig interjected, "We were delayed! Oh, and thanks for bringing up the pee wine story. I feel like I should rinse my mouth again." He took a sip from the wine sack and spit it out. "The locomotive crossed the road pulling a string of cars over a mile long. Twenty minutes later, the caboose of the long, slow-moving freight train cleared the road. We watched the sole light on the yellow caboose wink out of sight as the train disappeared around a bend." Unlike railroad crossings in populated areas, there are no crossing gates or lights in most rural areas. The trains themselves have lights on the front of the locomotive and the back of the caboose, but few, if any, in between. While the caboose's light faded out of sight, the women were in Tara's Bluebird, hurtling west, anticipating a night of partying.

"It was a moonless night," Tara continued. "Swaths of stars faded in and out behind a line of fast low clouds. We were passing a bottle of wine from front seat to back, singing and speeding on Route 105 with a good buzz. The road turned into a blind curve and everything went black. In an instant, the windshield was filled with the broadside of a boxcar exploding into view. The boxcars were all dark, it was like the train was invisible. My headlights shined on the slow-moving freight train a few yards away. I cut the wheel hard to the left to avoid plowing head-on into the train. The car went airborne as we sailed over the embankment. The Bluebird landed nose down, perpendicular to the road from where it launched.

No one was hurt beyond a bump or bruise. There's that saying again: God protects drunks and babies. We were loose of mind and body and rolled with the impact. Struggling out of the car, I was dazed; we staggered to our feet. The stars spinning around my head mingled with the twinkles above. When my vision cleared, all thoughts of partying in St. Albans were banished to the realization of the moment. There was nothing and no one else anywhere in sight.

We climbed up the embankment and watched the rest of the train chug its way west. Near total darkness was interrupted by an occasional spark, lighting an otherwise invisible freight car clickety-clacking across the road. We sat down on the rim of the embankment hoping that when the caboose passed, help might be in sight. At first look, we only saw fields of cow corn dashing our hopes until Ronni noticed a light in the distance. Dusting ourselves off, we walked, limped, danced, sang, smoked and drank our way to a farmhouse a mile away."

Craig finished the story. "We jumped to action when we got the call and picked them up twenty minutes later. We made sure they were all okay and marveled at the vertical Rambler, then returned to Leigh's apartment to tend wounds and de novo partying.

We returned at first light with a tow truck and pulled the Bluebird out of the ditch. The Bluebird would fly again with a few new scratches and dents."

"Mom, did the Bluebird really fly? I wish I was there."

"Yes it did, and no you don't, honey. That was very scary."

## Somewhere on I 89

Hugh and Fern woke up in Burlington. They couldn't get a ride out of the city last night, so they grabbed a few hours sleep behind some rocks near the onramp. The ferry trip was awesome, catching the last light of the day and the lingering colors in the sky over Lake Champlain. Unfortunately, there was no sign of Champ. Hugh told Fern about the legendary Lake Champlain sea monster and they scanned the water for the entire trip. They brushed grass from their clothes and went back to the road. No sign this time, thumbs out; they were on their way to St. Albans, at first light.

## No Return

I asked Skye about Sally, who I hoped would also return. She gave me the bad news; Sally made up with her boyfriend and she would never return. Well, good for her. Sally asked Skye to tell me she did plan to come back. I sat back by the fire remembering being awakened from a dream that was not a dream. The crackling fire returned me to the present; thoughts of Brook came to mind.

## 8

# COED COMPANION

*"Don't walk behind me; I may not lead.*
*Don't walk in front of me; I may not follow.*
*Just walk beside me and be my friend."*
*~ Albert Camus*

### Summer 76—Johnson College

A few weeks after my second Dairy Festival, I learned that Johnson College was offering classes on Vermont's ecology and field biology. I was all about trees, plants and wildflowers. With my knapsack packed, I set off to Johnson for two weeks at the dormitory. I had been to many dormitories as a visitor, often the girls' dorm, but never was I in a dorm of my own. My short-lived college time was at a commuter college. The dorm experience was interesting. We each had our own rooms, but the rooms were assigned at random without regard to sex. Young men and women shared the same hall and used the same bathroom. The bathroom was huge with private toilet stalls almost like separate rooms. There was a row of about a dozen showers with opaque glass doors, which offered some privacy. At first, everyone was shy. But as the time progressed, cautious proprietary behavior lapsed. At times a young woman would step out of the shower with a towel around her waist but walked around with breasts bare. Some more adventurous men and women stepped out of the shower naked before wrapping themselves in the towel. It was like being at the swimming hole. It was the mid-seventies, after all.

Studying a field guide was great; I owned several. However, it was wonderful to have an instructor who knew her stuff. On one occasion we drove up to Hazen's Notch, which is a mountain pass. Our instructor Marjorie was in great shape, about five-ten, with a svelte athletic build, mesmerizing light blue eyes, with long blonde hair, pulled back in a braid. Wearing cut off shorts, a button down shirt with the shirt tails tied in a knot, exposing firm tanned abs, she was shod in LL Bean hiking boots. Describing every plant and tree that we saw, she led us up the mountain. "The trail we are on is running through a climax forest, consisting of deciduous trees, including yellow and paper birch, wild cherry, maple, beech, ash and oak. This mountain was once covered with coniferous softwood like fir, spruce, pine and cedar, which were cut down by earlier Vermonters who clear cut most of the state. This is a hardwood forest now, but stands of evergreen trees still exist up near the lake."

Our destination, Sterling Pond, was an alpine lake which I thought was just a lake at high altitude. When we arrived at the lake, steep cliffs appeared to rise up from the shimmering crystal clear blue lake water. Huge swaths of coniferous trees grew up to the water's edge. Their reflections looked back at them from the surface of the water.

Sterling Pond

What a treat it was to have plants pointed out and described by someone so knowledgeable. We walked along the alpine lake for a while, then started our return trip back down the mountain. The group was spread out and then a young girl, maybe seventeen, five-foot-five, with flawless porcelain white skin and an elven face with long brilliant flaxen hair down past her waist. stopped to look at some wild flowers and asked Marjorie what they were. Before Marjorie reached her, I said "I think they're painted trillium."

"It's beautiful," she said. "I have seen purple trillium, but this is new to me. What's your name? I'm Brooke."

"Bob. Good to meet you," I said, shaking hands.

Marjorie stepped up and said, "He's right, but the official name is Trillium undulatum." We walked together the remainder of the trip down the mountain. The rest of the group moved ahead.

The next day in the cafeteria, I was sitting alone, eating a Vermont cheddar cheese and sprout sandwich with sliced apple. I noticed Brooke as she came in with her own lunch and I waved hello. Her face lit up as she walked over and sat with me. We talked for hours, and every day after that. She was a vegetarian but more strict than my on-again-off-again self. I told her about the farm, and we talked about plants, animals, life in general, and where we each came from. I mentioned that we were going to raise rabbits for food she had a hard time with the idea. She asked me, "Have you ever heard the screams of rabbits about to be slaughtered? Well, I have—last year on a school field trip. Those screams still haunt my dreams. I became vegetarian right after that." The imagery of Brooke's story was so vivid that rabbit screams played in my mind for a long time. Brooke told me she was a high school senior. She did not drink, do drugs or eat meat. Well, we had one thing in common. I just turned twenty-one and thought I was too old for anything romantic, but we did hold hands while walking around campus and shared a good night kiss.

Ents of Old

A few days later we walked through an old cemetery, boasting Revolutionary and Civil War monuments and weather-worn tombstones dating back to the 1700's. The trail from the cemetery led us to a stand of virgin trees that were over two hundred years old, which were part of the cemetery once, maybe that's why they survived. Their trunks were massive; at that time they were the largest I had ever seen. Brooke, Marjorie, Sheila and Gunter, two other classmates, and I with arms stretched out, holding hands, were unable to complete the circumference of the behemoth. There were dozens of such trees reaching over one hundred feet toward the sky. One of these behemoths had fallen over. It was like an elevated superhighway spanning the primordial forest.

We moved through the forest and into a swampy area, a cranberry bog. Marjorie explained, "A bog is an accumulation of dead plant material, often sphagnum moss known as peat. The peat is several feet thick and floats over the surface of the water.

"Look down. You're standing on a raft of peat." Sheila and a girl named Jenny jumped back. "Don't worry it's six feet thick and anchored to land. You'll be safe," Marjorie advised. "Keep walking out to the middle but stay away from the edge, it's only a few inches thick out there. Those low plants along the edge are the cranberry bushes that give the bog its name. They thrive in acidic soil, like the blueberry bushes to the left."

I was saddened when the class ended. I met some good people, but leaving Brooke was hard. We hugged and kissed—she gave me her phone number. Without a phone, I could not reciprocate. I would see her again.

## Dairy Day 1977

In anticipation of Dairy Day 1977, my last, it was time to call the number in my wallet; time to contact Brooke. I hadn't spoken with Brooke in a few months, since we had no phone. Brooke came up to the Phunee Farm a couple of times. We explored the land and rock-walked the Lucas Brook. She, a country girl, was used to skinny dipping; but she was still in high school at the time, and when we reached the waterfall we decided not to take a swim.

"One night we should go skinny dipping in Lake Carmi," she said.

With a swallowed disappointment I responded, "Yeah, maybe later this summer." We lingered and cuddled by the waterfall, then walked hand in hand back to the house, taking the brook trail. As we walked along the trail, sunlight broke through the canopy, haloing her flaxen blond hair in ethereal light, glowing like an elven princess. Platonic can be very hard. I saw Brooke a few times after that. There were sparks, but no ignition. We remained good friends.

We were still worlds apart. She graduated from high school a few towns west of Enosburg Falls. I left the farm earlier than the rest of the Phunee farmers and drove for about forty-five minutes to pick her up. She lived with her family, so I got out and went to the door to meet her father, Jerry. He was taller than me and forty pounds heavier, with a dark complexion and a thick head of dark hair. When her mother came to the door, it was easy to see which genes dominated in Brooke. She introduced herself as Leslie, and she looked much like Brooke with the exception of green eyes and large breasts. Being cute I said, "Hi, Leslie, I didn't know Brooke had a sister. Is your mother home?" She beamed at the compliment and from my smile and demeanor, she knew that I knew. We headed to my car waiting in the driveway, with Jerry and Leslie watching from the door.

The Enosburg Dairy Festival had indeed arrived. It was June, and like everyone else around, we were here to shake off the gloomy winter and have fun welcoming the fertile summer. We made it to Enosburg where the festival was in full swing. We ran into my crowd who were already aglow with the nectar of the day. I wandered around with Brooke, going from event to event, stopping to listen to music or dance. We checked out the winning bull and tasted samples for the pie contest. At some point, we met up with Brooke's friends who looked like little kids, young and naive. I was only four years older, but lived a much different life. Many of her friends did not imbibe, but some had paper cups with sudsy beer.

The previous year at the festival, all of us Phunee farmers got wasted. Deep down that was part of my plan. However, Brooke was as straight as an arrow. A few of us were dancing around close to the bluegrass band and when the band took a break, conversation somehow shifted to raising rabbits. I could hear the rabbit screams through the expression on Brooke's face. I thought about our agreement to raise animals. We set out to be old school farmers, but being vegetarian farmers proved to be a conundrum. The scales had tipped from the Zen spirituality of "harm nothing" to the real world of animal husbandry. I was reluctant, because when you raise animals, if you're in for a penny you're in for a pound.

I watched all of my friends dancing and hooting, beer in hand, a buzz growing, while I was sitting around with Brooke's friends, watching the festivities. The bluegrass music had everyone dancing a circling hoedown. As I watched the dancing circle, I noticed a dude dancing with a wild-haired boy, dancing crazier than us with frenetic moves like a Whirling Dervish. I led Brooke in their direction. We struck up a conversation. When we took a break, Brooke went back to the table but I stayed, talking about the Phunee Farm and the extension we were building. The "Dervish" told us he was a carpenter, and offered his help. I took one hit from the pipe he offered. He said he had a camper and could sleep in the driveway. I wandered off to find Brooke. Plans were made to meet him at the farm the following afternoon.

I looked around the table, at the high school kids, most having just graduated, and thought, "These people sure are young." I wanted a joint; I wanted a beer; I wanted an adventure. I would get up every now and again and wander around, meeting up with Tara, Hugh or other friends from Enosburg or communards we met from all around Northern Vermont. On each trip, I found time for sip of something or a puff of something. I was getting a buzz on. Things got a bit melancholy between Brooke and me—after the memory of rabbit screams, me getting buzzed and the call of the wild.

She knew I was getting buzzed and she knew I wanted to go to a party at Tom's and I knew she did not want to go. I made sure she had a ride home and I went to the party at Tom's. Brooke was with good friends and in good hands; nonetheless, I always felt bad about leaving Brooke, who I never saw again. "Cad" comes to mind. We were still worlds apart.

## 9

# CAMPFIRE TALES

*"Light a campfire and everyone is a storyteller."*
*~ Joseph Gebbes*

We lingered by the fire for hours telling stories. Craig and I talked about our adventure upstream and our cross country misadventure. They both winced and shivered when we relayed the story of the spider. There's something about spiders. We agreed that walking through the forest at night was difficult, especially barefoot. The fire was going strong with plenty of wood to keep it going. We told them of the blackberry bramble and we were all so buzzed we almost went back there to find some—munchies.

### Homebrew

Skye cracked-open the last quart. "This is powerful stuff. It's like white lightning but smoother and fruitier."

"Yeah, we got the recipe from the monks, but it was a group effort. We made about thirty gallons, mixing hops, malt, Karo syrup and citrus fruits. We saved or scrounged brown and green quart bottles, which lined the porch window for a while. The afternoon sun shining through them looked very cool."

"Yeah, we saw those bottles when we pulled up. Fae thought the green light was magical. She danced around in the light cast on her dress, singing, 'I'm dancing with the fairies.'"

"We used that vintage bottle capper we got at the auction in Enosburg. Tara, do you remember that potluck box we bid on for five dollars?" I asked.

"We wasted a few bottle caps until we got the hang of using the capper," Craig added.

Three things happened over the months we waited for the beer to finish fermenting. Poorly sealed bottles rudely announced themselves. A loud pop resounded as fermenting beer under extreme pressure forced the cap careening off the metal wrapped chimney, ricocheting with a metallic pinging then twanged or thudded between the ceiling and closet walls. In an instant, the smell of citrusy fermenting homebrew permeated the air. We lost a few bottles this way and, harsh as it was, we salvaged what was left in each bottle. The second thing would be our impatience. After checking the bottles for the least amount of sediment, opened the murky "green" beer and poured it through cheesecloth into our waiting glasses—good buzz, mouth-puckering harsh sour taste. Our patience was rewarded when the beer made it to the end of the cycle. The liquid cleared to a delightful amber hue with a fruity nose.

It was as powerful as moonshine hidden behind a citrusy bouquet. One quart could knock down your average big drinker. In fairness, Tara and Skye, both big drinkers, had no problem. Craig tried to keep up with the women. I was a lightweight and took small sips.

Fae fell back to sleep wrapped in a cocoon of blankets. Tara arranged the nest, a safe distance from the fire, soon after we met up with them. Fae wanted to stay up and sit around the fire, but she succumbed to the sandman once again. Her little eyelids fluttered, struggling to stay open, then—pleasant dreams.

## Water Witching

There are many forms of divination, from tea leaves to entrails, but one at least has gone mainstream in the country. I witnessed the use of a divining (water witching) rod to find water. It's something almost anyone can accomplish, but some are much more gifted than others. The word rod is used in the broadest sense. It can be as simple as a supple branch from a tree, willow or other such tree that likes water.

I met a few people proficient at the practice. One guy made a fancy divining rod that was carved and honed smooth. I saw another guy cut a branch about two feet long from a nearby tree and split the length of the branch leaving about ten inches intact. In each case, they were hired to find water. The first guy was hired to find a leak in a water line buried under ground, and the other was tasked with finding a good spot for a spring.

Their process was similar. The first guy took hold of his fancy diving rod and held it in front, as he walked the length of the area where the water line was buried. As he walked, he held the rod lightly, in his hands, and to my amazement as he approached what turned out to be the source of the leak the rod moved in his hand. When he was over the exact spot of the leak, the rod was pulled by an unseen force toward the ground pivoting in his hands. They dug a hole at the spot indicated and found the leak in the old pipe caused by a large root crushing it against a huge rock five feet underground. In the other case, the diviner was an amateur but had a good knack for finding water. He took the simple branch he cut from a nearby willow tree and, with one end of the split branch in each hand, he rotated his hands so that the tip of the branch rotated toward him covering the full arch of a circle. He walked forward with the rod in what seemed like an uncomfortable position. The rod started to move forthwith, but slightly. He said, "Yep, you got water here but it's deep. If you want it here, you're gonna need to drill down far." He kept walking and circling the area, the whole time the rod moved almost imperceptibly in his hand. After about an hour, the homeowner was giving up, and was almost resolved to bring in someone to sink a modern pipe.

He continued walking, now outside the original target area. The rod started to move up and down, as the diviner moved his arms side to side. I was thinking that his hands must be cramping up from holding the stick so long. When he reached a small stand of poplar trees, the rod shot to the ground, pulling the diviner's arms with it. He said, "Dig here about five feet and you will have your spring." While the diviner sat back and watched, we all started digging. When we reached about three feet, the ground was wet, and after another foot, the water rose up to fill the hole almost reaching ground level. The diviner was wrong; it was four feet down.

## Illegal Alien

Jim was at the Phunee Farm for a few months when he told us that his cousin from England was having trouble getting into the country. Geoffrey couldn't get a visa because of a burglary conviction. Jim's mother begged him to try and find a way for his cousin to attend an anniversary party for his grandparents. Jim knew Geoffrey could get into Canada and asked if there was a way for him to get to us, since we were so close to the border.

Jim's story sounded plausible, but it was hard to tell with him. We played along and researched a route for him to take. We rode over to Sutton and went to the organic food store, then explored the area. Jim took note of the route and contacted his mother with the info. No big deal, his cousin would be staying for a week. Despite this, we tried to keep our distance, when Jim got word of his cousin's arrival in Montreal.

The whole idea of this was intriguing, naughty and maybe even nefarious. Jim was, after all, smuggling a foreigner into the country—one with a criminal record who had already been blocked by the State Department, no less. It was 1976, and the fear of enemy combatants or terrorists was beyond anyone's vernacular. Intriguing indeed. You might think it was something out of a spy novel how the arrangements were made. Jim received a letter from his mother that was coded with flight information about when his cousin would arrive in Montreal. A time and code word for speaking to Geoffrey in Canada followed. Further cloak and dagger information would be received when he got to Sutton. The absence of a phone line at the Phunee Farm was a complication. Jim planned to be near a phone booth at designated times. Remember them? The Richford Luncheonette had two classic phone booths with wood framed glass doors set into the far wall that offered privacy. Besides, they served good food.

When the call came two days later, curiosity got the better of me and I accompanied Jim on his foray along the border to seek out his cousin. Much of the route was occupied private property but we had directed Jim's cousin to a three mile stretch that was a mixture of dense forest and overgrown pasture land. We didn't know where he would emerge or how long it would take him to find his way through the Canadian forest. Geoffrey was instructed to purchase a map at the bookstore in Sutton. The same Canadian road map we bought to plot his course. It was not the best map, but we narrowed the area where he would emerge to two or three miles.

We drove from the farm to the East Richford Slide Road, then turned around and repeated the route. Still treating this excursion as a spy novel, we didn't want to appear suspicious. So on the second trip down the West Jay Road, we went all the way to East Richford and gassed up at the ancient gas station. Returning from our third trip, we saw a sandy haired fellow wearing an English walking hat, a torn tweed jacket and English style slacks, that looked a bit worse for wear. He was lean and almost six feet tall with a knapsack on his back. He looked out of place on this dirt road, which drifted into and out of Canada. Way to fit in, bro!

Geoffrey was walking on the West Jay Road for about twenty minutes before we met up with him. As we approached, we noticed the scratches on his hands and face. Blood was still oozing from the deepest cuts. He had emerged just east of the old schoolhouse along a wooded section of the road. Our dead reckoning route worked well, but we calculated a spot further east.

"You look like you've been through the war, Geoff. What happened?" Jim said as we greeted him on the road. Geoffrey responded, "I had a lovely trip to Sutton. I bought the map, like you asked, then walked a few kilometers before I reached the dirt road that led to the border. I was approaching the turn for the dirt road when I spotted two Mounties cantering toward me. Before they noticed me, I dashed into the woods and dropped down behind a huge boulder. I watched them move along but they didn't go far. The blokes dismounted and stopped for tea. I was between the road and border and out of sight in the forest. When I moved away from them I almost fell off a ledge. I climbed down a steep cliff and got banged up some. I saw the road while I was coming down. I ran for the road and was gobsmacked. Ripped my jacket, I did. And look at my hands. I got scratched up."

His last obstacle was a dense thicket of thorny black raspberries. We were all relieved to put this clandestine episode behind us. He spent the night at the Phunee Farm and left with Jim the next day. As promised, he returned to the Phunee Farm with Jim two weeks later, who drove him to Canada.

## Blowdown

"Did we ever tell you the story about the blowdown?" I asked. "Two years before moving to the farm, a storm blew through the valley from the northeast. The storm triggered a microburst, also known as a blowdown, which sent powerful storm winds straight down, crushing and snapping acres of trees like the hand of God smiting the deciduous. A few hundred yards beyond the power line cut, the terrain was surreal. Hundreds of twisted, cracked and mangled trees were entangled by an unimaginable force of nature, extending beyond the horizon. We weaved our way through the carnage, walking along the branches and trunks of the fallen trees, for a few hundred yards high above the forest floor. We were like kids in a new playground, exploring an alien world. Traveling through this mangled jungle gym, we climbed high above the understory walking or shimmying up the severely canted trees leaning into and through each other. We sat looking down, high above the forest floor, smoking joints and enjoying the sunny spring day. This was the first form of tree walking we developed.

## Carnival

Tara told us about her carnival adventures. She went on to say her uncle had a knife-throwing act at a downstate carnival and sometimes with a traveling circus. At fourteen, already full-figured, her hips filled out the sequined leotard she wore. Accentuating her thin waist, the leotard was cut high along her upper thighs making her lean young legs appear longer than they were; seductive and clad in nylon stockings she cut quite a figure; calves and ass tightened by her sparkled high heeled shoes. The red shimmering leotard, cut low for her age, rested beneath a sparkling bright sequin vest highlighting her ample cleavage. Tara was the target for the knife throwing act. Her uncle made her a sexual object looking older than she was. Hey Rube, there is nothing like a beautiful girl masquerading as a woman to attract money from passersby's and gawking older men.

The show was successful and Tara made much more money than she could have at home. Her parents, believing they were doing a good thing, sent her to the uncle to work the summer and school holidays. The uncle, a talented knife thrower, had nicked her once or twice with his patented, trademarked knives. Good money. He gained notoriety in Europe, dazzling crowned heads with his projectile prowess. Tara was robbed of much of her adolescence, and with it, her innocence. She went on to describe that her uncle was a wretch of man, who plied her with drugs and alcohol and used her in ways no uncle should. Seeds of addiction took root in her life.

We sat quietly for a long time as the exciting first part of her story had us all in the thrall of childhood dreams and the magic of the carnival. The steadiness and nerve she displayed as a young teenager—to have long sharp knives thrown at her. This was compounded by the knowledge that the remarkable skill of the knife thrower was often impeded by his drunkenness, as he let the well-balanced knife fly. The magnificent image of this experience was brought crashing down by the lecherous nature of the uncle; his addiction was not enough for him, he needed to visit it on the innocence of his niece. The thought of this intrusion on a beautiful young girl, now just four years older, sitting with us by the fire, hung in the air; we leaned over to hug her.

When the pall cleared the air, I changed the subject, turned toward Craig and said, "Let's tell them about Faught Mills."

## 10

## FAUGHT MILLS

*If you cut down a forest, it doesn't matter how many sawmills you have if there are no more trees.*
*~ Susan Hugh*

The beavers were active since a big storm blew through a day earlier. Sitting in the lower level of the barn, the cross-buck barn doors opened, the view of Pinnacle Mountain was obscured by the heavy rain. Windswept water battered the house and flowed down the driveway like a river. The staccato pounding of rain on the roof was thunderous. A barrage of blue-white bolts of lightning danced through the valley like a nature-choreographed laser light show. A resounding crack and shower of sparks down valley ignited the conflagration of an elm tree struck by a bolt of lightning—a magnificent crescendo for the night show.

The volume of water falling from the skies that night overwhelmed Lucas Brook and flooded part of the beavers' dam, washing away part of it and pulling at the logs that made up their home. A testament to the engineering prowess of the beavers, the dam and lodge were damaged, but stayed intact. The water level was so high and the raging water was so powerful, the force of the water moved the old bus a little, wedging it up against a grotto of trees that saved it from being washed downstream.

The beaver pond was bigger than we had ever seen it. It was mid-morning and it was unusual to see the beavers during the day. We kept our distance, but our view was better than National Geographic. There were two that we could see, their light brown fur plastered to their bodies as they swam with sticks in their mouths held in place by large teeth. One was pushing sticks into the dam to slow the water from rushing out. The other was swimming in and out of the lodge bringing out sticks and forcing them into the upstream side of the lodge. Most of the dwelling was underwater with air-lock-like passages opening into something like a moonpool, effective in keeping predators out. The two beavers, working together, packed mud with their broad paddle-like tails sealing the breach in the dam. They never stopped, "busy as a beaver."

Beaver Pong and Lodge - Lucas Brook

We wanted to see what changes Lucas wrought on the valley. Prior to the storm, Lucas Brook was quiet beyond the beaver dam. The beavers had diverted a portion of the water, flooding the area below route 105 when they created their pond. The main branch of the Lucas, moving volumes of water, sodden from the rain, was raging. When the Lucas jumped its banks, it carved a new channel through the valley, excavating portions of the Lucas Flats. We found our next surprise a few dozen yards downstream. The raging brook unearthed a wooden sluice, surprisingly intact, which we found close to an exposed foundation of a large old building. A few feet further down was another smaller foundation and others became apparent as we progressed further downstream. It was then that we noticed it, nestled half in water and half buried in the dirt, a hulking rusted boiler tank from an old steam locomotive. We were intrigued. What is a railroad locomotive doing here?"

The way the foundations were clustered together, the larger foundation in the midst of the other buildings must have been a business, suggesting this must have been an old settlement. Craig made sketches of the things we found. Energized by the discovery, we devised a plan to find out more. Somebody must know about this. We questioned our neighbor Cedric, who remembered stories about an old saw mill down on the flats a long time ago. Another neighbor told us that the old locomotive steam boiler was carted from a railroad yard down Burlington way. We were onto a discovery, so Craig and I collaborated on an archeological project for our Vermont history class.

Craig picked it up, "We followed up with word of mouth contacts and our trail led to several octogenarians, and after a bit more sleuthing, we met Jake, a wizened white-haired man in his nineties. In all of Jake's years, he never left the state and never went further than Enosburg Falls— remarkable. We told him of our quest and were delighted when he said, "That old place, I haven't thought about that in years. I used to work there when I was a teenager." Looking at each other in triumph, we sat back smiling, while Jake told us the tale of the saw mill.

"Back about ninety or so years ago, a fella named Thomas Faught (pronounced Foy) was logging the Lucas valley. I'm thinking that Ole Tom Faught built the mill in 1885. He was a real go-getter. After his saw mill, he built two rooming houses and a general store for the crew and even a factory to mill the rough cut boards into finished lumber. He did real good 'cause he was the first person in town to own an automobile, but that was many years later.

I remember my daddy saying what a big deal it was bringing the equipment in. The blades for the saw mill and all the other machinery were mighty heavy. It was like a parade of wagons, most pulled by two teams of oxen. The whole town was out to watch. I was just a tyke; mostly I remember stories. Three of them wagons were loaded high with these big wooden crates. One of 'em had big flat crates standing on edge in the wagon; that one was pulled by three teams of oxen. The last cart was the strangest; this Faught feller trucked in a big old locomotive engine steam boiler. Us townsfolk all stood there wonner'n what he'd be doin' with that big old black steam boiler. Wasn't I mighty surprised later that summer when he used it to build a bridge? You see, they needed to get their crews over to the other side of Lucas Brook so they could get to the timber up there on the steep slope of North Jay Mountain. What a sight that was. What was I saying? Oh yeah, well, it wasn't so easy getting those wagons over to the Lucas Flats. The trip along the river weren't bad, but moved real slow. Most of us followed along. Twere just a few miles anyway, and them-thar wagons didn't move so fast.

The slide was awful steep and they almost lost one of the wagons when the oxen bucked. Good thing the whole town was watching because the men ran over to help push it over the crest. I was still a kid in my short pants, but my folks let me stay up to follow the wagons, being it was such a big thing."

Craig stopped for a slug of home-brew, so I continued. "Jake went on to tell us that he had worked at the saw mill until sometime around 'the end of the first big war,' as he put it. By then all the trees in the area were cut down.

The men worked long, hard hours clearing the mountains with broad axes and bucksaws and hauling the logs down the mountain with teams of oxen. The finished lumber was loaded onto oxcarts and west to the railroad depot in East Richford. It was a dangerous place to work and a lot of guys got hurt real bad and a couple got themselves kilt. There's a cemetery out there somewhere."

Craig added, "We looked for signs of a cemetery and found it behind a stand of birches straddling the border near the Slide road. It was overgrown and many of the old tombstones were broken or knocked over." Jake continued, "They dammed up the brook and made a millpond so they could float the logs into the mill. The dam diverted water into a spillway then into a sluice that turned the big paddle wheel that ran the saw mill. My first job was helping to build the spillway and sluice."

My turn again, "By our figuring, that dam would have flooded out that hollow where the beaver dam is today and could have flooded all the way upstream past the old bus.

Jake's memory was primed and he was pouring out stories of the time, "The mill workers made about eight dollars a week. They got paid in supplies from Tom's store but got some cash to boot. Most of 'em spent a dollar at Queen Lil's place over in East Richford. See, it was built right smack on the border. The whole area was dry back then and Lil made a fortune selling liquor. Liquor was available in other places like the Prince of Wales over in Abercom, Canada; fancy place that was. Some of the men would go to a shack on the border called "Bucket of Blood." Queen Lil's real name was Lillian Minor Shipley, and in 1910, she restored a three-story hotel-saloon that straddled the border with Canada. Men would go in on the state side and do their drinking on the Canadian side; nothing the government could do about it. When she had trouble with the law stopping regular deliveries of booze, she had a pipe laid that brought liquor underground to her building where it could be bottled for sale.

But, you see, Queen Lil's was the only brothel. If you wanted women with your booze, you went to Queen Lil's. When she moved back to Richford from Boston, she brought them painted ladies with her; but she also painted a few local women. She had a wild personality and packed a pistol to keep everyone in line. With her thirty rooms, bar and restaurant, she supplied women and song to the men of Faught Mills and the old Baker's Mill in East Richford. I'll bet you boys didn't know that back in the 1920's Richford was like Las Vegas on the border. It was a hopping place back in the day."

We told Jake that we were living at the old Mackenzie Farm; he went on with a sly smile. "One of the men who helped him set up the mill brought his family over from Swanton. He wanted to start up a dairy farm. Years of logging had cleared the forest all the way up to the end of Lucas Valley. Mackenzie's farmhouse and barn were built with some of the first lumber milled at the new saw mill. The whole house was sided with the wood from the packing crates used to protect the saw blades and other machinery. That's the house you young folks are living in."

Queen Lil's

Craig went on. "Jake had given us more information than we expected, and now we had learned something new about the Phunee Farm and about the foundations we discovered. He also gave us a circa 1905 photograph of him, as a youth, posing in front of Tom Faught's sawmill. We mapped out the old settlement as part of our project, when we get back to the house I'll show them to you." We both chimed in, "We had rediscovered Faught Mills. Cool."

Craig finished the story in a narrative. The mill kept growing and so did the population of Lucas Valley. Our closest neighbor, Cedric Morse's grand dad, was one of the first pioneers to settle, along with Gross and Beret. Back around the turn of the century, there were hundreds of people living in our valley. Most of the small farms were bought by the Gross and Morse families, who are still farming today. The rest went to Atlas Plywood or realtors. West Jay Road, "The Slide," was the only way through until the state put in route 105 in 1959.

## Three AM

Fae was still fast asleep; we were all getting tired but were still pumped up from the day's adventure and motivated by the stories. We considered just staying down at the beach until daylight, which was now a few hours away, but the chill of the damp night air took hold. It was not cold by any measure, and probably warm up at the house, but the chill in the air at the damp beach drilled into our bones. We built up the fire with our remaining wood, then Skye broke out the bottle of Jack. The sour mash had a way of warming the bones. The fire and the bourbon helped, but we slipped our clothes on to get more comfortable. Craig wished he had his guitar, but we sang a few campfire songs we remembered from scouts anyway. Corny.

Now dressed, we spread out for more firewood. I got back to the fire first with an armload of wood, Tara stayed back to tend the fire and check on Fae, in her blanket nest. Craig and Skye showed up a few minutes later dragging what appeared to be a small dead tree. We were set with wood for the rest of the night, cozied around the fire and told other tales.

I finished building up the fire since it was still a few hours until dawn, stories were told, and the lingering effects of the potent home brew and the bourbon capstone crept up on all of us and took its toll. One by one, we drifted off to sleep huddled together sitting near the fire, holding each other up with counter pressure like a human roman arch.

Maybe it was staring at the fire, or the stories told. Perhaps it was the daylong reminiscing, but ironically, warm as it was, I dreamed of my first night at the Phunee Farm.

11

# ARRIVAL–FIRST NIGHT

*"It is the life of the crystal, the architect of the flake, the fire of the frost, the soul of the sunbeam.
This crisp winter air is full of it."
~ John Burroughs*

I watched in disbelief as blood dripped onto my blanket. Anticipating the start of an adventure, I awoke snug in my sleeping bag beneath a space blanket and a pile of other blankets, knowing the encompassing warmth would be short-lived. Sleep still clouding my eyes, throat dry, thirsty, I reached for the glass of snow-melted water unfinished from the night before. "Ouch! What the hell was that?" I pulled my arm back, reacting to a sudden stinging pain. Looking at my nightstand, I could see the shattered water glass-shards tinged red, the glass-shaped ice, colored rose-pink. Blood dripping onto the blanket froze on contact with the wool. Time slowed; my arm, exposed for a moment, paled from the extreme cold. Exhaled breath condensed to frost, dropping imperceptible ice crystals to the floor like tingling glass. The wound began to gush.

It was the dead of winter in February 1975; my first night at the farm, frigid air capturing the room in an eerie stillness, my bedroom twenty degrees below zero. Frost painted the window panes with snowflake-like tendrils, obscuring the view of Pinnacle Mountain, distant to the northwest in Canada. It was past eight AM; the sun still below the eastern mountain peaks had yet to dawn. Here in the valley, daylight was slow to arrive and quick to leave. Gusting wind tormented the glass, interrupting the silence.

Throbbing pain brought my awareness to the blood gushing from my hand. Stirred to action I sat up. The loud crackling of the frozen space blanket harmonized with the rattling window as I pushed back the blankets. Unzipping my mummy bag, icy cold air rushed into the void. Standing, I caught my foot on the tight confines of the tapered sleeping bag. Stumbling, I stood naked in the bitter-cold room, awake, the haze of sleep instantly expelled from my eyes. Cold as it was and beginning to shiver, I wrapped a rag around my hand. Exposure to the severe cold caused the blood to slow before I finished. Dizzy, my shivering increased; fumbling with stiff fingers, I struggled to wrap the wound. The rag reddened with blood as I dressed into my thermal underwear, jeans, shirt and sweater. The shivering became spasmodic. Pulling on my thermal socks and military-issued combat boots, I struggled to ready myself for my first day. Sitting back down on the bed, I pulled the blankets over my shoulders until the shivering and dizziness passed and drifted into thought.

## Igloo and Snowflakes

We conditioned ourselves for this brutal Vermont experience with winter camping, long before our northern adventure was conceived. A year earlier, we camped at a favorite spot outside of Claryville, New York, after we hiked two miles into the Catskill forest through knee-deep snow, dragging our supplies on two sleds. At four degrees below zero the grenadine for tequila sunrises froze solid. Compared to my first Vermont night, this retrospective experience proved to be balmy. Camped at the fork of the Donovan Brook and Neversink River we pulled large sheets of ice from the frozen brook and constructed an igloo-like structure with a campfire in the center sheltered from the blustering wind. Backlit by the full moon, our ice igloo shone with a translucent blue-gray luminescence, in stark contrast to the surrounding darkness. Trips like this taught us how to survive in a cold-weather environment. Winter camping, much like my first night in Vermont, is counter-intuitive. When sleeping at night, the fewer clothes the better. My brother Danny and his friend Ted were camping with us, but they piled on extra clothes before climbing into the sleeping bag. Big mistake, they were freezing all night because the frigid night air took advantage of the sweat that built up within their clothes. Neither of them had decent gear as I discovered when Danny pulled out a few blankets, one of them with an electrical cord. They crawled out of their makeshift sleeping bags hours before me and started the fire. I had stripped down to my underwear and was toasty warm all night. Danny discovered that the eggs had frozen solid. In frustration he threw one at a tree knocking off a big chunk of bark. The remaining eggs thawed, I woke to a hot fire, breakfast and coffee waiting.

I witnessed the biggest snowflakes of my life on that trip. Some were several inches in diameter, each with its unique six-sided geometric design; an indelible memory.

## Warmed

As I warmed under the blanket, I attempted to lace up my boots—no easy feat. Blood seeping from the makeshift bandage ran down my finger and dripped onto the floor. My head clearing, body heat reestablished, boots unlaced, I gave up trying. Shedding my blankets, I went downstairs. The house was familiar yet foreign. I walked into the kitchen and found my first aid kit inside my knapsack; I was a Boy Scout, prepared, and trained for medical emergencies. I removed the bloodied rag and saw that the cut was deep. I didn't think it would need stitches; I was a fast healer. Good thing, considering the nearest hospital was forty-five miles away on the other side of the mountains. We were snowed in.

The arctic temperature helped staunch the blood flow, but there was a consequence. The first aid cream had frozen solid. The bandages were so stiff they were unworkable, as was the white adhesive tape. I rewrapped the wound with a handkerchief from my pocket. I thought for a second, and then with reluctance stuffed the cream, bandages and tape down my shirt. The subzero skin contact was like a blue-white flame burning my skin. When the shivering stopped, my six foot one, one hundred and thirty-pound ectomorph body had shared enough heat to thaw my medical supplies. Fumbling, fingers stiff from the cold, I attended my wound, a clean slice. I dabbed on the cream, applied butterfly bandages, then wrapped it with gauze. We had a long day ahead cutting firewood, and it was essential to wear gloves, so I was careful to keep the dressing thin. It still made wrestling with the boot laces harder, but my boots were secure. I went back upstairs for a blanket.

Coffee! I melted some snow and started the coffee perking. Not so fast, this simple task was problematic. The propane was frozen. Once again, I shared my body heat. Wrapped in my blanket with the icy canister I waited, remembering the first time I saw this place.

## First Sight

When Byron and I pulled into Richford, we weren't sure which way to go. Byron pulled to the curb across from an old church. I got out and asked two guys for directions to the old Mackenzie farm. The men, pleasant Vermonters in their fifties, had no idea where it was. I thanked them, turned to Byron and said, "They don't know where the funny farm is." Overhearing this, the taller of the two men responded, "Funny farm, why didn't you say so?" Take this road out of town about eight miles and turn left onto West Jay Road. It's the first right after the bridge." I knew it was referred to as the funny farm, but I didn't know why. Who knew it would be local knowledge? The directions were spot on.

Cresting the driveway hill, the view was spectacular. The valley was ablaze with autumn color, and the house was humming with activity. Craig and his girlfriend, Leigh, moved in a month earlier. We stayed a few days. I was hooked and planned my return.

Autumn raced into winter long before the solstice. Leigh found the bitter-cold-blended-season and rugged life hard to endure, but she did. That is, until the car accident sealed her fate, leaving her with a broken jaw. She and Craig moved into an apartment in Enosburg Falls. My plans to join Craig were already in motion and, while waiting for me to arrive, he made trips to the farm to feed the goats whenever he could borrow a car. The house was otherwise empty. Three months later Hugh and I arrived at Leigh's apartment in Enosburg.

Bob, Craig and Leigh

## Household Awakes

Wrapped in a wool blanket, working in the frigid kitchen, I filled a large stock pot and the coffee pot with snow and connected the thawed propane tank to my Coleman two-burner camp stove. The blue flames were mesmerizing. I willed the heat toward me. Craig and Hugh smelled the coffee and came into the kitchen wrapped in their blankets. Noticing the bloodied rags and my bandage, Craig said, "What the hell happened? Are you all right?"

Hugh asked, "Why didn't you call us to help?"

"It looks worse than it is," I said and explained.

Despite injury, extreme cold and related adversities, we were like little kids at Christmas enjoying our new digs. Overnight, a fresh layer of snow covered the valley. I knew it would be cold but was shocked when the outside thermometer read thirty-five degrees below zero. The mercury plummeted to the bottom of the tube. The wind, steady at twenty miles per hour, gusted to over thirty. It was cold enough to pop the nails out of the clapboard. The effective wind chill on human skin was sixty-seven below zero. Every gust sent chilling drafts through the subzero room sending me back to my bedroom to grab another blanket.

The old Acorn wood cook stove was beautiful—but useless without firewood. Its small firebox was icy to the touch. The stove in the cellar held trace-lingering warmth in the ashes. The last vestiges of heat leached out of the cellar and dissipated through the kitchen, returning the room to winter's chilling grip. Dishes left for weeks in the sink, still wrapped in ice, found no benefit from the evening fire. The squeezing crush of ice shattered a few glasses and cracked plates. Supple gear brought in from the warmth of the car the night before lay against the wall frozen stiff, caught still as they sagged to the floor, gelid air arresting gravity's pull.

Dressed in multiple layers, we Long Island transplants paced around the room wrapped in our blankets. The hot coffee chased the remaining sleep from our eyes and warmed our blood. Relishing the warming coffee, we spoke in awed, hushed tones at the intensity of being in this valley fresh with snow.

## The Day Before

We woke up early in Enosburg. The village struck me like a modern-day Currier and Ives print. The blizzard of snow that dogged Hugh and me the entire ride from Albany gave way overnight to crisp, clear deep blue skies with a few high, wispy clouds. There was no wind, but the brisk minus ten-degree air was like a smack in the face. Deep-walled paths led from street to store. It was easy to imagine the cars parked, with keys in the ignition and engines running, were horse-and-carriages. Back to reality, I cleared the snow from my car.

Craig, Hugh and I left Leigh's apartment and drove east under a deep blue sky. Cloud-shrouded mountains on the horizon portended a weather change. As we arrived in the valley, snow-filled clouds clung to the mountains like a heavy gray awning. A light crystalline snow swirled, wafting on a gusting breeze. We left Enosburg under the bright sun of early morning but we drove into a still-dawning sky.

Silhouetted against the eastern horizon, the weather-worn house appeared ghostly through the mist of light snow. Stalactite-like icicles hung from the eaves. Some of the larger icicles reached the ground, appearing as stalagmites rising from below. The porch door swinging in the gusting wind slammed against the porch wall dislodging smaller icicles from the eaves which plummeted like missiles and disappeared into the deep-drifted snow. The air was frigid, and the dawning sun cresting the surrounding mountain peaks offered no respite from the cold.

The noise of the car engine and tires spinning on the ice alerted the goats that wandered out of the barn and started down the driveway. Fishtailing most of the way up the hill, swerving to avoid the goats, my car slid to a stop in the space between the farmhouse and our huge red barn. A dream come true.

Exiting the car, engulfed by the biting cold, we were anxious to enter the house. The heat from the car was a fast-fading memory as we slipped and slid up the slight rise to the porch. A coating of fresh snow covered the low porch step and hid the packed ice beneath. The porch floor was glazed with ice, making the short distance to the kitchen door treacherous. Struggling to remain upright, we made it to the door and turned the doorknob. Despite no lock on the door, it wouldn't budge. A layer of ice and snow covered the door, painting it and the entire porch with an icy glaze, reminiscent of the Ice Palace scene from the movie Doctor Zhivago. As if living a scene from that movie, we pushed hard on the frozen door several times before it opened, then hastened into the kitchen.

The kitchen was as cold as it was outside, a coating of frost covered the inside of the window and expanded to the walls. Unwashed dishes sat frozen in the sink. Springing to action, we built a fire in both stoves. Much to our chagrin, there was almost no firewood for the two wood stoves, a Magee Beacon parlor stove down in the cellar that we called "Maggie" and an old Acorn Wood Cookstove that occupied a prominent place in the kitchen. A sudden epiphany was disconcerting. There was not enough wood to keep the wood stoves burning through the night.

We settled in for that long cold first night, thankful to have some wood to take the chill from the air. Grateful to have electrical power, at least we had lights. We sat in the kitchen, huddled at the pantry trapdoor above the Magee Beacon stove and next to the Acorn, soaking up and savoring the heat of the fires. In time the room temperature climbed above freezing while a bottle of blackberry brandy helped to warm us from within. Outside, the temperature plummeted. The light breeze that met us earlier started to rage and pummel the house with snow. The snow, crystalline from the intense cold, peppered the house like an angry sandblaster. Dusk approached as the early afternoon sun dropped below North Jay Mountain. Full dark was swift. The wind-driven snow became so dense and fierce that despite the porch light beckoning in the absolute darkness, the huge barn just thirty feet away was a specter in the night. We stoked the fire with the rest of our wood and moved to our respective rooms. A new storm was brewing.

## New Paltz Hitchhikers

Hugh and Fern were getting closer. After awakening on the side of the onramp, they caught a ride in a semi to St. Albans. It was early morning when they arrived. A half hour later the second ride got them as far as the Franklin turnoff on 105. They waited almost an hour, overlooking fields of ripe cow corn, when a pickup truck stopped. Meanwhile, the Bronze beach bards were just awakened by Fae.

# 12

# FIRE & ICE

*"Some say the world will end in fire, some say in ice."*
*~ Robert Frost*

Resolved to cut firewood, we vowed never to let the woodshed be barren again. Donning our heavy winter parkas, mittens, gloves, scarves, hats and balaclavas, we gathered our tools and stepped out into the breach. The sun rose above Burnt Owl Ridge, creeping into a clear sky. It was almost zero with a promise of ten degrees and, as the morning progressed, the wind died down. The gods smiled on us.

Adjacent to the house, a deer path rounded a large boulder, reaching high above the snow like a small mesa with edges chamfered smooth. A hundred yards up the hill, beyond the boulder, was a solitary dead elm tree, a victim of Dutch elm disease. We had few choices this late into the winter and, considering our immediate need, the three of us trod up the hill, which steepened just before the crest. Despite being a light powder, it was a difficult climb through the knee-deep snow. The iridescent snow sparkled, the night's wind whipping the snow around the boulder in concentric multileveled rings like an ever-changing Zen meditation garden. The depth of the snow varied, depending on obstacles in its path. The quintessential elm was about sixteen inches in diameter with five main branches rising to the sky from which a multitude of smaller branches radiated into a fan-like array.

The three of us were lithe, suburban youths who eschewed sports; and although we were far from weaklings and despite our survival motivation, we lacked a deep reservoir of physical strength. Breathing heavy, tired, we paused at the big rock. "Hey Craig, are you sure this is our best option?" Hugh chimed in, "Yeah, this is hard. Some workout!" Craig responded, "I wish! This is the best we got now. The snow is over five feet deep in the woods." Forging through the final waist-deep snow, we reached the tree. Exhausted we had yet to use a saw. Time for a joint!

We were dressed for the cold. Craig and I were both wearing military-style hooded parkas, the kind with fur around the hood. His was real, issued to his father decades earlier by the Air Force, and was superior to the one I wore. Mine was a copy bought at a surplus store, but they were both warm. Hugh wore two sweaters under a dark green hooded jacket, but his Norwegian genes helped make up the difference. My face was covered with a dark balaclava, Craig wore a knit hat with a full face mask and Hugh's face was wrapped in a green and blue striped scarf.

Keeping your core warm is important, as is trapping the heat escaping through your head; but the extremities were most difficult to protect. The body will sacrifice extremities to save essential body parts. We all had decent gloves worn under an insulated waterproof mitten shell. The finger portion of the mitten hinged back, freeing the fingers for finer tasks. Earmuffs were also essential. My combat boots proved to be better than I expected, and Craig's Wolverine hiking boots and Hugh's work boots were up to the task.

We sized up the tree and then cut the flat part of the notch near the snow line, next cut ten inches above the first at a downward angle until the two cuts meet. The wedge fell to the ground, with a little persuasion from the ax, leaving an open notch facing downhill. The notch is used to direct where the tree will fall. Keep in mind that most of this was theory when we started. Craig and I had cut down small trees before but this was a big tree, with many variables we knew nothing about.

We picked a spot above the first cut on the opposite side from the notch and started the final cut. When it reached midway, we heard the creaking begin, followed moments later by a resounding crack. The kerf widened. Craig pulled the saw from the tree saying. "It's going over. Run!" We all pushed through the snow away from the tree's fall. Novice mistake, we should have devised a better escape plan, our pace was slowed by the deep snow. The elm was not so impeded. As the kerf opened further, the tree leaned into the notch, building up speed. Halfway into its downward arc, the tree twisted toward us. The shadow of the elm's fan crossed overhead as we struggled for safety. Still, within the range of the upper branches, we surged forward, adrenaline pumping; then the elm, with its final vertical act, twisted away from us hanging in the air for an endless moment, and then crashed down through the snow a safe distance from where we stood. Branches disappeared into the deep snow, breaking on impact.

The unknown risks associated with cutting down a tree this size could have killed one of us. In time we learned how to gauge the weight displacement of the upper branches. This time we were lucky. The elm fell downhill as we had planned, but one of the big main branches pulled the tree, dropping into the deepest snow.

Despite our preparedness, cold and snow found its way into our gloves and boots as the morning progressed, resulting in constant pacing and thrusting our hands into our pockets or inside our coats for body heat warmth. My hand, throbbing from the wound and the intense cold, made my turn at the saw more difficult. We struggled to remember that cutting firewood heats you twice. Can I still feel my toes?

Using bow saws, ax and hatchet, we trimmed off everything above the snow line. Whoever wasn't sawing or chopping pulled the cut and broken branches free and stacked the long leggy branches to the side for the trip back down the hill. Some of the thick main branches were submerged in the snow, making them difficult to cut. We failed to bring a shovel so we cleared the snow by hand. The laborious task of dragging the smaller branches down the hill came next, but smaller may be a misnomer. Some branches were six inches in girth and others eight feet long. We could have made them smaller but that would have meant more trips. It was easier going downhill, plus we benefited from the tracks made on our uphill climb. My hand was throbbing. Time forged on, and multiple trips up and down the hill were exhausting! Sweat from the exertion was like a conduit for the cold; I could feel the start of a body-shaking chill. I wanted a fire.

Back at the house, the first phase done, we were presented with a final problem. How do we get the remaining twenty-foot tree trunk down to the woodshed? The first order of business was to cut up some smaller branches and get a fire started in the Acorn."

Hovering by the Acorn stove, the kitchen still below freezing, we took a long break, smoked a cigarette or two, melted some snow, made some coffee, smoked a joint, ate some oatmeal and pondered our plight. Warmed by the sun, now past its zenith, the kitchen window was clear of frost. I looked through the window at our path through the snow and said, "Flume."

Hugh replied "Flame? You want another joint?"

"No, I said flume! Look at the tracks we made bringing the branches down." I continued, "We need to go up and down the hill a few times and connect all of our tracks to make a flume. Then we can drag the log into the flume and slide it down the hill." A new plan devised, we lit up another joint.

Back to the top of the hill, we were exhausted from the multiple trips up and down. The western sky was ablaze with reds and oranges radiating from behind North Jay Mountain. It was two PM, the sun soon to set; time to get moving.

"Not a bad flume," Craig said, as he tied the rope to one end of the log. Rope secured, we lifted, pulled and strained to no avail. The log was heavier than we could manage and we needed to cut it again, but cutting through the horizontal tree trunk was easier. As I pushed the saw back and forth through the log, getting into the Zen of the task, it was easy to imagine being back in another time, at the end of a long two-man saw, sometimes called a "misery whip," working in rhythm with my fellow sawyer, cutting through a huge log. Wanderings like this distracted me from the penetrating cold. After clearing the compacted snow, we finished cutting, leaving two ten-foot logs.

Dusk darkened the sky and the temperature dropped back below zero. Frostbite was becoming a real concern. My feet and hands felt numb and were getting hard to move. Despite headgear, hood and knitted ear band, my ears felt like they getting ready to break off. Conversation was difficult with faces wrapped, the wind increasing and teeth chattering; we worked in silence. Re-tying the rope was more difficult because of our brittle hands and the crusting surface of the fast-freezing snow. The three of us on the rope repeating our earlier effort, managed to get the log to move. Craig was in the lead, Hugh and me in the middle; we dragged the log into the flume, and started down the hill. Our plan was for the log to glide through the flume like a bobsled, but the front end dug into the snow like a plow. The flume wasn't big enough for all of us and the log, so Hugh and I trudged through the snow alongside while lifting the log to keep the leading edge up and out of the snow. Craig walked in the flume at the front, pulling the rope with all his might.

The snow along the trough varied in depth from exposed windswept grass to waist deep. Deceptive sections sculpted by wind shielded terrain vagaries—like deep depressions—from view. We built up momentum when we reached a shallow area and the log picked up speed. Just as it started to slide free in the flume, Hugh and I stepped into a snow-covered depression and sank into the deep snow falling forward losing our grip on the rope. The log, inertia-broken, sped through the flume, scant inches from my left ear as it almost emasculated Hugh. The speeding log threatened to take Craig out at the knees, but he reacted like a cat when he heard us yell, "Craig! Watch out! Jump!" He dove to his right, burying himself in the snow. Speed building, the log slid over a mogul and became airborne, dropping back down and then rocketing through the flume, breaking through the brush at the driveway's edge, skidding across the driveway and burying its leading edge into the berm on the opposite side. One log down!

The temperature had dropped again. Friction from the first log propelling through the makeshift flume generated enough heat to melt the surface snow that refroze and glazed smooth, making a fast path for the second log to rocket down the hill, with just a few pushes from behind. Darkness was encroaching when we got the second log and the tools back to the woodshed. It took some work to dislodge the second log from the snow berm at the edge of the driveway, then drag it up the ice-covered driveway. Déjà vu!

We cut up some of the smaller branches and, desperate to get warm, started a fire in the Magee Beacon Parlor stove, down in the cellar crawl space. The larger task of blocking and splitting the wood still lay ahead. "Maggie" was hungry and burned through the branches in no time, requiring the larger quarter-split wood. She was quite demanding.

When we finished cross-cutting about ten blocks, we resolved to buy a chainsaw. They were invented for a reason; if they had such tools in days of yore, they would have used them, too. We huddled above the trap door in the pantry floor, enjoying the heat rising from Maggie below. We also got the Acorn cook stove blazing. Still had to split those ten blocks; I love splitting wood. So I did, throbbing hand be damned.

## Artesian Spring

With enough wood stacked in the shed to heat the house for a few days, we were still in the woods, so to speak. The water was frozen solid; hence, all of the snow-melted water. Our water flowed down from a gravity-fed artesian spring up the hill behind the house. Maggie did a good job pretending to be a furnace heating the cellar, but the recalcitrant pipe refused to thaw. Light failing, night encroaching, we grabbed a couple of flashlights and a crowbar, then traipsed through thigh-deep snow up the hill with hopes of finding the spring.

Craig was there the previous summer, so he had a good idea where to look; and it was marked well enough. We found it buried under a thin layer of snow next to a high snow drift. It took some time and effort to dig out the snow and free the heavy wooden door from its icy bonds. Struggles to raise the door revealed a thick layer of ice on the top of the makeshift well. Clearing a hole through the ice cap and shining the flashlight revealed the inky water's surface about a foot down, but did nothing to pierce the dark abyss, so we abandoned the task. Securing the trap door, there was nothing else we could do at that end. We trudged back to the house and warmed up again and stoked the fire, and then broke out the toolbox.

We devised a plan B on the trip back from our unfruitful mission to the spring—blowtorch. I had a full tank of Mapp gas with a torch head that I used for sweating copper pipes. New problem: the gas had frozen. With the tank near the stove, it thawed an hour later. Taking turns descending into the crawlspace, we held the torch flame on the galvanized steel pipe protruding from the foundation wall. Stoking the fire was another job that went along with the pipe thawing. The Mapp gas had almost run out when Craig yelled from the kitchen, "I see a drip!" A few minutes later the water broke through the ice dam in the pipe, flowing full force. We learned two things from this experience. Never turn the water off in the dead of winter, and always have backup Mapp gas in case someone does. Night had fallen and darkness prevailed, and we were all spent.

More oatmeal mixed with grape jelly, some blackberry brandy, another joint and more cigarettes followed. By the way, grape jelly and Quaker Oatmeal was our primary diet for days to come. It was nice to make coffee without melting snow first. Settling in for the evening, we rested with the anticipation of a fire burning through the night.

So went the first twenty-four hours at the Phunee Farm."

## Reinforcements

Trooper Neil recounted the story and his concerns, Nick's gaze still burning in his mind. "You know, Ted, I'm not sure anymore. They may be just what they say. I think I am buying her story, but we need to check it out." The two troopers approached.

Trooper Neil said, "You can stand up now. Just keep your hands where I can see them. What's your name, miss?" She replied, and introduced Nick, who was more relaxed now and said, "What's going on, Neil? You pointed a gun at my woman, and I didn't think cutting through here would get me shot. Look, I won't drive through here again."

Trooper Neil was now thinking about the ribbing he would get for calling out the cavalry for a couple of hippies taking a shortcut. It was then that the assault vehicle pulled up with a group of motivated drug enforcement troopers acting like they were hitting the beach at Normandy. Neil approached the captain and explained the situation.

The captain said, "Stand down, men." Then, turning to Nick, he said, "Your name is Nick, right? How far did you say your log cabin was?"

Nick lightened up a little, saying, "It's less than five minutes by truck or about a twenty-minute walk." "OK, Nick. Pick up your keys and move your vehicle onto the grass, then get into the four by four. Mia, go and sit in the back now." Mia did, and felt uncomfortable with the steel mesh cage separating the seats. When Nick got in, the captain said, "OK, direct me to your cabin."

It was more like three minutes when the log cabin came into sight. The captain's expression of approval nearing wonder showed he was impressed. The workmanship was impressive; the logs were interconnected like Lincoln Logs. He was a little older than Nick and had his own back-to-nature perspective. He built a log house from a kit when he moved up to Vermont from New Jersey a few years earlier, but it was modern with factory-hewn logs. He told Nick and Mia his story, while he looked around.

"You did a helluva job here. Would you mind showing me the inside." Nick was still reeling from the gun incident but Mia said, "Sure, I would love to." Twenty minutes later, they were back at the interstate. After Trooper Neil was updated by the captain, he turned to Nick and Mia and said, "I'm sorry, folks, you fit the description of someone we are looking for, and when you popped out of the woods I thought you were them." He held out his hand and Mia shook it. Nick relented and did the same.

Trooper Neil said, "If you promise to stop using this unauthorized entrance, we will let it go this time. We will be watching." Six weeks later the interstate crew installed a barrier blocking the clandestine road.

13

# WINTER'S GRIP

*In the depth of winter, I finally learned that there was in me an invincible summer.*
*~ Albert Camus*

Time moved at sloth speed in the shadow of our mountain. Many long nights were spent discussing philosophy, political theory, poetry, astrology and religion. Religion was a big component of our impromptu forums but from a spiritual rather than dogmatic perspective. We discussed and debated the Bible, Bhagavad Gita, Kabala, Tao, Wicca and Zen, and esoteric topics such as ancient astronauts, wizards, dragons, time travel, alternate universes and grade B sci-fi flicks like Invasion of the Neptune Men. We were also Trekkies. Come to think of it, I lent my copy of the Starfleet Manual to the farmer's son up the road and never got it back. My penchant was Wicca, occult and all things mystical.

Pragmatism ruled most of our time, theoretical discussions notwithstanding. We prepared for spring, ordered seeds from catalogs, studied gardening, local trees, wildflowers and edible wild plants, and researched our orchard of apples and plums and learned about raspberries and currants. We schemed ways to make money but needed little since we were renting the farmhouse, barn and five hundred acres from Cole Larsen, a real estate agent. All of this for the exorbitant cost of twenty dollars per month. He was holding this land for the future benefit of his children, and having us live on the land helped protect his legacy. Water was free, but a challenge to keep from freezing, and the electric bill came in at under ten dollars every other month. You gotta love hydropower. Firewood was almost free—of coin anyway. Cutting firewood required a substantial physical effort. During the day, we foraged for firewood until we built up a safe supply. It was hard to determine if a tree was dead in the naked winter. Such was the deal with the landlord; cut only dead trees.

The winter was long, cold, hard, wonderful, and sometimes scary, as our biggest objective was survival—literally staying alive—even if we were oblivious to the potential danger at the time. In retrospect, we pushed the envelope of survival to its apex, sliding through life-threatening experiences protected by our youthful idealism. Maybe the adage "God protects babies and drunks" also extended to potheads. Youth is far removed from the fear of mortality or serious injury. The nearest hospital was forty-five miles away, an hour's travel if the roads were plowed; and we did not have a phone to summon help. We were indestructible, harboring few fears of injury—or worse.

*Danger lurked on the edge of civilization.*

We heard the blood-curdling bleating. Craig looked out the kitchen window and saw the white goat lying in the snow. We rushed outside but in the seconds it took to get there, it was over. We could see large blood-filled tracks in the snow near the goat and drag marks from the driveway. Its neck was broken when a predator ripped its throat, blood was still spurting. Craig drew his buck knife from its sheath and ended the suffering goat's life. We had no firearms. We had never seen one before; we surmised it was a Bobcat, based on the description in the Field Book. This was the second goat we lost in two weeks. On ground frozen solid, we built a pyre. It smelled like a barbecue but burned to a fine ash.

The fearful screams of a chicken got us all running. We cornered the barn to see gray and white speckled feathers floating down to the ground. It could have been another rat snake, also known as chicken snakes, but we suspected a weasel. One of the dogs killed something, on the hill near the upper barn doors, but the yellow bib on its chest pointed to a mink. It wasn't alone; we suspected a small company. How they found a way into the hen house was an enigma. The hen house was in a corner of the barn with thick cement walls and floor. Two smaller chickens, exotic silkies, were taken first. The next to go was the gray speckled Plymouth Rock in that brazen daylight attack we witnessed. The dogs got two more mink and the carnage stopped. All was good until one of our roosters met his demise. Bloody tracks by the barn door implicated a red fox we saw poking around. We were on the edge of wilderness, the last homey-house in the valley, and more susceptible to wild things.

"I was wondering where the silkies went," Tara said, "but it looks like you have more chickens than the last time."

Craig said, "Yeah we got a couple of Rhode Island Reds and a few Leghorns from a farm in Richford. But those silkies were cool. They were named for their silky fluffy plumage, but their real claim to fame was their green-tinted low-cholesterol eggs."

"Craig, were the 'silkez' the white ones with the puffy heads?" Fae asked. "I liked them best."

"Yes, I'm sorry, Fae. Do you want to go see the new chickens?

## Cars at Thirty Below

It snowed every day with few exception and, at times, the thermometer dropped to forty-two below zero. Add in a thirty-mile-an-hour wind and the wind chill factor rivaled Antarctica at eighty below zero. On days like these, exposed skin could have become frostbitten in minutes. Some tasks required the removal of one or both gloves, necessitating multiple trips to the warmth of the fire to bring blood back to our fingers. We tried to avoid it, but life on the land forced us into the maw of that kind of weather. We might even drive somewhere, that is, if we could get the car started and drive it out to the main road and back again.

The first part of the driveway was a town-owned road which was plowed, but many times it wasn't and we would be snowed in for a few days. Being snowbound was incompatible with our hand-to-mouth budget and our ability to keep the pantry stocked. More than once, circumstances forced us to trudge eight miles into town for supplies. Several times we were picked up en route, hitchhiking. One driver commented, "I turned on to the Jay Road and started the climb, and thought I saw something up ahead. Looked like some kind of big critters. My eyes been failing me these last two years; but as I got closer, I was taken aback seeing you boys. Your legs were below the snow and I thought you 'was' a couple bear out of hibernation. "Well jeezum crow, whatta them boys doin' out in this snow and 'oice'?" We almost always got a ride home.

Climbing the steep driveway was a challenge every time we came home. Preparation for the ascent started the moment after turning onto West Jay Road. Down the hill over the bridge, fishtailing through the right turn, then up the steep icy slope, while white-knuckling the wheel attempting to stabilize the swerving vehicle, until finally cresting the hill where the driveway turned hard to the right before straightening out to a gradual rise. We learned how to control the wild erratic fishtailing that ensued after we slid into the bank a few times.

Speaking of cars, they liked the subzero weather less than we did. In time the cars were fitted with a dipstick heater. Every night we connected an extension cord to a plug that dangled from the grill. The tank heater was effective for cold weather starting, but we had no such luxury the early part of our first winter. We shoveled hot coals from the wood stove into a long-handled frying pan and place them under the oil pan to thaw the oil enough to start the car. It was so cold one time that a car parked overnight in the driveway slid down the hill when the ground under it flash froze and a vicious wind gave it a hard shove. Breaking the inertia, the car built up momentum and inched from its place between the house and barn, sliding downhill into the orchard. We were lucky that time. More than one car was held captive by the embrace of the deep snow until the following spring. We became experienced snow drivers.

## Unemployment

When I arrived in Vermont and transferred my New York State Unemployment Insurance, I was required to seek employment every week and complete a form listing at least three places where I looked for work. Every week I attempted to find a job and would physically appear at an establishment and ask if they needed help. They never did. I made minimal effort, but there were no jobs to be found. My check came in handy when I first arrived and went a long way to help us get started, especially that first spring. I arrived in February but started collecting checks sometime in March. Once a week I mailed my creative employment-seeking form to the Unemployment Office in St Albans. Like clockwork, my check would arrive in the mail the following week. One week I retrieved my envelope from the mailbox, anticipating a vanilla milkshake at the Richford Luncheonette, but there was no check in the envelope. In its place was a notice of defect and a directive to report to the Unemployment Office.

Oh no, I thought. Was I getting nailed for the creative forms I submitted? It was my third check, and I was already in trouble. Would they hit me for filing a false instrument? On my last day to appear, driving through blinding snow with visibility less than twenty feet, we took the forty-five mile drive to St. Albans. We crept into St. Albans two hours after we left the Phunee Farm. Why did I wait until the last minute? I parked the car and Craig and Hugh went over to a luncheonette to get some coffee and wait. I went into the office thinking I was in New York, expecting to queue one of the many officious counter lines to respond to my rebuking letter. This was not New York. There were no lines, just a receptionist who greeted me politely and asked how she could help. I showed her the letter trying to hide my nervousness and wondering if I was in trouble. She read my notice, smiled and said, "Oh you got one of the red line letters. Please take a seat over there." I sat while she put my letter in a red labeled folder and walked it into an office.

I heard my name called, well attempted, no one ever got it right, and I went into the office. A stern looking plump woman about fifty with blond-gray hair pulled into a bun said, "There is a problem with the form you sent in". Here it is, I thought. She handed me the form I mailed in with an ostentatious red line underlining the box labeled "Sex." "Honey, you forgot to fill in your sex." What? I thought. She handed me a pen. I wrote "M" in the box and handed it back. "One minute please," she said, as she started to write something. At this point, I was relieved, since there was no mention of my job search creativity. Then I thought, did I just drive two hours, with another one and a half to get back, because some bureaucrat was unable to intuit that Robert was an "M?" The woman leaned over toward me with something in her hand and said, "Be more careful next time, dear," as she handed me a handwritten unemployment check. Sometimes, you've got to just love the system. Four months later, the unemployment checks ended.

## Snowshoes

There was also time for solitary exploration, deep snow notwithstanding. Snowshoeing proved to be an invigorating exercise, and also cathartic. The snow was deep above the thick ice sealing the beaver pond for the winter, and yet I traversed the snow's surface, being careful to avoid the many gnawed tree stumps that poked out above the snow. Dozens of tree stumps rose above the surface of the pond, remnants of the trees fallen by the beavers and used to build their dam and lodge. My snowshoes disbursed my weight well, such that I sunk scant inches into the covering snow. I wandered further out toward the snow mound covering the beaver's lodge in the middle of the pond, where dead trees left in place by the beavers rose fifteen feet above the lodge. These trees were utilized by the beavers to support the lacework of sticks and twigs that formed their lodge. Most of the lodge was underwater, but there was a space above where the beavers slept, like a moon pool on ship allowing Scuba divers access from under the vessel. I enjoyed a rare view of North Jay Mountain's peak and Lucas Brook flats while standing above the frozen beaver pond nestled in a small vale below the highway. The ribbon of Route 105 was still covered with unplowed snow. I turned at the sound of motion to my left.

When I set out from the house, I had options that would have been impossible at other times of the year or even now without my snowshoes. Cutting across the field, I felt like I floated above the thicket of brambles on the western edge of our land. Although we were renting, we felt it ours because of the spiritual kinship we had with the valley, forest and brook.

The morning air was crisp on a late March day. An early snowfall lay like a pristine blanket, unfolding in the valley ahead. High clouds floated against a deep blue sky. I plodded along in complete solitude, striving for oneness with my surroundings. The penetrating silence hung in the air. Startled by my approach, a white snowshoe hare came scurrying out from its cover. The subtle shifting of a red tail hawk's wing tips broke the silence. With a whoosh of forced air, the raptor plummeted toward its unwary prey. In a flash, the hawk's sharp talons struck the scurrying hare and carried the writhing hare back into the sky. Splotches of blood stained the snow where the rabbit's tracks ended. I stood for a while watching the hawk fade into a tiny spot in the distant sky. This was a natural occurrence in the balance of the food chain. The quiet of the day resumed as I moved on, my steps approaching silently.

Standing on the beaver pond, I was startled from my reverent observations by the sound of movement moving below the snow and to the left of where I stood. My presence had awakened the dormant beavers. They don't hibernate. I could see the snow pushed up near the lodge as a groggy but wary beaver poked through the snow. Doing my best to present a non-threatening posture, I backed up with a slow steadiness and continued away from the pond. The beaver, satisfied by my retreat, withdrew back into his lodge—which was a good thing because they can be formidable when threatened.

I worked my way back over the Lucas Brook Bridge, stopping to appreciate the snow-covered ice that capped the brook, eight feet below. The translucent blue ice was like a sculpture rising high above the splashing water, frozen in motion, forming twisted tendrils of ice. I started up the hill toward Route 105, gazing at the undisturbed snow. Following the perimeter of our land, I crossed the road and started up the mountain slope. I looked back to see the wide tracks of the snowshoes leading back to the beaver pond. Cautious, I continued uphill into the forest, staying atop the deepening snow. Sheltered from the melting sun by the dense canopy of naked branches, the snow could reach ten feet deep.

Plotting my course farther up the mountain listening to the movement of unseen woodland creatures and the gentle rustle of the wind in the trees, I heard a new sound intruding. The quiet was shattered as they approached. I could see the snow thrown high into the air. Although distant from the road, I was pelted with snow as I watched my trail surrender to the deafening scraping of two giant highway plows. I watched them blast through the stop sign heading west toward Richford. They disappeared from sight long before their cacophonous diminuendo.

Once the forest returned to silence, forest creatures began to roam again, having sought shelter from the din. I rested under a small conifer, hoping that its branches would spare my head and hold their load. Secreted in my coniferous sanctuary, I joined in the restored silence of the forest. I looked up the slope as a small herd of deer led by a six-pointed buck traversed the slope upwind from my position and unaware of my presence. There was a certain majesty to these deer, like a court following their regal leader. I took several snowshoe treks, but this was the most rewarding as regard to fauna.

## Creature Comforts

Creature comforts during the winter were minimal—in fact, they never became robust. We had no phone and the idea of cell phones was closer to Star Trek communicators than reality at the time. We had electricity, a small two-fuse electrical box. Considering our remoteness, it's remarkable we never lost power. The bathroom was a real challenge with its quasi-indoor plumbing. The tub had no hot water and the cold water froze in the winter. This meant the tub needed to be filled with buckets of cold water warmed on the Acorn wood cook stove. You don't need much water for a sponge bath. Showers were a dream. Our toilet was quasi-flush. It flushed by pouring in a bucket of water. Boiling water was sometimes required to clear the frozen bowl that, although frozen, never fractured. The harshness of winter hygiene encouraged us to visit friends with modern conveniences.

# 14

# ENOSBURGIANS

*The glory of friendship is not the outstretched hand, nor the kindly smile, nor the joy of companionship; it is the spiritual inspiration that comes to one when he discovers that someone else believes in him and is willing to trust him with his friendship.*
*~ Ralph Waldo Emerson*

Visits to Enosburg were our main link to the northern Vermont social world. Most of the people we encountered that first winter were transplants from Long Island or New Jersey. We often stayed overnight at Leigh's apartment on the second floor above the Ben Franklin store. The capacious bathroom with its seven-foot clawfoot tub was a savior in the deep of winter. Tubs, as a rule, made me feel cramped but I could stretch out and submerge my whole body in this one. This respite from sponge baths was always welcome.

### Leigh

Leigh, through her effusive personality, was the glue that held many of the people, places and things together in the social fabric of Northern Vermont. I met her in my freshman year of high school. We were part of the same crowd of friends that frequented the "mansion" in Rocky Point. Leigh started seeing Craig. I remember discussing my new found Wiccan religion that involved being skyclad. Leigh found that hard to conceive of, saying, "If I was naked in a room with Craig I would have a hard time keeping my hands off of him, even if there were other people there." Modern Wicca had been introduced to the United States a year earlier by Raymond Buckland, and it was hard for people to fathom the nakedness and stigma following centuries of defamation.

Back in our hometown, the drinking age was still eighteen. Leigh and a few friends became regulars at an "old man's bar" in the village. They served nickel beers; how could you go wrong? Leigh was friends with Byron. Many nickels later, I got to be friends with Byron who owned a house a few towns north with an extra room. When I moved in, I was still working at a well-paying factory job making Naugahyde Upholstery Vinyl until I got laid off—unemployment.

## On the Missisquoi

Tom's house sat about fifty feet from the Missisquoi River on the outskirts of Enosburg Falls. The front porch faced the river. Many hours were spent watching the river flow towards Lake Champlain. I would sit daydreaming in a comfortable wicker chair imagining a stick I tossed into the Lucas Brook was floating by. During the winter months, the river was iced over. Surface ripples appeared flash-frozen, surrendering their kinetic motion to a frozen stillness.

In the spring, we sat on the porch, wrapped against bitter winds, waiting for the ice to break. The eerie creaking and the powerful sound of cracking ice were forerunners to heaved ice sheets breaking up as the floe quickened. Like a ritual, we would bet on when it would break. Sitting on the porch with beers in hand, we toasted the river and cheered. The river's pent-up energy forced destructive sheets of ice downstream, pulling trees out by their roots and into the melee, redefining the river's banks as it pushed flotsam and yanked detritus into its grip as it raged downstream. Huge trees raced by along with building debris that dared to stand in the river's path.

Tom moved up from New Jersey and bought the house, where he lived with Ginny. Tom was an oil burner mechanic. He worked hard every day and when he got home, he would blast Bruce Springsteen and other rock musicians; he drank his beer, smoked weed and gobbled prescription barbiturates, soon to fall asleep. Ginny, who once embraced a similar lifestyle, moved on, moved out and moved in with Leigh.

Friday nights we gathered at his house. The crowd of backwoods denizens, ages ranging from three to thirty-five, woke up on the floor to Saturday morning cartoons. Scooby Doo ruled the morn. We shared festive breakfasts, warm beer and leftovers. Tom's house was a haven for us in many ways, providing any tool we needed, a warm place to sleep and the shower, of course. He installed two hot water heaters feeding two separate shower heads, one at each end of the tub. Heaven! Back at the farm, it was more like winter camping every day. In time, he would help us update the plumbing and electrical systems at the farm. I learned a lot from Tom.

## Mitch

I met Mitch eating breakfast at Carney's, a renowned local restaurant. One morning, I was telling Minnie, my waitress, that I left my wallet in the apartment, when Mitch walked over and paid my bill, saying, "Hi, I'm Mitch. I've seen you around the building."

"Thanks, Mitch. My name is Bob. I can pay you back in a few minutes."

"Nah, forget it. It's on me."

"Well, I appreciate it. Thanks again. So what brings you up to God's country?"

"I went to high school with this guy Bruce Gorsy, who's been up here a couple of years. I was looking for a change, and he told me about an apartment here in Enosburg. He's a real character. I knew his girlfriend Ronni when we were six."

"Hold on a minute. Do you mean Bruce—of Ronni and Bruce?"

"Yeh, that's him. How do you know him?"

I said, "I think we have a common ancestor." We sat down for more coffee and shared stories of our arrival and backgrounds. I told him about Melody Mansion, and the people I followed to get here.

We shared an interest in things occult. I mentioned I was reading about palmistry when he proceeded to take my hand and described what he was doing while he read my hand. After breakfast, he invited me to smoke a joint. The apartment building was above the Ben Franklin store, two doors down Main Street from Carney's. On the way upstairs, we ran into Leigh and Ginny coming down. There are no coincidences.

When I introduced Mitch to Ginny, I could almost see the sparks igniting between them. Mitch brought her up often while we talked. He lent me a few books on palmistry, formally known as chiromancy. I spent my free time studying back at the farm. Winter offered ample time to do so. Mitch was a master, and I did my best to glean as much information as I could.

I was a wannabe believer in such divinations, unconvinced but open to the practice, yet skeptical of the practitioners. The information Mitch read from reading my hand softened my skepticism. Palmistry is much more than just the palm. It includes the whole hand, fingers, joints and, of course, the lines on my palm. Each finger, joint and part of the hand is associated to an astrological sign. Palmistry and associated astrology are the result of millennia of recorded observations. Mitch was skilled enough to read an ink print of a palm without ever knowing or seeing the person. I never got to be that good, but I did improve.

## Buckland

"Say, Mitch, Do you know anything about Wicca?"

"I know a little. My ex-girlfriend was Wiccan."

"Not something I hear very often," I replied. Then I thought, finally, someone I can talk with, and said, "Can I tell you about my experience with Wicca?"

"When I was in high school, Raymond Buckland, a Wiccan High Priest, narrated a slide show about modern witchcraft. Pictures of naked people in a high school auditorium were provocative. Slides bared a coven's naked ceremony, 'sky clad' as they considered it. This was a big deal; Buckland brought the religion out of the shadows. The nature-based religion caught my attention. I studied religion all senior year and read the Bible several times, but became disillusioned with the Catholic Church and the many other organized religions I studied. Buckland's presentation opened my eyes to a whole new perspective on religion."

## Occult Shop

When I returned from the Air Force, thoughts of this religion stayed with me. I set out to find Buckland and traced him to a neighboring town where a museum of witchcraft was located. I arrived late. He had moved to New Hampshire months before. A lead took me to The Occult Shop about twenty miles away, a small eclectic shop with an aura of mystery. The shop was dark, with effective, eerie lighting. Ethereal music played in the background behind a compelling aroma that filled the space. Globules of milky white frankincense and brown gold granules of myrrh were burning on round charcoals in a brass chalice brazier, filling the room with a church-like scent. My experience with incense was with the cone or stick form. Sandalwood was the favorite of my crowd, but outside of church, I had never seen or smelled incense burning on charcoal in an ornate burner, known as a 'censer'. The store was stocked with items from unique gifts to tools for a Wiccan coven, an astrologist, a student of the occult, or just the curious. I put myself into the last group.

The shopkeeper was Mortie. I explained my quest and he told me he worked with Raymond Buckland and that his wife and he were ordained as the High Priestess and High Priest of a Gardinarian Wiccan Coven. He invited me to attend a "pagan group," the first step to becoming a Wiccan. I carved wooden wands with intricate Celtic designs and sold several in his store. We became friends and Mortie asked, "Why don't you come to my fiftieth birthday party. Bring a date."

## Glenda

I met Glenda while I was living at Byron's house. She went by the name "Dormouse" and always considered herself to be a witch. Brought up in a wealthy family in a prestigious village, she had a difficult past. Addicted to heroin in the '60s, she took to prostitution to support her habit. Glenda's childhood best friend was Byron's ex-wife Maggie, "Mad Maggie" as she was known. I invited her to the party after I explained the background, she was psyched to join me.

We arrived at an ordinary house in an upscale suburban neighborhood and walked in the door then went down a few stairs to find a not so ordinary party. Everyone was naked! "Come on in," someone yelled, "and take off your clothes." This was a new experience for me and I looked at Glenda as if to say, "You OK with this?" She nodded as she unbuttoned her shirt; a moment later we stood naked in a room with thirty-five other naked people of all shapes, sizes and colors. Nary a man was erect, this wasn't about sex.

I was eighteen with a woman who was twenty-eight, and despite our age difference and her sordid past I had developed a crush. We were naked together on our first "date" with many strangers. There was no uneasiness; no one felt the need to cover up. The openness and oneness that flowed from a shared nakedness with nothing to hide were freeing and empowering. Despite the overall energy in the room, I was aware of her nakedness, this was someone I had courted. She was thin with alabaster white skin and small but well-proportioned firm breasts.

We were sitting next to Sheba, a black woman, and her seventeen-year-old daughter Venus, and the contrast between them was stark. Many were overweight, others were in great shape. Aside from Venus, everyone was much older than me. The music was great, and Mortie loved my gift, Thai sticks, perhaps the most powerful weed I have ever encountered. The following week Glenda and I joined a pagan group comprised of many of the folks we met at the party and began to learn about Wicca in earnest. A few months after that I parted from Glenda and arrived at Leigh's apartment, as a clandestine pagan initiate.

## Mitch and Ginny

A short time after Mitch bought me breakfast, sparks ignited between him and Ginny, and they married. Mitch's friend John, a chemist from New York City, took over the apartment in Enosburg. John had a bad temper but we became friends after Mitch moved down by the river with Ginny.

One of the things I remember most about that house was standing in the dimly-lit galley kitchen, preparing instant coffee. The water came to a boil and someone went to pour the water into the cups. Ginny cautioned that the water must boil longer, "If you don't let the water boil long enough you will get foam in your cup. I hate foam in my cup." I never noticed before but, to date, I always let the water boil a little longer. At some point during the move from Enosburg to Burlington they found God, became "born again" and to my Fahrenheit 451 horror, burned all of Mitch's books. I was grateful that I still had several in my possession. What a loss of knowledge.

## Gregg the Guru

The second year I went to the Dairy Festival, I met and befriended the legendary Gregg, a funny farm original. Self-known as Gregg "Caterpillar" Guru, he was a student of eastern spirituality and, at the time, took a vow of silence. He wore a chalkboard on a rope around his neck, communicating via terse phrases. We had many philosophical discussions about life and spirituality, with me doing the talking and reading his slate.

Gregg rented a storefront on Main Street in Enosburg. His quaint apartment with dim lighting and the prevalent aromatic smell of incense peeked at the pedestrian traffic on the sidewalk through a veil of sheer curtains that allowed us to see out, but obscured the view of the passersby. I think the incense was for both the soul and to cover the smell of burning reefer. He wrote a book of spiritual observations with sketches and parables. To my surprise, he gave me the manuscript to take back to the Phunee Farm, where most of it was written, to review, study and comment on.

When I knocked on his door to share my thoughts, he was gone to parts unknown. That was the last time I saw Gregg, but not the last time I would cross his path. We heard he returned to Long Island and was arrested the following summer for violating New York State Penal Law section 220.05, possession of marijuana.

When not hanging out in town, the Enosburg crowd often found their way to Kilgore Trout's Saloon. We Phunee farmers were regulars, and Tara and Skye were legends.

# 15

# KILGORE TROUT SALOON

*Trout called mirrors 'leaks' . . . If he saw a child near a mirror, he might wag his finger warningly, and say with great solemnity, "Don't get too near that leak. You wouldn't want to wind up in the other universe, would you?"*
*Sometimes somebody would say in his presence, "Excuse me, I have to take a leak." And Trout would reply waggishly, "Where I come from, that means you're about to steal a mirror."*
*~ Kurt Vonnegut*

### Venus on the Half Shell

Kilgore's was started in the early '70s, by five Harvard graduates. The Harvard Crimson quotes Kenneth Cross, "There are an amazing amount of crazy people here. It's a small town; you know everybody. Education doesn't give you a whole lot to do, and the problems of the city bummed me out, so I came here. You create your own interests and follow them."

Happy to report on behalf of all of the Phunee farmers, we were among the crazy people. I could relate, but for me, it was the suburbs that bummed me out. The name Kilgore Trout Saloon alluded to the

Kurt Vonnegut character, Kilgore Trout, but also the Trout River that ran behind the saloon. Kilgore's was a cross between an old western saloon and an Irish pub. The back corner was set up for kids with games, movies and other activities. Sometimes I would hang with Fae and the other kids back there. The bar itself had the quintessential brass foot rail and polished wood bar top with an antique cash register centered on the back counter with huge mirror above it reflecting back the numerous bottles of alcohol arrayed on glass shelves. We rarely reached the top shelf. Multiple copies of Venus on the Half Shell, written by Kilgore Trout, were displayed next to the register, like an ode to its namesake.

## The Car Knew the Way Home

Kilgore's was fifteen miles south of the Phunee Farm, and most of the trip could be completed using dirt roads. This allowed the car to drive us home when we were in varying states of inebriation but sufficient to navigate the dirt back roads. What was that old joke? A cop pulls an old Irish priest over for driving erratically. He says, "You look mighty drunk, Father, what are doing driving tonight?" "Well, officer, I was much too drunk to walk." We were young, it was a different age, and driving while inebriated was not on anyone's radar. Locals, emigrant hippies and law enforcement folk alike found their way home from many an establishment, party or buddies' house while under the influence of hops, the grape or grain, without much attention. The sparse country roads, as well as the nature of the times, were also factors. That all changed years later when the nation cracked down on "Driving While Intoxicated." The fact that your car was sober would no longer be considered relevant.

My old Dodge knew those country roads well. On more than one occasion, but notably one time, a bunch of us packed into the car and drove to Kilgore's. The Dart had two front bucket seats, center console and a back seat that fit three. We packed in seven, getting the ride started with a few quarts of Labatt's Blue and a joint before pulling up to the parking lot. Hugh claimed two tables in the corner, and we all sat, waiting for the band. "The Green Mountain Boys" bluegrass band was playing. By midnight the place was full to capacity. The band finished playing at two AM so we all loaded in the Dart. I was driving, Hugh riding shotgun, Tara on his lap, Ronnie, Craig, Bruce and Pepe in the back seat. Jason came over to the car and said, "My car is dead. Can you give us a ride to Pat's cousin's house. It's just three miles; dirt roads all the way."

"Sure Jason, but there's no room in the car. Can you sit on the trunk and hang on?"

### Them Fargo Brothers

On St. Patrick's Day in 1976, the country folk band, "Them Fargo Brothers," played their first gig at Kilgore's and billed them as "Them O'Fargo Brothers."

The snow had yet to abate up in the mountains. We were looking forward to seeing the band and hoped the snow would stop before showtime at eight PM. The snow slowed around five PM, so we geared up and got ready to drive out into the waning snow. Plenty of time. Craig was working in the barn, so we flicked the lights on and off a few times to get his attention. Route 105 had four inches of powder when we reached the stop sign. A seasoned green Dodge pickup was coming down the hill, heading toward Jay. We turned right and passed the truck on the slope. At the same time, we were getting ready to leave for Montgomery, Them Fargo Brothers were traveling on Route 105, cresting Owl Ridge toward Montgomery. They were on the road for three hours, driving in from New Hampshire in a 1971 Ford van, drinking beer the entire trip. They pulled over to the side. The van sunk into the deep snow. Stuck! Two hours to show time.

We arrived at the saloon early, the band arrived late. While waiting, we wandered in and out of the bar and onto the chilly porch when the Ford van was towed into the parking lot. They ran onto the front porch of the Saloon where we were sitting and were met by Gordon Cross and Tom Murphy holding a tray full of shots of Jameson Irish whiskey. They retold the story of a long drive and confessed the beer run for the ride caused them to stop and pee and how they were stuck for about an hour. They could see the lights of a farmhouse blinking on and off through the barren trees and were starting to trek toward the house when a communard driving an old green Dodge pickup truck helped them get a tow truck and pull them out. It was clear from their story that they got stuck less than a mile from the Phunee Farm and we chuckled when they mentioned the blinking lights.

## Back at the Campfire

"You gotta be shitting me. Them Fargo Brothers, really," Skye said. "Sally, Tess and I used to follow Them Fargos when they played in Connecticut. I loved them. Sally met her boyfriend at one of their concerts."

"Well, I used to like them." I joked.

## 16

# BACK FROM THE BEACH

*The echoes of beauty you've seen transpire,
Resound through dying coals of a campfire.
~ Ernest Hemingway*

Hours later, propped up around the warm ashes of a faded fire, we were awakened by Fae, still wrapped in a blanket, humming, playing and prodding at Tara saying, "I'm hungry." Waking to a symphony of birds, dawn light creeping through the forest, brushing the forest floor off our clothes, we rubbed the sleep from our eyes, then packed up.

Climbing the narrow trail, we stepped out of the dark forest onto the logging road and into a bright sky. The sun crested the ridge behind us, casting a golden hue over the valley. Morning dew glistened in the fields rolling down to the Lucas. We walked in quiet reverence, not exactly hungover, but perhaps we should have been. Fae got tired of walking so I transferred her to my shoulders. "So, Jelly Bean, wanna help me make some pancakes after we clean up back at the house?"

Fae said, "Yes, can I mix the batter? I like them with apples."

"Of course you can. We have plenty of apples but you have to help me pick them from the orchard first," I said with a tickle, earning another giggle. We reached the porch and opened the kitchen door, arms full and talking breakfast.

## Coiled

The cellar door was open when we left for the Lucas and we thought nothing of it. Stepping through the door with our view of the floor blocked, we didn't see the black snake curled in the middle of the kitchen floor. The black eastern rat snake was two inches thick with a bulge just beyond its head. Startled, it lunged then pulled back into a defensive coil of at least six folds, then raised its head like a king cobra lulled from a woven basket. It all went so fast as we opened the door, stepped in, and looked down. "Holy shit, "Craig said, stepping through the door first, dancing away from the hissing serpent. We moved away. Sensing our retreat it uncoiled to its six-foot length, then slithered under the sink and down along the sink drain pipe into the basement. Fae said, "C'mon, guys. Let's see where it goes." Then she ran outside; I was right behind her.

Skye climbed onto a chair, "Ewww! Snakes. I hate snakes. They skeeve me," she said, shivering. "Make me creepy all over."

We ran outside and saw the snake winding its way across the driveway and into the tall grass. It must have chased and caught a mouse as evidenced by the bulge close to its head. We sealed the holes we found under the sink and made it a point to keep the cellar door closed henceforth.

"Breakfast is ready. Fae, leave the snake alone. Come to the table, please," Tara said. Then, sitting down, she continued, "So, boys, the kitchen looks really good. I mean homey, not like last years boys' club."

"Yeah," Skye said, "It looks like a woman's touch. What gives?"

"It's a long story," I said. "Did you see the woodshed? Let me back up a bit."

## Wake Up Call

A week ago we had a reckoning. We'd done a fair amount of partying with our guests all summer, and we were behind with cutting firewood. We needed to change our mindset from partying hippie youths to active woodsmen readying for winter. On the way to Aubuchon's hardware store in Richford, we came across a man standing near a beat-up Toyota Land Cruiser on the side of the road with the hood up. We stopped to see if we could help. He was rugged-looking—about five foot seven with a muscular build, a dark, weather-beaten face, around thirty-five, and sported a thick auburn mustache with a short haircut.

"What can I do for you boys?" The man said in a jovial manner, speaking with a New England country accent as he spit out tobacco juice.

He was a mechanic working in his driveway. "Mighty white of you to stop," he said, introducing himself as Nick. "Me and my woman, Mia, moved up a couple of months ago. You boys want a beer?" Then he yelled, "Hey, Mia, we have company, get me three beers."

Mia, an attractive sturdy woman, about thirty with dark curly hair, pleasant round, friendly face with a wide smile and obvious Italian features, met us at the door with three bottles. She greeted us warmly.

The small, tired kitchen felt vast with the aroma of Italian cooking filling the air. When we walked in, we were met by two large German Shepherds. The male was a huge dog named Zeke with the biggest square head I had ever seen on a dog. As I passed by Sally, the other dog, I patted her on the head and scratched her ears. Nick, showing concern, stepped over and said, "You're lucky she didn't bite your hand off. She can be a bit feisty. You're OK with me if she likes you."

Nick praised Zeke as he told us of a skirmish with two men outside the house when he first arrived. Zeke, sensing Nick was in danger, tried in vain to get outside. The door was closed and the lower windows were shuttered. His instincts inflamed, Zeke jumped through the upper sash, breaking the glass and plummeting twelve feet to the ground below and sprang into the fray. He offered no more details of the ruckus, but it was safe to say that Zeke ruled that moment. They were renting the first floor of the house, the outside of which could be described as dismal. We left after two beers, invited them up to the farm, gave them directions, and continued on our way.

When they arrived at the farm for the first time, Mia fell in love with the Acorn wood cook stove, saying, "Oh, that brings back memories. I used to bake bread in a big old wood cook stove, at my grandmother's farm. Oh, by the way, I wasn't sure if you were vegetarians so I made an eggplant parmigiana for dinner."

"Thanks, Mia," Craig said. "If it tastes anything like it smelled at your apartment, we are in for a culinary treat. Yes, we are vegetarians."

We set her up with hockey stick scraps and seasoned maple, split small for the Acorn's firebox. She started the fire and put dinner together while we were outside talking firewood. It was obvious she knew her way around a wood cook stove. Nick loved the fact that there were no neighbors, saying, "Nice hideout you got here." Then he took notice of our meager attempts at gathering firewood.

Autumn was fast approaching, and only three cord stacked in the woodshed. Outside, we had a pile of logs and a few blocked. An eight-pound splitting maul was leaning up against our main chopping block, with another axe blade driven deep into the surface. Our steel splitting wedges were scattered around. Nick commented, "Decent setup you got here, but ya know, you shouldn't leave the blade in the block like that, it'll dull the edge. You're gonna want that kept sharp 'cause I bet it gets mighty cold up here. You folks are gonna need some serious wood before winter sets in."

Craig and I looked at each other, but we didn't say anything about our fun, soul-searching summer. Craig said, "Yeah, we are behind schedule, but we have time," and thought, the hippie B & B was closed.

## Schooled

Nick asked, "You guys got a good chainsaw?" I reached into the woodshed and took out my sixteen-inch McCulloch. While we talked, he leaned on the back hatch of the 1973 Land Cruiser, chewing tobacco. He looked at our saw, spit and said, "That's a decent saw, looks like you got one of the last good models. They're not what they used to be." He turned around and motioned us over and opened the hatch. It was like a logger's candy store. In the back were two sixteen inch Homelite chainsaws, an eighteen inch Poulan and a top of the line, monster twenty-four inch Stihl chainsaw. It was evident that they had seen some serious use. There was a box with bar oil, two-cycle engine oil, and five gallons of pre-mixed gasoline, several wrenches and files. A thick chain was coiled in the back corner. With a devilish grin he pulled out the monster saw, spit out his chaw and said, "So, you want some help?"

Nick was a woodsman, reinforcing our initial impression. He talked of his time logging in New Hampshire and about a log cabin he built in Sheffield, Vermont on property that abutted the interstate. It was well off the beaten path, miles from the nearest accessible paved road. We just kept getting more and more enamored with this mountain man guy. I suppose, in future terminology, we developed a "man crush" and were blinded to any signs to the contrary. I wondered why they left Sheffield.

Nick was ready to tackle the rest of the pile. "What say we cut some wood," he said, putting down the big saw and grabbing one of the

Homelites. Craig and I grabbed each end of the nearest log and put it into the log rack. Nick stepped over to one of the bigger logs on the ground and pushed it with his foot so it rolled away from the pile. With the log on the ground, holding the saw in his right hand, he pulled the starter cord with his left and the saw roared to life. The man moved like a machine down the length of the log cutting a little more than three-quarters of the way through the log, spaced every sixteen inches. When he cut the last section, he rolled the log with his foot bringing the uncut portion to the top. Then he slid the tip of the chain into each slot and lifted up with the saw, freeing each sixteen-inch block from the log. Before I completed my first cut, he finished six.

Nick advised, "Those racks are great for cutting the smaller logs. Stack them up as high as you can and bring the saw down through the whole pile and you'll make quick work of it. But leave the bigger logs on the ground and cut them the way I just did." Impressed, we felt like we just met a mountain man and possible mentor to the wilds.

Mia yelled out that dinner was ready. While she waited, she tidied up the kitchen and organized as she cooked. We stalled her a couple of times because we were so close to finishing, but she won out and we went in to eat with two logs left. The dinner conversation was all about firewood, chainsaws, logging and eggplant parmigiana, and how homey Mia made the kitchen look.

## Apple Pancakes

"So Fae, do you like the apple pancakes?" I asked.

"They're my favorite. Can I have more?"

Craig said, "I'll get them. I think it's gonna be another hot one today. It's already warm. Do you want to go to the swimming hole later?"

Fae jumped up, "Can we, Mom? Please, Mom."

"Finish your breakfast. Maybe after lunch. I need to take a quick nap first, then I want to go into town."

"I'm down with a nap," Craig said.

Skye nuzzled up to Craig. "You want company?"

"Well, Fae was the only one to get a good sleep in, but I have a second wind so I'll hang out with her. Wanna help me in the garden, Fae?"

"Okay," Fae said half asleep.

"What time is it anyway, Skye asked?"

Craig checked his watch and said, "It's 8 o'clock. When did we leave the beach?" Fae was already asleep, and minutes later everyone else was down for a nap.

Two hours later everyone woke up. Everyone but me that is. I cleaned up the kitchen and read for a while, too restless to sleep.

Tara said, "I was thinking about bringing Fae into St. Albans to see my mother for a few hours. Skye, did you decide if you're coming?"

"I need some stuff from the store, so yeah. When do you expect to get back here?"

"Hopefully in time to go to the swimming hole, but we have to be back before it gets dark. I don't want Fae to relive Craig and Bob's night trip."

"I'm gonna try for some sleep. What are you up to, Craig?" I asked.

"I think I'll hitch a ride to Enosburg if that's alright with you, Tara." They packed up and drove off in the Bluebird. I went to my room.

## In the Bed of a Pickup Truck

The 1959 Ford pickup, in good shape for a Vermont vehicle, pulled into Enosburg. Hugh's ears must have been ringing; his name was invoked many times throughout the day. They hopped out in the center of town and went into Carney's Luncheonette straight away. They were serving breakfast, and they hoped it would be ready. Fern couldn't wait. Hugh could not stop talking about the famous raspberry pie. They walked in and Hugh said, "Hi, Jenny, smiling trees to you. Have you seen Tara?"

"No, hon. She left here a few months ago. So, the usual for you, Hugh? You're in luck—the pie is just out of the oven."

"Extra big pieces today, please. It's Fern's first time. Oh, I'm such a shit. Jenny, this is Fern." Hugh sat with his back to the window, so Fern could look outside.

Just as the pie was served, the Bluebird pulled over near the Ben Franklin, three doors down the road, and let Craig out. Then it continued to St. Albans.

# 17

# WALKING STAFF SAGA

*As he lay on the mountaintop, the great eagle Gwaihir came up and bore him to Lothlórien, where he was clothed and replenished, and given a new staff by Galadriel.*
*~ JRR Tolkien*

### Ah-Ha Moment

I lay in bed tossing, unable to sleep, my bedroom hot and muggy. My head was spinning with everything that happened since we went rock walking yesterday. Reminiscing and telling stories all morning left my mind swimming with fragments of tales yet to tell. I looked up at my new walking staff leaning against the door jamb as a ray of sunlight lit the staff at an odd angle, illuminating the wide crown and showing me a path. "That's it," I said aloud, jumping out of bed. In my mind's eye, I visualized the steps needed to create the final product. Walking to the barn, I hoped I could finish carving my staff before everyone got home. Maybe even take it out for a spin. Removing the bark was quick work with my drawknife, the old tool I got at an auction. The original idea came to me last night when I found my staff high up in that dead maple tree. I'm no Michelangelo, but like him, I can often see a finished carving inside the wood. After that, it's easy: just remove the extra wood. I carved my moonbeam symbol, a crescent moon pierced by a suggestive moonbeam, in high relief, achieved by removing the surrounding wood. Elemental Celtic runes were carved along the shaft. A small pipe was added at the crown as a final touch. When done, my staff was six feet one inch long, equal to my height and arm span, or so says Leonardo Da Vinci's Vitruvian Man. A work of art that served me well for many years.

## Value of a Staff

An incident a few years back was a great exemplar of a walking staff's value. I was hiking Slide Mountain, the highest in New York's Catskill Mountain range, with Craig, Leigh and others, including my friend Jordan who was more of a suburb-city guy than outdoorsman. The weather was warm for a late spring camping trip, despite the remnants of snow along the trail. Reaching the crest, we climbed atop a massive boulder, the size of a house, rested and hydrated while enjoying the view.

Our thirst slaked, canteens empty, we followed a trail to the best water I ever tasted, which flowed from a rock crevice a hundred feet below. The trail became icy and steepened just before turning hard to the left. Directly in front of me was a fifty-foot drop. I stood at the edge making sure everyone knew about the danger casually leaning on a simple staff I found. Jordan was last in line looking at the view when he slipped on the ice and started sliding toward the drop. He was building up speed on the slick ice as everyone tried to stop him but they lost their own footing on the ice slick. He slid past each of them and was racing toward the drop. With little time to react, I thrust my staff between two big rocks and braced myself as Jordan's legs cleared the edge. He reached up and grabbed hold of my staff, his feet and most of his body dangling over the edge. White with fear he worked his way back to his feet, his face already reddening with anger. He remained silent as we filled our canteens and returned to the top. When we reached the top, he turned and shouted at the mountain, "Fuuuuck." Such is the value of a walking staff.

### Big Black Surprise

My new carved staff in hand, I checked the time—one PM—plenty of time to try it out on its maiden voyage. Contemplative, I walked in silence. David Carradine's character, Kwai Chang from the old Kung Fu TV show, came to mind; he could walk on rice paper without tearing it. The quiet crunching of stones beneath my feet, the muffled crack of small twigs and the crinkle of dried leaves complimented the beat of my heart. One with nature, I moved up the mountain, gazing at my surroundings, mindful of each step, each stone on my path and each twig leaf and branch around me. Like a lure to a fish, I was mesmerized by a small leaf reflecting sunlight as it spun down from high in a birch tree.

Moving with quiet deliberate steps, absorbing the tranquility of the forest, I stepped onto the first of several flat dry rocks across the flooded path before me. As I moved to the second rock, it pulled out of the mud creating curious sucking sounds, slurp-gurgle. Intrigued by the sounds breaking the silence, I leaned on my staff and teetered back and forth on the rock, thwerp-flurp. The deep tones were meditative and calming in a strange way, like a Gregorian chant.

The sounds attracted another's attention. I looked up from my teetering stone and ten feet away a black bear stuck his formidable head out from behind a tree.

The bear sauntered onto the path toward the sound and me, six feet away. I stopped, my tripod stance frozen; looking toward the bear, I was calm. I had no fear, saying to myself, I can't believe I'm actually seeing a bear. I was staring un-menacingly at a three hundred pound predator. We both stood there, like statues in the forest, my noisy rock silent. Avoiding direct eye contact, I looked up and projected my thoughts, it's cool. The bear looked back at me and I could swear he returned the same thought. With that, Ursus turned and started up the trail. Keeping the rock quiet I turned and started walking back the way I came, my pace quickening. I looked back and noticed the bear also quickened his pace, in the opposite direction. Slowing now and resuming my walk in silence, it was difficult to stay mindful of the moment. My head was spinning with excitement, a spring in my step as I thought of *The Jungle Book's* bear Baloo and started singing *zippity do da*, as I danced and bounced back down the trail.

## The Bluebird Returns

The gang returned home as I dashed down the trail back to the house. Tara parked the Bluebird and everyone got out and Fae said, "Can we go to the swimming hole now, Mom?"

"You bet, Jelly Bean. You've been such a good girl. Go see if you can find Bob."

"He's not in his room, Mom. I'll go look in the barn."

Craig said, "I'll come with you, Fae."

"Not in the barn," Fae said.

Skye spotted me, "Look—he's bouncing down the road like something is chasing him and he has a big stick."

I leaned on my staff, hunched over trying to catch my breath—more from excitement than exertion. "You're not (gasp) gonna (gasp) believe (gasp, wheeze) what just happened (pant.)"

"What happened?" everyone asked with concern.

"Let me catch my breath." Beaming, I relayed my story and everyone was psyched. We had a reason to celebrate; did we need one?

"Wow, you're walking staff came out great. Now I understand what you were saying last night,"

Thanks, Craig, "Check out this feature."

Skye came over, "Is that a pipe." Wow, that's very cool. What are those symbols?"

"Celtic runes, actually. They are elemental sigils; this one is earth, next air, then fire water, energy and power," I said pointing to each symbol going down the staff. "Moon signs, a pentagram and other Wiccan symbols are on the back."

"Mommm, are there bears by the swimming hole?" Fae asked warily. "I don't think I want to go near a bear. They're scary."

"No, Jelly Bean, they're up higher on the mountain. Who's ready to swim?" In truth, bears go wherever they want.

# 18

# VISITOR LOG

*And for those who were dancing were thought to be insane by those who could not hear the music*
*~ Frederich Nietzche*

## Hippie B & B

We were living the dream. An amazing adventure of wondrous exploration, fun, friends and family, but not like our childhood dream. Tending the gardens and animals, cutting firewood and upgrading the house and barn were all consistent with our dream; but visitors and partying were consistent with being twenty-something. When it warmed, visitors from home, hitchhikers and transplants arrived. Contrasted against the intense winter brutality, the summer shifted our focus from survival mode to the splendor of the summer play. The summers were robust with company, some staying the whole summer, others for weeks or a day. In reality, we were less like a commune and more like a hippie bed and breakfast. Unlike a traditional B&B, we offered a mountain to sleep on, work-for-meals-plans and extended stay options. We didn't always know who was coming and were ofttimes surprised when a hitchhiker stayed for weeks. At one point, we had over twenty people sleeping on the land, in the house, barn, tent or yurt.

## Skunked

Even with the harsh winter conditions, our sturdier friends from Long Island braved the elements and came to visit. The first stalwart to arrive was Byron, making his third trip. He drove up in the middle of a wicked March snow storm in his friend, Chet's, 1974 Silver Corvette. On the road for about twelve hours, they traveled on clear roads the first part of the trip and the car flew most of the way up the Northway. The blizzard started before Plattsburgh. Corvettes were not designed to travel in deep snow or ice. Grueling! They crawled, spun out, slid their way through and when roads cleared, they started smelling something bad. They were two hours away, when Byron said, "Holy Shit! What's that smell? Chet, pull over. I think we hit a skunk."

"Nah, let's keep going. I don't want to stop now the road is open; we can air it out." The smell persisted an hour later. They stopped for gas and walked around the car but saw no sign of blood or fur, so they kept driving. They pulled up to the house just as they could no longer stand the smell. Jumping out of the car gasping, they grabbed a small box and a big bag. The small box contained some sweet smelling high-end Columbian weed and the big bag had two bottles of coke, a bottle of rum and a bottle of Jack. When Byron slammed the passenger door, a chunk of ice behind the front wheel fell to the ground along with the remains of the skunk. They gasped, savoring the fresh air.

It was a short visit, but rich with a reward for us. The company alone was great. Our weed supply was Vermont homegrown or, if lucky, we smoked commercial weed, a third of which was seeds. The seed ritual took place with every new bag. Shaking an album cover, the seed rolled off. They came in handy. Chet raised the bar. He was my Long Island source for exotic weed, which we knew as Columbian, very brown tasty weed with fewer but much more powerful seeds which we treated like gold.

The night's snow abated, leaving a fresh coating glistening in the morning light. "Oh, my freak'n head! What's that damn racket?"

"It's the town alarm clock, Byron."

Chet moaned, "Somebody turn it off."

The loud scraping faded, replaced by the rumble of the snowplow driving back down the driveway. Despite drinking and smoking into the morning, a few pots of coffee had our eyes open by the time the sun climbed over Owl Ridge. Bill and Chet were ready to go.

## Jose

I met Jose in my junior year of high school on the day he transferred from the Bronx. He was a tall gregarious guy of Puerto Rican descent with a perpetual smile who acclimated well in a predominantly white school. Always laughing or at least in a good mood, he was a big ladies' man, outgoing and witty. He came up to the farm a few times, always with a different woman.

His first visit was with Natasha. It was a hot July day and no one else was home, so the three of us went down to Lucas Brook. Before her feet touched the water, she was naked. We followed her lead and rock walked for the afternoon with a splash in the waterfall pool. I learned Tasha loved to be naked and had an amazing physique, with perfect breasts and a well-sculptured slim figure to match. When we got back, Jose said "Isn't she beautiful? She told me she wanted to have sex with you. Do you want to have sex with her? She loves it." I was stunned. "Really?" We went to my room. Jose went for a walk.

Once, while on leave from the Army, he came to visit, driving his beat up yellow 1966 Volkswagen Bug. He was visiting with Joan, a cute, thin girl with swaying hips, small breasts and short curly auburn hair —and always with a sultry smile. It was late March with snow trace scattered throughout the valley; the mountain peaks were still capped white. We drove into town so Jose could use the phone and check on his status back at the Base. He hung up the phone and turned toward us, his face ashen, saying, "All leaves were canceled." I needed to be back at Fort Hood yesterday. My whole battalion was ordered to deploy to Fort Chaffee in Arkansas, for Operation New Arrivals—Vietnamese refugees. The Vietnam War was about to formally end. "Holy shit! I think I'm AWOL!" he lamented.

A night of partying, on the road at dawn, plenty of time he thought. Surprise! It was late March in the mountains of Northern Vermont and we woke up the next morning to a foot of snow and reports of blizzard conditions all over New England. Jose, Joan and Hugh left a few hours later in the VW bug, with visibility down to a few feet. Snow was falling at a frightening rate.

We got word about their trip south a few days later. On the way to the Northway, they got stuck in a ditch twice, the second time they thought they were stuck for good. They trudged through the deep snow to the closest farm and pleaded for help. The farmer, a patriot, appreciated their plight. After an eternity of waiting, he pulled them free with his tractor.

Freed from the ditch, the windshield wipers broke from the weight of the snow. They rigged a system to operate the wipers by tying a rope to each wiper. For the next hundred miles, Jose pulled one way then Hugh pulled the other. They drove the rest of the way through the blizzard with the windows opened a crack. Jose was two days late getting back to base; but they loved the story, and then demoted him one stripe.

## First Guns

Andy, Scarlett and Samilia were some of the first to visit, after the valley greened. Driving in Scarlett's Chevy van, they arrived with Long Island delicacies such as bagels and hard rolls and, of course, exotic weed. Samilia's brother Qamar, and his friends Nick and Jon, pulled up behind them in a white Pontiac LeMans. Upon arriving, they removed the inside of their car doors. Hidden within were five handguns—two Saturday night specials, a 38-caliber Smith and Wesson, a chromed 45-caliber Colt revolver, a 9-mm Glock automatic and a small 25-caliber automatic Derringer. The back doors were loaded with boxes of ammunition. These were the first guns to find their way to our farm. We hated guns and the violence they represented. In time, we learned that they had a legitimate place on a farm.

For this trip, they wanted to do some target practice. The vastness of our surroundings made it easy. No big deal. We gave them a wide berth. They owned the guns and wanted the practice. Why? Because they were criminals! I met them once before and they bragged about their prowess with burglarizing factories and other businesses. They were prepared to use those guns in the course of their crimes. Two days later, they left after hiding their weapons for the return trip, I never saw them again. Andy, Scarlet and Samilia stayed the rest of the week.

## Rescues

Byron returned a few weeks after Andy and company left. This time he had two rescues with him. No not dogs: Deidre and Luthor. Deidre was seventeen and six months pregnant. Luthor was a good-hearted kid who made a bunch of bad decisions, but he was not the father. Their arrival and request to stay changed the farm dynamic quite a bit. We became big brothers to the seventeen-year-olds. After getting them set up with Social Services, they brought food stamps and WIC cheese to our diet. The baby was getting close to term; they wanted to get married. So with Craig acting as minister, we painted our faces, joined in a big circle and married them. It wasn't legal, but it was real. Not long after the wedding, Deidre made up with her mother. Byron came back and transported them back to Long Island. We never saw or heard from them again.

Hugh, Tara, Bob and Paul at the wedding

## Shocking

Anka, Maria, Hank and Larry arrived in Larry's 1972 Chrysler van a couple of weeks later. Anka, a native of Germany with a sturdy frame and cheerful face, helped me pass my German Regents in high school. Hank was a year older than me, Larry two years younger. They were as skinny as we were with long thick hair, quality freak flags. I was a little jealous, my thin rat tail ponytail was unremarkable. Maria was tiny, less than five feet tall with a dark Mediterranean complexion, long dark hair and friendly eyes.

One evening, a storm imminent, air charged, some of us stopped playing Frisbee and went into the kitchen. Hank, Larry, Anka and Maria continued to toss the disc between the house and barn, hoping to get in a few more throws before the rain. It was like a bomb exploded. Preceding the rain, a bolt of lightning struck the barn with a thunderous, earsplitting boom. I was standing in the kitchen when the main charge hit the barn's metal roof.

The barn's lightning rods glowed and dissipated the charge through the grounding cable, fizzling into the dirt. Through the open kitchen door, I saw a zigzagging blue static charge, like in a cartoon, jump from the barn roof to the house, hitting the metal-jacketed chimney.

My ears ringing, I watched in amazement as the brilliant blue spark wrapped itself around the chimney, like a ferocious blue snake slithering around the chimney's metal column through the kitchen and grounding into the dirt-floored crawlspace. I looked around and saw that everyone's hair was flying toward the ceiling from the static charge. The hair on my arms tingling; I rushed outside to see if everyone was alright. The force of the lightning was explosive.

Maria was entering the porch when she was thrown through the door and into Hugh, pushing them both against the inside wall, their long hair entangled together, floating up toward the porch's ceiling. Larry and Hank were furthest from the blast and landed on their asses, while Anka was thrown backwards and lay like a turtle on her back. As the static discharged, the guy's hair was settling to their shoulders while Anka's hair settled to the ground like a frizzy strawberry blonde halo. She sat up brushing, the driveway from her hair. She would have been in big trouble if this happened after the accident.

Two weeks after Anka left the farm, she went camping at Giant Panther Ledge near Slide Mountain with Andy and friends. She wandered away from the light of their campfire to answer nature's call. It was pitch dark; she didn't need to go far for privacy. Stepping behind a cluster of rock maples, she turned, squatted and fell backwards over a twenty foot cliff. She was immobilized, her back broken. Andy went looking for her when she didn't come back. He found her, then ran down the mountain in total darkness, burning his clothes as he did so he could find his way. He was near naked when he reached help. Anka recovered many months later and returned to the Phunee Farm the following spring to visit.

One of the best compliments I ever received was from Larry who, after hearing me describe our sanctuary on the mountain and our spiritual direction, commented, "Wow, Bob. You are like a priest of nature the way you talk about this place."

Hank was nodding his head, saying with reverence, "Yeah, I feel that too, man!"

Later that summer Maria sent a letter to Hugh. A small envelope with iconic drawings of mountains and Hugh's symbolic smiling trees were drawn on the lower left side of the envelope. The colorful letter was addressed simply Hugh, Richford, Vermont. It was delivered.

### Geno / Marta / Clara

Sometime later that summer Geno arrived with Marta and Clara. Geno was an entrepreneur who realized the early demand for marijuana. He did well, invested and went legit. He once asked me to deliver a guitar case to a friend a few towns over, which I did. I shouldn't have, but I did. There were six pounds of commercial grade bud in the case and one was for me. Marta was one of the hottest girls in high school, blonde, thin, tall, long-legged, flawless light complexion, well formed, great person, and Geno's new girlfriend. Clara was similar to Marta but with a darker complexion and deep-set dark eyes.

After hearing about it, the girls were anxious to check out the waterfalls and swimming hole. Geno opted to stay at the house and catch up with Hugh. I led the girls down to Lucas Brook. Barefoot, they picked up rock walking fast. We dallied at the waterfall, listening to the brook play its tune, splashing into the pool. Climbing up the root ladder we made our way to the swimming hole.

When we got to the water, they both stripped down naked. Neither would be considered busty, but perfectly proportioned to their lithe physiques, small firm breasts, tight abs with long Rockette-like legs. I joined them swimming, then we lingered on the sun-washed rocks. We rock walked with clothes in hand, until we reached the waterfalls, where we dressed before descending the root ladder. Back at the house, an anxious Hugh and Geno were waiting. Geno held out his hand, displaying a clear plastic bag with orange powder and a rolled up one hundred dollar bill—organic mescaline. Might as well snort in style. We did. I suggested a hike up to the old Bell house.

Our path took us through a stand of young maples, mixed with birch and poplar, that grew fast and straight as the forest went about reclamation. Twenty five feet tall, two to three inches thick at the base, they were limbless half way up. We were in no hurry, ambling along enjoying the peyote-weighted color perspective, laughing and dancing among the trees. Everyone was wearing cutoff shorts and hiking boots. The men were shirtless and the girls braless behind flowered peasant blouses. Lying on our backs in the deep grass under the tall slim trees, I saw a vertical pathway.

Feeling energetic, I jumped to my feet and shimmied up the nearest maple, and when it reached a tipping point, the tree started to bend. Reaching out to a nearby poplar, I pulled myself over, wrapping my legs around it. I found that by moving up or down and leaning, I could control the speed and inclination of the bending tree. Looking through the trees, I saw another tree within reach, so climbing higher and then leaning to the right I was able to snag the next tree and move along like a monkey through the trees. At first, the others didn't know what to make of it, and then one by one they started up the other trees.

Encouraged by the mescaline, we discovered a new form of tree walking such that we shimmied and swung in the trees until we noticed the irritation on our bare skin from the tree bark. Distracted by the added energy, enhanced colors and altered perspective of the psychedelic, it took some time for us to notice the problem. Raw reddened skin was evident the next day. This new sport was repeated in the future without the mescal assist, but we made sure we wore jeans.

We made it up to the Bell house after the tree walking adventure. The house was small and there was little left of it. High above the Phunee Farm, the view was spectacular. They all left the next day. A week later, Geno wrote to tell us that he bought the Bell place. Like I said, he was taken by the view. He did well.

## Rick and the Border

Opting to take the scenic route along the West Jay Road, driving on Route 105A at Rick's usual high speed, music blasting, we just finished a joint. I told him to take the next right, but the volume was so loud he didn't hear me. We had already started to cross the Missisquoi River Bridge by the time I looked. We were in no-man's-land, between the US and Canadian border, with no place to turn around. Oh no, not again. Rick's instinctual reaction was to stop—bad idea. He turned around and proceeded toward the US border. Why not? he thought. We never went into Canada—worse idea. Eyes from both border stations were on us the whole time. There was no opportunity to ditch the weed we had in the car.

As soon as we pulled up to the borderline, a seasoned border guard told us to get out of the car and go into the office. He asked us for our IDs and directed us to empty our pockets on a chest high white counter. I took out my wallet, removed my license and placed my wallet on the counter. Then I put my keys, lighter, cigarettes, a few nuts and bolts and wrench next to it. Rick did the same; he was in a panic but did his best to stay cool. Border guards in this area had gotten used to long-haired hippie types since the hippie invasion. We were free to go. Before Rick drove off, the guard leaned down to Rick's window. I thought Rick was gonna freak. The guard said, "Next time you find yourself between border posts don't stop and turn around, you dumb shit." Had we just kept driving, the Canadian border guard would have tipped his hat by way of welcome, maybe ask where we were heading, and we would have cruised through. We could have driven up the road apiece and turned around.

When we stopped in no man's land Rick said, "Take these joints, and keep them low." I tucked his and my joints into my sock alongside my black combat boot, a souvenir from my short stint in the Air Force. I'm glad I forgot about the five tabs of paper acid behind the spare key in my wallet. No knowledge, no stress, no worry. These were planned for after dinner.

## Raspberry Pie

Carney's raspberry pie did not disappoint. When Hugh and Fern finished feasting on pie and coffee at Carney's, we were sunning on Lucas Brook. The neighborhood roads did not offer any hitchhiking opportunities, so they slow-walked the mile and a half to Tom's house, only to find the house on Missisquoi Street empty. They curled up in the wicker chairs on the porch, watching the river flow by and, despite the four cups of coffee they drank, they fell asleep.

# 19

# IT'S MAY, IS IT SPRING YET

*There is something infinitely healing in the repeated refrains of nature—
the assurance that dawn comes after night, and spring after winter."
~ Rachel Carson*

### Vernal Equinox

As I understood it, spring started at the Vernal Equinox. The snow and cold didn't agree. Winter lingered well beyond the equinox as spring's march to summer progressed at a labored pace. March came in like a pride of lions, so did April. Believing we cleared the worst of the winter at the end of the third month, we pursued one of our schemes to make money and ordered earthworms. We prepared trays of loamy soil enriched by manure. It was cold when our package of worms arrived in the mail. Craig opened the box and we saw dirt. Underwhelming! We placed the box near the Acorn stove. Returning later the warmed soil was robust with slippery writhing earthworms. Craig yelled, "Yeehaw! We're earthworm ranchers!"

We envisioned our starter worms reproducing exponentially so we could sell the wriggling masses of annelids back to the company we contracted with, or maybe sell them as bait for fishermen at area lakes.

April arrived but winter cold returned with a tame vengeance. The temperature dropped to ten degrees, well below freezing. April Fools! The earthworm habitat froze solid along with the worms and with it our hopes of cash. We sucked at earthworm husbandry.

The snow melted, the spring rain came, and a new phase began. Spring thaw, dirt roads and rain are a bad mix. Mud season! The hard-packed dirt was brutalized by plows, salt and winter; and when it thawed it became a puree of mud, riddled with holes, trenches and gullies. Cars would slip, slide and swerve driving down the driveway and up West Jay. Some roads could swallow a car in the deep, viscous mud. Getting out of a vehicle to push a vehicle free of the mudded bonds was like stepping into brown taffy. The suction sometimes pulled a shoe or even boot from your foot. Time progressed, the rain abated and the wind and sun dried up the roads. The valley awakened. Trees showed signs of budding, the grass greened, wildflowers opened and the ubiquitous scent of spring filled the air. Manure spreaders, colloquially known as "shit spreaders," were feeding the fields for the soon-to-be-sown crops of cow corn and hay.

We broke ground in the garden we inherited out beyond the orchard. Our first garden was laborious—hand-turning the soil and augmenting it with manure, fish emulsion and compost, black gold. We started our vegetable and cannabis seeds in moistened paper towels. Once germinated, we transplanted them into pots. The young plants were then moved outside for increasing time frames or hardened-off. By late May, we were planting seeds of cold-resistant plants such as lettuce, beets, spinach and peas into the loose garden soil. Zucchini and other squashes would need to wait for another few weeks. It was well into June before it was safe to put the seedlings into the garden. Around the same time, tomatoes, eggplant and peppers were ready to harden off and the cannabis seedlings were about a foot tall. They went into a secret garden. A camouflaged trail led to a clearing amid a stand of poplar trees, which provided cover for this clandestine crop which required the regular portage of water.

## Mysterious Find

Spring also meant we could work in the barn. While setting up the summer workshop and cleaning up the barn, we found something very interesting.

It was powerful—hidden in a dark corner, behind a pile of wood and rusted metal. We were scroungers at heart and we explored the pile as we cleared the area in the barn. The dimensional lumber was perfect for building a new workbench. We kept getting distracted by the old metal stuff, like the old maple sugar buckets, some with tree taps inside, and several types of milk pails. Most intriguing was the gear teeth from the baler and other machinery. I found a classic, tubular metal head and footboard for a child's bed. Little did I know that I would restore it for Fae weeks later. After moving most of the pile, Craig said, "Check this out. Is this some kind of door?" The wood was aged, but there was no sign of any hinges. It looked like a trap door. It was dark in this subterranean corner of the barn and it was difficult to make it out. We wondered if it opened to a tunnel.

"Hey, Craig, I'm gonna get a flashlight." Craig moved the rest of the pile before I got back with the flashlight. Shining the light in the corner, what looked like a door was large, flat and secreted in a recess tight against a wall. The age-darkened wood and square cut nails suggested it was old. Vertical slats framed with a narrow border and diagonal brace was a classic door design. Seeing it was unattached, we realized it was an old crate, about the size of a large art portfolio. We tried to move it, but it was so heavy we tilted it to see the other side. The backside looked the same but the top corner of the crate was missing. Lettering on the top edge, *'ht Mills' * East Richford Vermont *  1902.* Some letters were lost from the missing corner, which revealed a glimpse inside.

"Hey, Bob, I think it's a box of old window glass." He called me over to see and said, "This is great! We can replace the broken windows on the porch. I'm tired of looking at that plastic."

"Looks like there's a lot here," I said, "Hey if there's enough we can double up some of the storm windows!" We opened the crate.

It wasn't window glass. Inside we found assorted panes of what looked like black glass; some pieces were broken. Puzzled, we pulled a piece from the crate and lifted it into a shaft of sunlight beaming in from one of the many breaches in the walls and roof. The glass looked old. It was stored on its edge for decades and was thinner on the high end. Many believe that glass is a semi-liquid which settles to the bottom and gets thicker but others challenge that. The debate goes on, but I put my faith in gravity and liquid rather than defects in the original pane.

The moment the glass crossed the mote filled sunbeam, it was clear that the glass was dark blue. It seemed to trap the light, allowing only diffused light through the glass. The meager light piercing the glass revealed tiny air bubbles within. Holding it up to the light, Craig said, "This looks like old stained glass."

"What else could it be?" I asked ."You saw the date on the box, so we know it must be old. You see that lettering on the box? Too bad that corner was missing, I wonder where it was from. At least we know it was some kind of Mill in 1902." The following summer we learned it was Faught Mills. I wonder what they used it for. "What do you think? Did you see those bubbles?" They were spread out in mesmerizing patterns.

Staring at the bubbles through the backlit glass, I was pulled in. "Craig? Would you hand me the glass for a minute?" The instant I touched it I could feel an energy run through me like a warm static charge. Holding the glass up, seeing my reflection distorted through the murky blue hypnotic pattern of the bubbles, I was transported for a flicker of an instant. Staring at my face for one moment, my reflection blurred, revealing nebulous distant vistas, memories and a vague understanding of everything. A nanosecond later, I felt a curious calm, my reflection returning. I put the glass down and told Craig what happened. He picked up the glass again. "I can feel a slight hum of energy when I hold it, but wish I could feel the rest."

"Craig, I think I know how you can. Have you ever heard of a scrying mirror? I got turned onto scrying in the pagan group I joined last fall. It is also called "seeing" or "peeping." It is a tool for looking deep into your inner self which, if you do it right and are lucky, can open a window into the past, present and future events—or even a portal to other planes of existence. Black mirrors made from obsidian are most common, often known as 'magic mirrors'. A scryer friend used a crystal ball, and another the still surface of standing water. The wicked witch of the west used a water scry to hunt for Dorothy. You know about Nostradamus right? He used scrying for many of his divinations.

I can make a couple of scrying mirrors with this glass, but scrying is not casual, there are a lot of rules. I am still learning about this stuff but, in essence, once a psychometric link is established, no one else should use it; the glass must always be clean; it should only be used for scrying; never expose it to sunlight or electric light, and store it wrapped in silk. It is also a personal tool for your eyes only. Let me build the mirrors, then we can get more into it."

I made several scrying mirrors with that blue glass, and working with Craig, we learned how to use them. I know mine worked as hoped.

## Lunar Eclipse

A full lunar eclipse was expected on May 25, 1975. The air was humming with energy; spiritual, magical, celestial and clear skies were forecast. We planned a big celebration. The day was warm, but we knew it would be cool at night, so we gathered wood for a bonfire.

Hugh was psyched about the eclipse and scored several bluish purple tabs of organic mescaline. It had been quite a while since psychedelic drugs had found their way here. The farm itself was no stranger to them. "Time's a-wastin," Hugh said. The sun was dropping in the western sky. We each gobbled up one of the magic tabs. From what Hugh said, they were dried and pulverized shrooms, you know - psilocybin. The real thing was better but was hard on the stomach. In pill form, you got the thrill of the ride with no side effects. The giggling and kibitzing started early, leading to prolonged laughing bouts providing more than a few distractions; might as well have fun.

The colors of the western sky blended and wove through the atmosphere in an overlapping palette of reds, yellows, oranges and blue. A zigzag streak of violet angled through the western sky like a bolt of lightning. There was even a hint of that light green color just above the horizon. The sky, magnificent in its own right, exploded in a surreal phantasm of a shroom-enhanced light show. When the sun, undulating as if breathing, dropped below the horizon, it was time to get the fire going in the back pasture. Lighting the fire, the show was about to begin. The colors of the western sky hung in the dim half-light of dusk.

The fire flared up and we danced around it with our mescaline-influenced, pagan-like dance moves. Then it started. High above the North Jay Mountain, a corner of the bright full moon began to disappear. The instant the earth's penumbra crossed in front of the moon the colors started. The brilliant white of the moon drifted toward orange-red. Imperceptible at first, a progressively bigger bite was taken from the lunar disc. Maybe it was the mescaline assist, but the colors exploded with swirling hues of purples, reds, greens, oranges and yellows. We soon realized the downside to our blazing fire—light pollution of our own making. Fire still blazing, we drifted away from the firelight and lay down in the spring grass. Hugh had his super-8 camera and filmed the whole event. Lying on the dark grass, we gazed at the lessening moon, earth's shadow now at antumbra engulfing the light of the moon, save a thin corona.

A halo surrounding the shadow of terra firma was shooting bolts of color into the night sky. As if in response, the moonlight-muted stars exploded into brightness. Frenetic, we jumped up dancing around the fire, hooting and hollering, laughing and singing. We smoked a few joints and were soon lying back in the grass away from the light, watching the earth's shadow move across the lunar sphere exposing the light of the moon.

We watched until the full moon returned, awaiting the next full lunar eclipse some thirty years into the future. The mescaline-aided colors were waning, but the night continued with weed, beer and liquid fire, a.k.a liquor. The moon returned in the wee hours of the morning, the light of dawn already brightening as we drifted off to an electric sleep. Ah, psychedelics! A magical night I will never forget.

## Blacksmith

Jake, a Willie Nelson lookalike, heard of our would-be commune and set out to find us. Unlike us to leave a hitchhiker on the road, we pulled over. Craig asked, "Where you heading, bro." He replied, "I'm looking for the funny farm, I think it's somewhere up this road." Craig looked my way and smiled, nonverbally saying, "OK, let's have some fun." "Why not, I thought, a little playful teasing never hurt anyone." So I said, "What's the funny farm?" He said, "I don't know for sure, but I heard tell of this group starting a commune and, you see, back in Louisiana I was decent a leatherer and blacksmith and thought I might fit in." Craig finished rolling a joint, which he lit, saying, "Well, Jake, you found it." His lean weathered face lit up with a big southern smile, accentuating deep lined creases. His narrow blue eyes widened as he said chuckling, "You boys were yanking my chain. I think I'm gonna like it here." We drove the rest of the way up to the farm.

After walking up to the waterfall, then returning downstream, we reached the bus. The circa 1940 GMC bus overlooked Lucas Brook. Jake said to himself, I could live here for a while. As if in a grotto, the bus was surrounded by a small group of trees. Its light green paint was fighting a losing battle with rust. The light inside the bus was sparse, but someone had done a decent job outfitting the bus as a residence or camper. Jake's eyes widened, which we came to see as a regular expression of interest or concern, as he asked, "I could live here for a while. May I?" It was obvious that Jake was moved by the energy of our mountain retreat. We were trusting and connected with this interesting guy. Craig said, "Might as well, nobody here, anyway." Over the following weeks, Jake made the bus a home. It was weather tight and he managed to score a kerosene heater. The summer was easy. When the cold and snow struck, he went south, for his stuff.

When Jake returned, he asked if he could build a small Yurt and use the bus for storage. We gave him the green light and he was off running. Spring was in full swing. Most of the mud had dried up and the rains had slowed before Jake got started in earnest. He worked like John Henry, unlike us pampered, skinny, Long Island hippie youths, who struggled to embrace the cruel reality of our chosen lifestyle. That said, we worked pretty hard, too. The difference is that he lived pretty hard. He became the man of the house at eight when, as he put it, "My pappy got 'kilt' by black bear fishing the bayou." There were no ice cream trucks or even many paved roads where he grew up. Jake was ten years older than us, but you would think it more like twenty with deep-set wrinkles around his eyes and a weather-worn complexion. He was wiry and strong with an indelible positivity, no matter how hard he worked.

## Asleep on the Porch

The Missisquoi River rambled past Tom's porch for hours before he got home at 4 o'clock that afternoon. He found Hugh and Fern sleeping on the porch chairs. At the same time Tara, Fae, Skye, Craig and I got back from the swimming hole, Tom walked over to Hugh and playfully kicked his foot. "Wake up, sunshine." Hugh jumped to his feet. Fern rubbed sleep from her eyes.

## 20

# NORTHWAY INCIDENTS

*Some journeys take us far from home.*
*Some adventures lead us to our destiny.*
*~ C. S. Lewis*

Most trips on the New York State Northway were calculated to the gallon of gas. My Dodge Dart took many a trip with bald tires, sometimes showing threads on the sidewall, something I would consider unimaginable later in life. At the time, mortality was not a strong consideration. It was about the quest, the zeal for a completed adventure. Sometimes the adventure was more about the trip than the destination, a fair comparison to life at large.

### Wind Shear

I was driving down to Long Island with Mitch before he got serious with Ginny and was reborn. It was snowing hard, accumulating an inch a minute. We were discussing palmistry. I never wasted the opportunity to learn from Mitch. His car had oversized snow tires that kept the undercarriage of his Lincoln Continental well above the building snow. He had no problem negotiating the snow-covered

Northway. A gale force wind was blowing across the road, swirling the snow as we drove. Sections of the road, cut through solid rock, were shielded from the wind. Passing the brief protection of the erstwhile canyon, billowing wind pushed the car hard to the left. This sudden push caused a brief loss of control as the car began to fishtail.

Several eighteen wheelers up ahead drifted in the wind and began to swerve and slide across the roadway. The shear challenged the most experienced drivers, despite the weight of the trucks. Two semis slid into the snow bank; one was jackknifed and the other was struggling to get free. Mitch learned to anticipate and adjust for the wind shear by watching the terrain ahead, an effective bellwether of the impending blast.

We were climbing a long rise with several of these wind shear situations, when up ahead a 1975 White Cadillac was traveling in the left lane, struggling with the rise as the snow was building up on the road. The car cleared the rock face and was pushed by the wind, swerving and fishtailing, and was soon spinning in full circles as it was pushed closer to the steep drop at the edge of the road. The Cadillac spun around to the left and slammed through the plowed snow mounds.

Mitch slowed as we saw this spectacle, and fearing the driver may be injured, pulled up behind the car. Stepping out of the car, we entered a new world. The penetrating wind whipped the snow into a blinding veil of tiny white ice shards pelting our faces. We risked getting stuck ourselves but we leaned forward into the wind and pushed through the bumper-deep snow. A woman about sixty was slumped in the seat leaning on the steering wheel. We walked up to the car to see if she was OK, and found her with Rosary beads wrapped around her hands as she said a prayer on each bead.

She was startled when she saw us as dual feelings of fear and relief washed over her. She collapsed in relief. Once calmed, we asked her to try and start the car; it started right off. Mitch scoped out the problem as I went back for a shovel. The wind at my back, I was blown toward Mitch's car. I took the shovel from the trunk and fought the wind back to the car. Taking turns, we removed as much snow as we could from behind the tires then asked her to put it in reverse. No luck. Mitch asked if he could try and she eagerly complied.

She stood off to the side of the road as I tried to push. Mitch waived me away then revved the engine rocking the car forward and back. The tires spun, sliding side to side, the car lurched and jerked free of the imprisoning snow, fishtailing onto the left lane of the Northway. It was too dangerous to dawdle in this lane so we made sure she was okay to drive. Mitch gave her some tips about where the wind would break through and we bid her adieu. The woman drove off and, as we went to follow, our tires spun. Adrenalin abated, and after a few spins and fishtails later, the rest of our trip was uneventful.

## Asleep under Fifty-Five

I was driving in my trusted 1965 Dodge Dart Supra, heading to the Island with Lily, Jim and Marion. Our preferred travel time was late at night. Everyone else was sleeping and I gobbled up the miles heading south. Getting tired, I turned up the radio volume and nudged Lily, riding shotgun, to help me stay awake. We were chatting about my experience with Wicca, which intrigued her. I invited her to join me at a pagan group meeting in a nearby town on Long Island and she was excited with the prospect.

I had a little crush on Lily, but we were just friends. I explained that we would be meeting naked and I was unsure how she would feel about that. Earlier on her visit, a few of us hiked up to the swimming hole and she was uncomfortable getting naked. She took her shirt off but clung to her shorts. Lily was a beautiful young woman two years younger than me. She had long thin blond hair, a fair complexion and firm, perky breasts. I looked forward to being naked with her, if only in the context of this religious experience.

The miles were ticking by when we noticed the erratic driving of a car a few hundred yards ahead. The car was traveling at about forty miles per hour, slow for the Northway. We thought the driver was drunk so we approached with caution. The car was in the right lane but drifted from the shoulder to the middle lane. Moving to the left lane, we were passing the car when we noticed an elderly man had fallen asleep at the wheel. He was fortunate the pristine gray Lincoln had a tight wheel alignment and the road was level and straight. The road ahead was about to begin a serpentine path, raising additional concern. I woke everyone, and we opened the windows as I got as close as I dared, matching his speed and drift. I beeped the horn while everyone else was shouting out the window. His speed dropped to an even thirty. I cut the wheel hard to the left, avoiding his car veering toward mine. He got so close that everyone had to pull their arms in the window. The car was moving all over the road; we thought the driver was going to kill himself if we couldn't wake him.

I slowed and pulled behind him still beeping my horn. I knew I was about to put my own passengers at risk, so with unanimous consent, I moved forward and started to tap his rear bumper with mine. The driver jolted awake on the third tap dazed, confused, and wondering what happened. Pulling up alongside the now awake driver, we yelled out the window that he was asleep. He mouthed a shaky "thank you" and held his hands toward us as if in prayer. We sped off to complete our journey.

When we reached the Throggs Neck Bridge, after pooling all of our funds, we didn't have enough for the toll. I went into the office and took an IOU. Neither the first IOU nor the last.

"That's for sure," Tara said. "I think we left every toll with an IOU when we went to your uncle's farm in Jersey."

## Stranded

Brilliant starlight filled an ebony sky in late September. I was traveling to Long Island, with Paul, who was our first extended-stay hitchhiker. Driving in my Dodge Dart, we were rolling through the Adirondack Mountains with just enough gas to make it home. It was a dark, moonless night about three o'clock in the morning, one hundred miles south of the Canadian border, in the middle of nowhere. As I was driving up a long, steep incline, the usually quiet Paul was reading from his Bible. We were discussing John the Apostle who, in his nineties, spent time in prison on the Greek Island of Patmos, where he was visited by the Angel Gabriel. He later dictated the revelation to Polycarp and Ignatius, who transcribed the visitation. I knew something about Revelations and have always been fascinated by the story.

We were having a great discussion when we noticed a car in the distance pulled over to the side of the road, flashers on and hood raised. We slowed as we approached the car, pulling in front of them, thinking we could at least bring someone to the next pay phone, or perhaps summon help on their behalf. A man was pacing, with concern written on his face. A woman and two young children were in the car. Whether that concern was for his predicament or the two long-haired guys getting out of my car was unclear. We exchanged greetings and offered our help. He visibly relaxed, fear falling from his face.

We walked over to the blue 1967 Plymouth Valiant to see if we could do anything. He remained wary of my long hair but thanked us for stopping and introduced himself as Bennie, revealing a slight Hispanic accent, then introduced his family. His wife and two girls smiled and waved; the girls whispered something to their mother in Spanish. His wife was an attractive Latina and looked a few years younger than him. He was a short Latino in his forties who spoke clear but accented English.

"What's the problem?" I asked.

"Think it's the battery," he replied. "We can help, then. I have jumper cables in my trunk."

I turned my car around so we would be head-to-head, then fished out the cables. Bennie said he knew nothing about cars and stepped back, watching. "Paul, connect the cables to the terminals on his car. I'll hold the flashlight. Make sure red goes to red, and black to black. Looks good. Here, hold the light. I'll connect the other end."

I started my car and let the charge trickle into his battery for a minute or two. He turned the ignition and the car started. The kids cheered from the back seat, and mom let out a sigh of relief. We chatted a bit before I removed the cables. The car ran a few minutes and I could see orange sparks coming from the alternator as it died. Now they were in a panic.

I was sure it was the alternator. Bennie was worried about how he was going to deal with it, concerned about his family out here in the middle of nowhere. Bennie was throwing his arms up and mumbling through his panic. Maria and Salina, the little girls in the backseat, started to cry. He looked at my car loaded with a few pieces of furniture and two bucket seats, and he calculated that he could squeeze in the back seat if he put the fancy clock on his lap. He asked, "Can you give me a ride to the next exit?"

Here we were standing in pitch darkness, in the middle of nowhere, in the wee hours of morning, stopped to help a stranded family. I smiled, then said, "You know, Bennie, I think this is your lucky night." As I walked to my car, Bennie looked at me with an unbelieving look, considering his predicament. I reached into my trunk so I could get to the box at the back, moved a starter and some radiator hoses then pulled out a used alternator that was standard in Chryslers. I picked up my toolbox and, with the alternator in my other hand, walked over saying, "Hey, Paul can you hold the flashlight?"

I always kept extra parts in that box in my trunk. The great thing about the car was the 225 slant six engine, one of the best ever made at the time. Great engine, lots of room and easy to work on. I replaced many a part en route.

There were two bolts holding the alternator in place that were easy to remove. I manipulated the alternator away from the fan belt and remove it, then, after connecting my spare alternator to the fan belt, I bolted it into place.

"Hey, Paul, Can you get the tire iron from my trunk?"

"Got it! What now?"

"Perfect! Slip it between the alternator and engine block and lever it back; get the belt as tight as you can. Great, done."

Another round with the jumper cables. "Fire it up, Bennie." The car roared to life. His wife Carlotta and the girls got out of the car, cheering. This used alternator would be good enough to charge Bennie's battery. It was imperfect, as evidenced by the tiny blue sparks. Bennie was grateful, and ran over to shake my hand as Carlotta and the girls came over to give us a hug. These folks had little, but he wanted to give us something if only for the providence of coincidence.

It was bizarre that we two ships in the night sitting on a mountain dark would cross paths, or was it, as Bennie put it, divine intervention. He offered half of what he had in his wallet. We took five dollars and loaded the bad alternator, cables and tools in the trunk. His wife sang our praises and the girls waved. I closed the trunk, we said goodbyes, turned the car around and pulled onto the highway.

Five dollars richer. Next rest stop—two cups of coffee, some gas—and we were speeding south. On this trip, Paul got out in Newburgh. We made a couple of trips together, but this was the most fortuitous.

# 21

# ENCOUNTERS & ESCAPADES

*In the garden place where man laughs, sings, picks flowers, chases butterflies and pets birds, makes love with maidens, and plays with children. Here he spontaneously reveals his nature, the base as well as the noble. Here also he buries his sorrows and difficulties and cherishes his ideals and hopes. It is in the garden that men discover themselves. Indeed one discovers not only his real self but also his ideal self. He returns to his youth. Inevitably the garden is made the scene of man's merriment, escapades, romantic abandonment, spiritual awakening or the perfection of his finer self.*
*~ Confucius*

## Phunee Farm Flag

It would have been cool, on the day the Phunee Farm flag flew, to attach the flagpole at the highest point. However, the pitch and height were too dangerous for a fanciful notion. The lowest edge of the roof was about thirty-five feet high; the peak another fifteen feet higher at a steep pitch. Hugh borrowed an extension ladder from a farmer outside of Enosburg so we could fix some of the bigger holes in the barn's tin roof. I think the ladder inspired Craig to make the flag in the first place.

Hugh was fearless. With a rope tied around his waist, he climbed the ladder like a chimp. When he got to the roof, he tested it with his weight. Assured, he walked, hopped and danced around hooting and hollering about the view. Hand over hand, Hugh lifted the basket loaded with tools, hardware, flagpole and the flag. Then, with death-defying moves he leaned over the edge. Drawing gasps and words of concern from the ground, he proceeded to secure the flagpole. We gasped anew as he reached out over the roof, uncaring of the roof edge. We all sighed in relief as he moved back to a more secure footing. Hugh attached the flag to the rope. Then with lots of fanfare, he unfurled the flag. It looked great—the Phunee Farm flag was flying.

It was cool, it was wonderful yet it was, on reflection, a dangerous folly that did nothing to advance our farming goal. It did meld with the essence of our artistic hippie life. Hugh stayed up on the roof checking for problems and patched a few holes while he dallied and enjoyed the view. Hugh sent the basket back down and we loaded his super eight movie camera so Hugh could document the view. We all breathed easier when he was planted on terra firma. Watching with pride, the Phunee Farm flag flapped in the breeze. I lowered the flag, then with ceremony, raised it again. The flag flew for most of the summer. We were bummed when the cord fouled and the flag wrapped around the flagpole. The flag tattered as the winds of autumn increased, an anthem perhaps to the looming fate of our dream.

"Craig, do you think the Kimmel projects are worthy of a story?"

"I do, Bob. No bull."

## Bovine Surprise

Craig met a wealthy Canadian businessman who owned a classy A-frame chalet in East Berkshire and was contracted to build a dance floor his daughter's wedding. I was brought in to help. Most of our projects used material that was scrounged, donated or rehabilitated. Kimmel said, "Give me a list of what you need and I'll have it delivered." We did. He did. The next day a big pile of lumber and plywood was delivered. Built in two sections, Kimmel was impressed with the dance floor and he reached out to Craig for a new project after the wedding.

The dance floor was destined to become the floor for a small cabin, in a nearby forested part of his land. Once again, the materials we needed were delivered to the site. There was a catch—a mudded field between the road and the forest entrance with dozens of black and white Holstein cows milling around, and an unseen threat. We hopped over the fence, picked up our tools and started across the field. Deep, viscous mud sucked our boots into the gooey fen. Halfway across, our arms full, we looked up to see a large snorting brown bull charging at high speed straight towards us. Slopping through the mud, hampered by the load, we made a clumsy fifty-yard dash for the far fence. We reached the fence and threw ourselves and gear over, landing in deep mud. I looked back through the fence and got a face full of bull breathing heavily an inch away.

It took a few days to complete the project but each time we crossed the field, one of us had the chainsaw ready at hand. On our third trip across the field, the raging bull came charging again. I hoped the finicky chainsaw would start. I pulled the starter cord, and it sputtered to life followed by its menacing roar. The charging bull stopped ten feet away then turned in another direction. Toro never bothered us again. The job paid well.

"That was some tale," Skye commented with a chuckle, " but you were misleading, Craig—clever, but misleading. You said "No bull. It sounds to me like you had plenty of bull."

## Ethereal Encounter

One morning, Tara and I took a ride over the mountains under clear skies with a following wind gusting gently. Planning on meeting some of Tara's friends at a party, we turned onto a small road heading south, passing small dairy farms along the way. In the distance, we saw a field with strange animals, so we pulled onto a dirt road to see what was there.

Tara took over, "A dozen llamas and long-haired goats were grazing in a small pasture. The farmhouse was eclectic, like a yurt and geodesic dome combo. They were definitely hippies. We crept past the house, rolling at idle, hoping to see someone outside in the garden or yard; but as we passed, there were no cars around and the house was quiet. We stopped near the pasture, got out of the car and leaned on the split rail fence watching the llamas. They were across the field, but the goats started to wander our way. We watched for a while, then time got away from us, and we were hungry."

"I really wanted to talk to those people. Too bad they weren't home," Tara finished. "OK, Bob let's go."

Back in the car, we followed a dirt road through a dense pine forest. The distinctive scent permeated the air as we drove. The dense canopy formed a mysterious tunnel as we meandered along the darkened road. A few more exploratory turns and we were back on a paved road, finding a store with a "Grinders" sign. We stopped and picked up a six-pack of Labatt Blue and two cheese grinders.

Arriving at the party, cars were parked everywhere, narrowing the road. With a full stomach and a light beer buzz, we parked and walked up to a two-story farmhouse, close to the road. A band was playing in a wide side yard, where fifty people in frenzied dance were well into an afternoon buzz. We parked the car and danced into the crowd. Almost everyone there was a local from far-reaching parts of northern Vermont. Tara knew a few people and introduced me as we danced through the crowd toward one of the seven kegs sitting in the ice behind the house. The beer was good, the music was loud; we had arrived.

Tara's friend Kenny came over, with hand clenched, and said, "Hey, Tara, I just picked up a batch of brown barrel. You want some?"

Reaching into his hand, Tara introduced me, "Sure. Sounds great. Hey, Kenny, this is Bob; he's a Phunee farmer."

Kenny responded, "Hey, Bob! I've heard of that place. It's on the other side of Jay Peak, right?"

"Yeah, we're at the end of Lucas Valley." Tara took the mescaline and handed one to me. Gobble.

These were "on the house" and I wished I had some dough to buy some for another time. The party was getting wild in a fun way as many of the revelers succumbed to the magic of mescaline. We were there for several hours, picking on some of the barbecue food. I stayed away from the meat, but the roasted corn, summer squash and beans worked well; no veggie burgers here. I wondered if they would run out of beer since the mescaline enhances your ability to consume alcohol. The sound of motorcycles drowned out the band.

Nine bikes pulled up close to the action and their riders, sporting colors, went straight to the kegs. The tenor of the party changed when the uninvited arrived. One of the bikers overheard someone talking about the party while they were in town picking up the kegs. Wild and fun soon turned rowdy when the newcomers started hitting on the braless, halter-clad women bouncing on the dance floor. Some of the women flocked to the "bad boys." Some of the women's boyfriends objected to the pawing of their women and a few altercations started. The bikers were outnumbered but yielded little ground. When a true round of fisticuffs started, Tara and I decided to leave before the Donnybrook advanced.

Still in the throes of color-enhanced vision, we drove off with a full cup of beer apiece and a few Labatts left in the car. Staying off main roads, we followed a maze of dirt roads for as long as we could. Twice we followed a road to a dead end, but we made it to a small paved road."

Tara interrupted, "Between the mescaline, the bikers and beer, that place was getting ready to explode. I'm glad we left when we did."

"Me, too," I said, "I'm no good in a fight, anyway. But that's not even the story.

As dusk closed around us, the weather changed and light misty fog filled the valley. Even without the barrel-aided enhancement, the fog made everything appear ethereal. Up ahead, coalescing from the swirling mist and fog, was the shimmering specter of a white horse, drifting along and then across the road. Believing I was having an amazing hallucination, I drove on, waiting for the horse to fly off like a winged Pegasus. I described my vision to Tara, who was astounded because she had seen the same specter of the white horse.

Hearing this, I began thinking we were having the same vision, when out of the mist, about thirty yards ahead, a real white stallion stepped into my path; I was driving slow because visibility was so bad. Swerving and braking, I stopped as we approached the beautiful creature. The horse sauntered to the side of the road, leaving me room to pass. I inched up. Just as we were nearing the majestic horse, he slowed. So did I, wondering what the horse would do next.

The stallion looked into the car as we passed, then, taking up a challenge, he began to trot alongside my car. He then bolted ahead, daring me to catch him. We were in a low speed race to the end of the field, when the horse slowed to a stop, then darted into the pasture through a break in the fence - the probable point of egress. I stopped when he darted into the field and watched as he bounded over a hill. Staring at the breach in the fence for seconds that felt like ages, we pulled over to the side of the road and pondered. Did we see what we had just seen, or were we sharing the same hallucination?

We sat there for quite a while discussing what just happened, as the fog folded around us and dusk faded to dark. Less than two minutes passed from when we first spied that ethereal white creature manifesting from the mist, to the moment the white stallion bounded out of sight. We stayed there, reliving those minutes in wonderment, for a long time. Before we left, we jerry-rigged the broken fence corralling the horse.

My last beer was hours before, and the brown barrel mescaline had run its course by the time I pulled back onto the road. To this day I never did remember the name or route number of that road. We found our way back to our familiar route 105, fifteen minutes from home, downhill. The memory of that night brings that spectral steed into my present.

Tara said, "I really thought we were having the same trip. That was a beautiful horse, especially with that fog swirling around his mane. That horse was amazing. I hope we trapped it in the right field."

Hugh came walking over and joked, "Sounded like a helluva trip. Can you get any more of those barrels? I just walked through the orchard. Those apples are almost ready, a few are, and the plums are great this year. He passed some plums around. "It got me thinking of another barrel. A fifty-five gallon barrel."

"What's the plan for tonight?" I asked. "Is anyone up for another campfire? We still have a fire pit out behind the barn so we don't need to go back to the beach. Let's keep it simple and eat first. Fae, I think we still have some marshmallows. I'll help you find a big stick if you eat a good dinner."

"Is it OK, Mom?"

"Sounds like a plan," Tara responded, "We picked up supplies while we were out. We should have everything ready in an hour. Skye and I will cook dinner."

"Fae, do you want to help me and Craig with the fire? We'll just set it up for now and light it later."

## Night Fliers

It was dusk when we finished cleaning up after dinner. Fae was upstairs getting changed when we heard her shriek. She was running down the stairs screaming. "Mom! There are things flying around up there, pulling my hair." Craig, Skye and I went up and found three bats. Yanking blankets from the bed and using them to make an artificial wall, we steered the frightened bats to the open window and into the night. "It's happened before, we should really get screens," I said.

"Is it always like this?" Skye asked.

"Not exactly, but yeah. There's often something."

Skye looking out the kitchen window said, "I see headlights coming up the driveway. I wonder who it is?"

## 22

## FOR A TIME REUNITED

*It is one of the blessings of old friends that you can afford to be stupid with them.*
*~ Ralph Waldo Emerson*

"Hard to tell who's coming. It's kinda dark, but from the sound of that rattling, I'm guessing it's Bruce," Craig offered. A few seconds later what was once a Chevy came into the barn's light. Pop-rivets and metal patches replaced most of the body. The driver's side door was held closed with rope.

"Who's that in the car with him?" I asked. Just then, the dome light came on. "Never mind. You can't mistake Hugh. Tara, can you make out who is in the back?"

"I don't know, but they're brave to ride back there. It's not too stable, and a little scary watching the road go by, through those holes in the floor. At least it's dry today."

"Could it be Hugh's girlfriend from school?" Craig asked, "I think her name is Fern."

Bruce came to a stop—a cloud of dust floated into the barn light—

and a piece of his fender fell off in the driveway. He climbed out through the window and picked up the rusted metal and tossed it in the back seat. He was exhausted from his predawn work wrangling cows at the Gilbert dairy farm and was still wearing his mucking boots. Tiny Fae was thrilled when she helped him run the cows into the barnyard earlier this summer.

Hugh helped Fern out of the back. He took in a deep breath, spun in a slow circle—his arm held out as if in flight—and said, "Phunee Farm air. Ahh, it's great to be back. Hey everyone, this is Fern."

We gathered at the bonfire, added more wood, and in moments the flames were six feet high. "Hey, Hugh, we've been telling war stories," Tara said, "Remember the Dart getting stuck in the ditch."

"Uh, yeah," He replied, "Not my best moment."

## Bruce's Story

Bruce, who had been unusually quiet, said, "Ayup. I got a good border story."

"Ya see, I was parked on a dirt road near the Canadian border with Jason. He and his girlfriend, Pat, were two of the original funny farmers. So we were driving dirt roads kinda just fuckin' around."

"That's a bad word, Bruce," Fae chided.

"Oops! Sorry, Fae. We pulled off the road at a secluded spot overlooking the valley and parked. Bullshitting and sharing a quart of Budweiser; the view was amazing. It was a beautiful, warm summer day and the car windows were all open, well, the ones that can open. The breeze was blowing the tall grass in the pasture next to us. Through the trees, cow corn rose above the tall grass. I just lit a joint and we were passing it back and forth. I was fixed on a pair of red-tailed hawks riding the thermals high above the purple splotched hillside in the distance. We were both captivated, far from civilization, enjoying the majesty of the soaring raptors." His voice dropped to a whisper.

"Bang! Bang! Bang!" Bruce said, suddenly raising his voice, then pausing for effect. Half of us jumped with surprise; the other half heard it before.

"Ayup, we did the same thing. We jumped, hitting our heads on the car roof. You can still see the dent in the roof where Jason hit his head. Anyway, the loud rapping on the car roof pulled us back to reality. I looked out the driver's side window and stared at the haunches of a large chestnut steed and a black boot attached to a Royal fucking Canadian Mountie. We never heard him. I was shocked. I thought we were still in the states. We were really stoned with a beer buzz, and pretty giddy.

So I said, 'Hello Mr. Mountie. Or is it Officer Mountie?' We broke into hysterical laughter which got the Mountie laughing.

Through a chuckle he said, 'What are you boys doing smoking weed on my road. Eh? You know I have to write you a ticket? Which one of you wants the ticket?'

It was my car so I said, 'Ayup, that'll be me.'

We laughed through the whole process. Who knows? He could have been there long enough to get a contact buzz. The Mountie was still laughing as he handed me the ticket, saying 'You can mail in the fifty dollar fine; but if you plead not guilty, it's unlikely I will make the trial.' He mounted his steed and said, 'You boys have a good day now, and from now on, smoke that shit in your own country.' The RCMP officer, still chuckling, cantered over the hill, and out of sight. So I lit up a new joint and turned the car around. I must have told this story twenty times and I betcha the Mountie told it a few times as well."

Craig said, "I heard that story a couple times, Bruce. I get a kick out of it every time. Tara, did Fae fall asleep? She looks like she's wiped out. Want me to carry her to the porch? You can see her from here."

"No, I don't think so. Tara answered, "I'm hoping she won't have nightmares after the bat incident. But Craig, would you mind getting a few blankets?" He returned with the blankets and Tara made another nest for Fae a safe distance from the fire. With that, Bruce, tending the fire, pulled out a burning stick, still wearing his farm day overalls and shit-shoveling boots, and started three doobies flaming.

I said, "As long as Fae is sleeping, I have a story that probably would cause her nightmares."

## Lost in Plain Sight

Things would go missing the first year or so at the farm, only to be found elsewhere in the house. Most of the time it was something small —a watch, a book, a list, pen or tool. Once it was a hammer. That time I walked into the house, placed the hammer on the table near the stairs and went into the bathroom. When I came out, the hammer was missing. I was alone in the house but called out, "Hugh, did you come in and take my hammer? Hugh, are you screwing with me?"

The kitchen door opened and Hugh stepped in, "Did you call me?"

"Hugh, this is weird. I was fixing the screen door on the porch, came in to pee, and put my hammer on that table." I pointed to the table by the stairs. "When I came out of the bathroom one minute later it was gone. You sure you're not messing with me?"

"You're shitting me, right? Hugh said. "I was outside with Craig in the barn. But you know something, I lost my pocketknife last week. I was sure I put it on my bed table. Then I found it the next day in the pantry. I figured I was stoned and forgot."

"You know," I said, "come to think of it, that kind of stuff has happened to me too, but I only realize it's missing the next day. I chalked it up to the weed as well. But this was one minute. Can you help me look?" We looked around the den and first floor.

Craig came in from outside. "Hey, what are you looking for?" We filled him in. "Same thing happens to me—little stuff, easy to forget or misplace. I thought it was me."

Peculiar, I thought. We all picked up the search. I never left the first floor, but Hugh did a cursory walk through upstairs, then I gave up, picked up another hammer, and went back outside. Later that night, Craig went up to his bedroom, plopped down on his bed and laid his head on his pillow and bellowed, "What the hell?" He came downstairs rubbing his head and holding my hammer. Now what?

The next day, Anka arrived, and with her, a bitter wind from the northwest. Our Magee Beacon Parlor Stove was burning hot. The wind was howling, and we were huddled on the couch talking, joking, laughing and just having fun together. Sitting there, having a grand time sharing joints and drinking beer, a book fell off the bookshelf and hit Hugh on the shoulder, "What the hell," he said, rubbing his shoulder. Moments later three more books fell down. They seemed to be launched from the shelf and landed on the floor beyond our feet. We all jumped up in surprise, saying, "What the fuck?"

Recounting the recent events, starting with the hammer, we came to believe that we had a poltergeist. What else could it be? Could it have been a gust of wind causing some deflection in the wall? The wind was blowing hard against that west-facing wall. We could have just misplaced stuff. Yet, if all that were true how did the hammer get under Craig's pillow, we wondered. And then Craig reminded us that, years ago, old man Bell hung himself up at the Bell House.

Anka said, "Hey, Mr. Bell, we got your point. You got me scared stiff. Can you leave us alone?"

There were no further incidents that night. I started reading up on psychic cleansing; some may call it blessing the house, others an exorcism. The next day the weather retreated from the howling winds of the night before. The sun warmed the valley air. I stayed home when everyone went into town. Why not? I lit a candle at each of the cardinal points of the house, defining its borders, filled my hanging incense burner, and walked from room to room, circling the house on each floor, clanging the loop of the chain against the side of the burner while filling each room with a blend of frankincense and myrrh as I recited the names of pagan gods and claimed my rights to the house and commanded anything or anyone to leave. Completing the process, I went outside with my incense burner and walked around the perimeter of the house, spreading a symbolic line of salt—completing the circle and forbidding unwelcome visitors to cross. What? I read it in one of my books. When everyone returned, they commented on the sweet smell in the house. I told them what I did and showed them my books. Despite some wary laughs, everyone slept well. By the way, stuff stopped disappearing. Maybe we just sobered up?

"No shit," Hugh said, Those books were crazy. Scared the hell out of Anka. But I really did stop losing things, seriously. How about you, Craig?

"Come to think of it, yeah. Anything I lost after that I could blame on myself," Craig said, smiling.

"That's some pretty crazy shit. You'll have to tell more about it sometime," Skye said. "Spooked me out," Tara whispered. Then said, "OK, enough of this stuff. I don't know if you're crazy or not, but that definitely spooked me again."

## Boom in the Night

Fern and Skye jumped when we heard the first boom. "What the hell was that?" A few minutes later everyone jumped when another boom sounded. It was like the sound barrier was broken. "Really, guys. What the fuck is that about?" Tara asked, joining the conversation.

I answered, "Interesting story, really. But you may not believe it." In March of 1976, we took a different kind of automotive repair class, at the home of Kendal Gross, an eccentric, retired guy. It was peculiar because it took us in a strange direction. He told us he worked for a secretive joint United States and Canadian project known as the High Altitude Research Program (HARP) which, according to him, was unique in the history of the space age. Ken said, "We made history there. It was the first real attempt to use cannons instead of rockets, to explore the upper atmosphere. We launched satellites. You see, I worked for Gerald Bull, who ran the project with McGill University, before funding was cut. We never managed to get those weather satellites higher than suborbital."

I whispered to Craig, "Do you think that's what those loud booms are that we hear at the farm?"

"Well HARP shut down in '67."

I shrugged at Craig. Oh well.

"I stayed on with Mr. Bull when he started his own company—the Space Research Corporation (SRC)—on six thousand acres of land straddling the border between Highwater, Quebec, and Jay, Vermont, just over that hill," as he pointed north over our shoulders.

Kendal loved to talk. "At the time we were using a sixteen-inch bore cannon with a barrel one hundred feet long. I think the ole Highwater Gun still holds the record as the longest big bore artillery piece in the world. I drove by there last year and the big gun was still on the grounds rusting away. This was the biggest, but we had projects in Barbados and Yuma. I went down to Barbados once. Got sunburned really bad." The story he told got more interesting, but we didn't know how much of this guy's fantastic story to believe.

Jules Verne Gun

When we focused on our main project, taking apart and rebuilding carburetors, we learned a lot, like setting needle valves. Distractions were plentiful as Kendal regaled us with tales of other research projects he was involved with, making us wonder if he was a conspiracy theorist. Who doesn't love a good conspiracy story?

He said, "The government was working with my company for a few years on the sly. They knew OPEC was getting ornery over there in Arabia. It wasn't my department, but I played poker with those guys. One time they snuck me to see what they were doing. They were building a carburetor that operated on water. The premise was that this high-tech futuristic carburetor could separate water molecules and run a combustion engine. The project ended abruptly and was hushed up when some men in black arrived and took all of the research."

We were intrigued; it was hard to believe, but we ate it up at the time. Hmm, thinking back now, I was able to validate most of his story. I have to wonder.

"So ladies," Craig continued, "now you know. Those booms are missiles from the 'Jules Verne' gun fired into a mineshaft two thousand meters away."

"Hey, Bob, remember Paul's reaction the first time we heard it?"

"Oh yeah, he fell through the plastic and off the porch. He looked like a turtle, but unhurt."

Tara asked, "Whatever happened to him, anyway?"

"Funny you should ask." Craig responded. "So much has happened around here, but we've only been talking about our first year. This summer had its own adventures, but that story really starts at the end of last year."

# 23

# YEAR TWO

*"You live life looking forward, you understand life looking backward."*
*~ Soren Kierkegaard*

We celebrated the Winter Solstice ending 1975 at the Phunee Farm then went south for the holidays and to make some money. Paul agreed to stay at the farm while we were gone and keep the home fires burning. Best laid plans... We lost contact with him and took the return trip north a few weeks earlier than scheduled.

## Abandoned

Seven of us arrived in two cars. The house, cloaked in winter's embrace, was eerily dark. Above, billions of stars watched from a cloudless ebony sky. The absence of smoke from either chimney was a bad sign. We parked close to the house; got out of the cars, turned off the headlights, closed the doors and our visitors learned what it's like to be inside a subzero freezer when the light goes out. Near total darkness, the house was a shade against the ice-slicked driveway. Thanks to our winterizing efforts last year, the porch was clear of snow. No light —the porch bulb was broken. I stepped through the door into a darkened room and was rewarded with light when I flicked the switch, illuminating a room in shambles.

Kitchen chairs were upended. Half-eaten food was strewn across the table and floor—and would have rotted, except for the subzero temperature. Icicles hung from dirty frozen dishes in the sink, which was itself a giant ice cube. A bedroll on the kitchen floor, littered with soiled underwear and clothing, made it clear that Montezuma found his way to the farm and exacted revenge. There was no sign of Paul. He may not have heeded our warning: Never Turn the Water Off in Winter. Frozen water combined with desolation and loneliness took their toll. Paul was gone, never to be heard from again. As we huddled around both stoves, the temperature crept above freezing. I tried to thaw the frozen pipe, that is, after I thawed the frozen gas tanks. Despite a valiant effort, the torch failed to free the ice dam in the pipe. The first northern experience for most, nobody was ready for a subzero Phunee Farm winter. Lack of water and the condition of the house shortened the visit.

Back on Long Island, I worked the midnight shift at a gas station, working on woodcarvings and playing chess with customers during the down time. Craig rented a room in Albany, working at a college, where he took a couple of gratis courses and recharged his yearning for formal education. He scored some really cool stuff, including two church pews and a three foot by five foot Guernica Picasso print that hung at the Phunee Farm for years. Another year would pass before either of us realized the pull of the quiet voices calling Craig back to the academic world.

The weeks passed. I worked, saved and tried to pick things up with old friends and the pagan group I attended a year earlier. They disbursed, following a dose of soap opera quality drama. I was connected to a new pagan group and a whole new set of friends. Hanging with old and new friends sucked up time.

I stayed on the Island longer than planned but earned enough money to pay the rent and electric bill for the year. I returned with a trailer, rototiller, and an assortment of other stuff. Jim asked to come back with me, which caused a bit of concern because Craig didn't trust him. I'll get to that. It was a delicate situation, so we worked out a trial run. Craig was finishing up the spring semester in Albany and would not return until May. A determinant factor, since I did not want to go back alone. I packed my Dart, hooked up the trailer, and headed north with Jim. We arrived at the farm, dragging the trailer behind us. After two fishtailing driveway attempts, we made it to the house, empty since early January.

## Mice

When we returned in earnest to restart the Phunee Farm experiment, the rodent issue reached colossal proportions. Two mice ran across the floor when we walked into the kitchen. What's a couple of mice; we saw two back in January. Six more ran along the chair rail in the kitchen, four others scurried into the pantry. They were darting under the table and stove. The house was overrun with dozens of mice, a veritable rodent resort. We could hear them running through the walls as if they were traveling on highways. The most amazing thing was a mouse we found trapped in a sealed Quaker Oatmeal container. You know the one; a round cylinder about six inches in diameter, with a tight-fitting cap. The Pied Piper was nowhere to be found, so our first order of business was to get some mousetraps and a cat.

I was allergic to cats most of my life so I kept them at a distance, but I met a tiny pure black kitten who I connected with. I named him Binah, which means "understanding," from the second sephirot of the Kabbalah. It is associated with the color black and the left pillar of Solomon. Binah proved to be an excellent mouser who proudly brought his kills for human inspection and accolades for a job well done. Binah, along with a black and white piebald cat named Zephyr, managed to rid the house of mice in a short time. The traps got the rest. One night Binah did not come back from a winter hunt. I searched for days looking for him but to no avail. A few weeks later, after spring sprung and snow receded, I found his remains along the road to bronze beach. He was a great cat—the only cat I ever called my friend. Farewell, Binah. May you return in another life.

## Little Gray Lies

When I met Jim in high school, he told me his grandfather was a sheik in Iran who owned thousands of acres of fig trees. His mother was a British woman with a delightful English accent; his dad was of obvious Middle Eastern visage. Over time, he showed me the hunting rifle he made with carved Birdseye maple stock. The woodwork was amazing. He talked of working with an uncle in a machine shop where he rifled the barrel from a kit he purchased. I was intrigued when he discussed the seaplane flights he took to remote Maine lakes for hunting in the wilds and trips to a Pennsylvania game preserve to hunt exotic animals. He pointed out the Bighorn ram's head with its distinctive curling horns hanging on his wall. I was told tales of other exotic animals—North American predators like bears and cougars that were captured around the country and confined in a huge preserve where the hunter was guaranteed a trophy. I was not a hunter, and thought it was like shooting fish in a barrel, but interesting stories, nonetheless.

Here I thought, was a well-rounded, worldly friend. And friends we had become. We were friends when my girlfriend and I got pregnant, friends when he met my larger group of friends that included his wife to be, friends when we went camping in the White Mountains—and we remained friends after the fall of the Phunee Farm. Two years later, when the Shah of Iran was exiled by the Grand Ayatollah Ruhollah Khomeini, he told me that his grandfather was from Iraq.

Long before empirical proof accrued, and after years of incongruous details, contradictory and suspicious information confirmed that Jim was a pathological prevaricator. There were dozens of incidents that caused Craig to be concerned. But Jim had become a friend, so I dealt with it. The trouble was that Jim was smart and did many good and cool things, but it was hard to tell what was true.

He wandered in and out of the Phunee Farm for about a year. Often returning with stories of amazing adventures, joining up with two different communes, building houses somewhere, or hitchhiking to Guam via the Crab nebula. I never knew what was true, but often knew what wasn't. One day he took off never to return, but he left without his ailing Basset Hound, Heidi. The dog was problematic. He was wise to leave, since he was not well-regarded by the new guard at the house. As things turned out, he may have suffered physical harm.

Tara said, "I never really liked that guy."

"I've known him a long time. He's OK. He does have a problem with the truth, though. I'm actually going down to his wedding next month. Bruce, can you help me get more wood to keep this fire going?"

"What are the chances of everyone being back here for Thanksgiving?" Craig asked. "We can have a vegetarian Thanksgiving." Little did we know. L"et me tell you about the Vegetarian Thanksgiving we went to last year."

# 24

# VEGETARIAN THANKSGIVING

*"I am grateful for what I am and have. My thanksgiving is perpetual.
~ Henry David Thoreau*

Thanksgiving Day arrived. We were invited to a small commune for a Vegetarian Thanksgiving Dinner on the other side of the mountains. The house was a big blue-gray two-story colonial. On the far horizon, the snowcapped White Mountains in New Hampshire were visible against a clear sky. Jackson was waiting outside near the front door, smoking a cigar and holding a bottle of beer. He had long thick auburn-red hair and a matching bushy beard. At six foot one, he was lean in loose-fitting overalls and a red lumberjack shirt, and as cold as it was, he was wearing sandals. A flower-painted VW bus with flattened tires peeked out from behind the weather-worn barn. Beyond that was a renovated sugar shack, dormant now, awaiting the sap flow in the months to come.

Jackson greeted us with a big smile, exposing a wide space in his upper front teeth. He sounded excited about the holiday and new friends, so with introductions all around, we went inside. The house was decorated to be functional rather than by the eye of a designer. A bow saw hung on the wall near the door. Quilts hung from a wall rack, on display now but ready to provide warmth with a quick tug; others draped on the sofa and chairs suggested a quilter lived there.

Hanging our jackets on the hooks under the shelf, we were led into a spacious working country kitchen. Jackson explained that he, Henry, Malinda, Mary, Nathan and Nellie shared the house. It wasn't clear who the couples were—if there were actual couples. Mary and Melinda were both of sturdy New England stock, big-boned with light brown hair and pudgy, friendly smiling faces. Nellie was the opposite in almost every way. She was thin, like Shelley Duvall, with a long thin face with big searching eyes and warming smile. Nate supported a handlebar mustache and Hank was clean shaven. Both wore torn jeans and homemade flannel shirts. My curiosity was piqued by the subtle smell of fresh lumber and sawdust wafting under the smell of burning wood. Nate showed apparent signs of woodworking with sawdust on his jeans and wood chips clinging to his boots, suggested a woodcarver. I was among kindred spirits.

Glancing around the kitchen I noticed a large well-used butcher block, about two foot square, set on thick squat legs raising it to counter height on the wall across from a beautiful, large blue Glenwood wood cook stove that was a little bigger than our Acorn stove. The cooking fire roared in the firebox, flames licked up through one of the larger holes at the back of the stove, which was exposed when Malinda moved a large pot from the stove top to the sink. Six other cast iron pots boiled, steamed and cooked. A vintage white country sink was on the opposite side of the kitchen and a classic gas range with a small oven was next to the sink. Nice to have a backup.

My hands were full with our contribution to the meal so I offered, "I've got a pot of miso soup and three loaves of fresh baked whole wheat bread." Malinda took the bread from me saying, "I'll put this in the warming oven, why don't you put the soup on the stove to warm it up." Craig, holding the zucchini and yellow squash au gratin casserole, asked Nellie if there was room in the oven. Nellie took the casserole dish and set on the edge of the stove saying, "A little full right now, the lentil loaf, stuffing and sweet potatoes will be out in a minute." Hugh brought in the beer and brandy and handed it off to Ken who put it outside the back door in the mudroom.

Kendra and Nate gave us a tour of the house. The stairway, with a shaky railing, was across from the small foyer. There were five small bedrooms on the second floor and a large bathroom that opened onto the hallway. Another room had been set up as a sewing room. There was another small staircase that went up to an unfinished attic with a high ceiling. One corner was finished as a stained glass workshop. A large oval window in the east gable offered a panoramic view of the White Mountains in the distance.

Back on the first floor, we followed the hall that led past the kitchen to the back of the house. It led to the mudroom which also served as a winter "decompression" chamber. The first-floor bathroom had an ornate giant claw foot tub with chromed pipes providing a shower. The old black and white subway tiles on the walls matched well with the tiny black and white octagon tiles. At the back corner of the house was an indoor winter workshop with a wood carving of a horse dogged down on the workbench. I knew I smelled sawdust. Across the hall from the kitchen was a dining room with an antique cherry dining room set. This was a great house, tired in many ways, but many notches above the Phunee Farm.

Our tour ended in the makeshift dining room. The living room, large as it was, was dwarfed by a fifteen-foot long banquet table that had been fashioned out of plywood resting on the dining room table and saw horses. From our seats close to the tall Round Oak parlor stove we could see the fire through the Eisen glass in the door. The fire was stoked and damped down for a slow burn that should take us through the meal. And what a meal it turned out to be. This Thanksgiving dinner proved to be the most different, exotic and delicious.

While we were touring the house, Bruce and Ronni arrived, followed by another group of communards. They all knew each other and had been to the house before. I recognized two of the women from the Kilgore Trout Saloon, but I had never conversed with them. They were from a commune near Montgomery Center; everyone else from that group had trekked off to various states to join the family for the holiday.

When everything was laid out on the table, the colorful dishes looked and smelled fabulous. Others contributed an eggplant parmigiana, a sweet potato gnudi with sage butter. Gnudi are gnocchi-like dumplings made with ricotta cheese with semolina instead of potato. The feast also included baked stuffed acorn squash, stuffed mushrooms, stuffed cabbage, garlic mashed potatoes, stuffed lentil loaf, broccoli, cauliflower and carrots, white cheddar cheese casserole, roasted Brussels sprouts, a four-bean salad made with red, white, navy and garbanzo beans in a sweet and tangy sauce and it was topped off with a tofu roast with onions, garlic and mushroom gravy.

Once everyone was seated, dinner started with Nellie leading the table in a chant of Thanksgiving gratitude, influenced by mantras of eastern philosophies. Her voice was songlike in its cadence which made it hard to follow along because it was so serene and sincere and we all wanted to hear her intonation, but we joined the collective gratitude. The meal's preamble continued with a toast; glasses were filled from a choice of homemade elderberry or dandelion wine, mulled cider or honey mead. After the simple toast, "To friends new and old, found, lost and remembered." The feast began in earnest as everyone dug in and passed the plethora of exotic vegetarian dishes around the table. For the next few minutes conversation focused on passing the food and then became subdued further as everyone began to enjoy the delectable, palate-pleasing celebratory banquet.

As the initial gorging abated, robust conversations followed. I asked about the woodworking bench I had seen in the back room and commented on how wonderful it was to have a warm workspace through the cold winter months. Both Ken and Hank were woodworkers. Ken was the woodcarver and Hank was more about furniture and general carpentry. It was easy to talk with both of them with much in common. I talked about some of the woodcarvings, including a teak wood sculpture of a hand rising up through a cloud holding a lightning bolt; a gift for Craig, whose nom de plume was Cloud Catcher.

We were of the same political mind, so stories of our efforts to thwart the Vietnam War were recounted. We Phunee farmers were young compared to most of the revelers at the table. Jackson, Mary and Henry lived in San Francisco during the Summer of Love in 1968 and were involved in a number of tumultuous demonstrations. Nellie and Nate were present during the assault on Ohio State University when the National Guard killed four students, just a few years earlier. They were in close proximity to the mêlée and had known one of the victims. Their story brought tears to their eyes such that we could all feel their indelible pain. Although not Merry Pranksters, Jackson and Mary found their way to Vermont in 1971 driving their lotus flower-painted VW bus. "I really loved that bus," Jackson said, "I think you saw it out behind the barn when you pulled up. But now it will serve a new generation. My nephew's, Philip and Donald, are coming up for it."

Ecology being my passion, I steered the conversation that way, as the prior conversation left a sad pall hanging in the air. Nearly everyone at the table had been champions of the environment in previous lives and we all cheered on each of our efforts. I talked of our efforts to foster newspaper recycling and elementary school education. They were all intrigued at how successful we were with our local village that gave us the town for an Earth Day celebration—and especially when, at age seventeen, I was appointed to a village board committee to institute glass and metal recycling in 1972. Everyone laughed conspiratorially when we all agreed that we may have been, at least on some level, unwitting pawns in Nixon's efforts through the CIA to diffuse the youth movement from the anti-war sentiment. Everyone also appreciated that same agency's efforts to distract the youth movement by spreading LSD throughout the country. Well, that didn't work that well for them. "What a long strange trip it's been."

Conversations continued through the meal after which the men moved onto the porch for cigarettes, cigars, joints, pipes and bongs. What struck me as ironic was the surprising adherence to the same age-old gender roles maintained by our parents and their parents before them. The women were expected to clean up the table and do the dishes and get coffee, tea and dessert ready. Then and now I counted myself among feminists, so this did not sit well with me. I cannot change the behavior of others, but I can take my own action. Discreetly, I slid back into the house and took a place at the sink washing the dishes and drying when done. I stayed focused on my task as the women chatted along. Having been in this situation before, I realized that when absorbed in my task I tended to be quiet and not engage in conversation. Consequently, my male presence was often forgotten by the women busy at their chores, which resulted in my hearing things better left unheard. Perhaps you could say it was, in part, a mild type of male bashing.

Most of us had either an orchard or access to one, so the apple dishes were abundant. Dutch apple pie, apple cobbler, baked apples; apple cake and apple cider doughnuts were among them. Cakes came next, including chocolate, carrot, spice and glazed Bundt. It was a good thing that most of us were skinny because, in addition, there were plates of cookies, cherry and peach pies and homemade vanilla ice cream. It was like a wedding Viennese hour sans sparklers. Fully sated, new friends made, invitations to return and offers to visit the Phunee Farm, we departed shortly before midnight with a few leftovers in tow. More than forty years have passed since that remarkable Thanksgiving feast and I have never enjoyed the holiday meal more.

# 25

## BREAD & PUPPET

*The news is designed to be benign, comforting. It creates images for easy consumption. The street parade is different, however, in that it makes the harsh facts 'real'—physical.
It's upsetting. It's in your face. It cannot be soothed simply by changing the channel."*
*~ Peter Schuman*

"Hey, is everyone pumped for Bread and Puppet? It starts on Saturday. I'm surprised I didn't talk about this already," Hugh said, "I mean about our ride up the Northway." He told the story of the painted VW microbus, then continued, "The dudes in the bus were going to Glover to be trained as puppeteers at B & P. Peter Schuman asked them to come up. He is friends with their uncle. They invited us to come early and help; it shouldn't be hard to find their flower painted van. I'm planning to go a day early. Anyone want in?"

"I'm in. Hope you ladies are staying?" Craig said.

## Bread and Puppet Theater

We spent the end of each summer experiencing the wondrous happenings of Bread and Puppet Circus in Glover. Bread & Puppet was started in 1963 by Peter Schumann, the radical theater with politically-themed puppets that became a symbol of urban anti-war demonstrations. In 1974 he bought a farm with a gigantic barn and a few hundred acres in Glover. The place was an unbelievable hippie and fringe folk festival. The puppet concept was inspired by eighteenth-century Sicilian puppeteers. The bread represented the belief that art should be as basic to life as bread. They provided free homemade bread served with aioli (garlic and olive oil) at each performance. The bread helped to create community.

Hugh went to Glover the first day of the pageant in 1975. He was so excited when he returned home that we all went back and camped in a farmer's field for a few days. The Bread and Puppet land was transformed from a dairy farm into an eclectic theater venue. The main event, Our Domestic Resurrection Circus was held in a huge natural amphitheater. Throngs of people sat on the grassy slopes of the amphitheater and went wild over the show. Hundreds of people volunteered to help with the production or operated the puppets, some of which were twenty feet tall and operated by four or five people. One of my favorites was a flock of giant white-sheeted puppet birds with a twenty-foot wingspan; one volunteer would operate the body while two more the wings. A dozen or more such birds flew all around the grounds, up and down the slopes of the amphitheater then circled back to join the pageant parade.

A twenty-foot tall tri-masted sailing ship using hundreds of yards of white fabric for the sails and colored cloth for the ship was the most amazing. At least forty people operated this ship. Hundreds of actors and puppeteers marched in a bizarre parade flowing into and out of the main area. The birds preceded and followed the ship with dozens of other puppet creations, all with a subtle or profound political theme. The show would go on for days, ending with a spectacular fiery night show. At night, dozens of volunteers lined the path holding flaming torches, like a Polynesian ritual, lighting the way to the pine forest where puppet stages were erected.

Buses, reminiscent of Keyes's Magical Mystery Tour, loaded with hippies and communards, flocked to this event. Farmers in the area opened their fields to campers for free at first, charging only for firewood. That changed as the crowds grew over the years, reaching thousands of enthusiasts and curiosity seekers, and became a cash cow for the neighbors. There were two separate events going on, the Domestic Resurrection Circus proper and the campground antics. Puppets and Dead Heads and a wide array of hippies danced around a perpetual bonfire, circled by the flowery painted buses, vans, cars and bread trucks. Throngs of people sang and danced around dozens of bonfires scattered over hundreds of acres. Looking over the campground from high on a hill it was like witnessing an ancient pagan festival.

The Domestic Resurrection Circus added a new theme, the Washerwoman, depicting the plight of women around the world. This became more poignant than I realized at the time. The campground scene, with fires burning through the night, was wild with dancing and partying. The crowd was twice the size as the previous year. It was hard to believe that only five days have passed since we met the ladies at Bronze Beach. Great reminiscing and fun times, but we did little to advance the firewood project.

"Hey, Hugh did you see your new friends' van? It may not be as easy as you thought. I counted fifteen flower-painted bread trucks, six buses and at least thirty flowered vans. What kind did you say it was?" I asked.

"No, not yet. It was a mostly yellow VW bus. There were white daisies on the front and flowers on the sides. Fern, do you remember what was on the back?"

"There was some writing but I couldn't make it out."

"Well, that narrows it down. I saw a dozen VW Buses. I'll help you look around when it's light tomorrow." I said.

We regaled each other with tales around the campfire.

## Apple Jack-Hugh's Tale

"Last year after Bread and Puppet, we picked a shitload of apples. Before that, we found our way to Cold Hollow. Eric and Francine Chittenden started The Cold Hollow Cider Press in an old renovated barn at the base of the Cold Hollow Mountains. Our paths crossed, as they were transitioning to a new enterprise. The process was fun to watch. Although the facility was a renovated barn, the apple presses felt like they were made to be there. The huge hand-hewn floor joists were low above our heads. The apple presses were located on the lowest level of the old barn. Bushels of apples were fed into a huge press. When October arrived, we surpassed the minimum of fifteen bushels required. Sorry, guys. I gotta pee, someone finish for me."

"I got it, Hugh," Craig said, "So we picked our bushels, a mixture of orchard-grown apples and variations of wild apples we found growing around the mountain and neighboring roadsides. So, Fern, did Hugh tell you he started picking before he began his first semester at New Paltz? He became manic about it; everywhere he saw a wild apple tree he increased our harvest. He went so far as to call home and tell his Mom he wanted to be an apple picker and presser. Hugh ducked out of school to come back to the farm, pick more apples and help bring them to Cold Hollow."

Tara picked up the story. "We were driving when he saw an apple tree on someone's lawn so he pulled over and picked a bunch."

"Hugh! You can't do that."

"Sure I can," he said walking up the front door as a middle-aged woman opened it. "Good day and smiling trees. Do you want these wild apples I picked from that tree over there? I'm collecting apples from all over to make apple cider."

"You can't fool me, young man. I bet you're making applejack," she said, as she smiled and winked at him. "Sure you can have them. Just leave some for the critters."

Hugh got back and finished the story. "Each of our twenty-five bushels was inspected before it was packed to be sure there were no twigs, sticks, rocks or debris of any kind and excluded tiny apples which could jam the press. When done, we produced fifty-five gallons of apple juice, filling a whole cask. Another several gallons were poured into glass bottles that we took home with us. Our plan was to turn it into Applejack, but by the time we raised the seventy-five dollars, a dear sum for us at the time, it was too late. The Cold Hollow Cider Press moved to Waterbury and closed up the Bakersfield location. Unable to add sweetener to engage the fermenting process, the cider turned to a fifty-five-gallon barrel of apple cider vinegar; a noble effort."

"Hugh was really bummed since he was the most aggressive picker," Craig added.

## Bobbin Bounce

Hugh said, "I saw the woodshed; you guys have been busy. It's a far ways from the bow saw days. I was just telling Fern about our first day at the farm, climbing that hill to cut down the elm. Fucking cold! Glad we found that slab wood; it saved our asses. Say, Craig, why don't you tell the story about the first day we found the slab wood."

"Sure. We made plenty of trips to the Maple Bobbin factory for slab wood, the discarded, outside rounded surface with one side made flat by the saw.

Five dollars bought all you could carry. How could you go wrong? The factory was loud, dark, dirty, dangerous and interesting. Maple logs were floated to the ripsaw; grabbed by the conveyor, cut four times; resulting in a long square log that would be cut into ten-inch blocks for further processing. The blocks were positioned under a sharp chisel blade attached to a hydraulic piston. This was treacherous work as the worker repositioned the square block, chopping it into many two-inch square blocks. Many of the workers were missing one or more fingers from improper timing with the chisel blade.

On our second trip, trying to get the most 'bang' for our five bucks, or as the case may be, 'bounce.' We mounded the slabs high over the sides of my 1960 GMC pickup and secured the load. The leaf springs groaned as we pulled out from the loading dock. Route 105 began a steep climb a half mile from the factory. What a ride. The heavy load caused the front wheels to lift off the ground and bounce as we headed up the steep rise. We bounced for about a mile. Rattled, we pulled over and offloaded half of the wood. After unloading, we went back for the remainder. Next slab trip, we aimed for a little less bounce for the five bucks.

## End of an Era

Three nights in Glover left us all grubby, smelling of smoke, and exhausted. It was just a week since regrouping at the Phunee Farm. Our window for bathing in Lucas Brook was closing as the night got cooler. When it was time to depart Glover, Tara and Fae left for points south. Skye decided to hitch home, so we dropped her off at the interstate just a few miles from Bread and Puppet. Hugh and Fern introduced us to Donny and Phil, who opted to stay and help where they could after the Circus. They seemed like good people but I didn't realize they were brothers. Something was very familiar. Hugh and Fern planned to catch a ride with them the next day. Skye never returned. Tara and Fae moved to Albany but continued to visit for a time. Hugh's time as a Phunee farmer lapsed. He and Fern moved out west. What I did not realize departing Glover was the finality of a way of life and the companions who shared it.

Craig and I went directly home. Nick was expected in two weeks. We relaxed most of the first day back, then hiked up the logging road and marked every dead tree with orange spray paint and did the same for every dead tree reachable from the Jay Road. With luck, everything will be cut before winter, but the bright orange mark would stand out in the snow. We must have marked fifty trees over two days and blocked, split and stacked the wood near the woodshed. Apple picking rewarded us with two bushels. The nights were getting colder and we were always concerned about an early frost. The social summer was over and time was ticking toward the equinox.

## Two Days after Bread and Puppet

Tara and Fae were back in Albany; Skye made it to her hometown in Connecticut; Hugh and Fern stayed in Glover an extra day. Donny and Phil proved to be solid new friends going an hour out of their way to drive them back to the farm. When I saw the VW coming up the driveway, I had a sudden understanding. An amazing coincidence, actually. They all got out of the van and I asked, "Do you have an Uncle Jackson who calls you Phillip and Donald?"

Hugh said, in recognition, "Holy frigging shit."

They stayed overnight and the four of them left the next day. We shared the story of our Vegetarian Thanksgiving with their Uncle Jackson. Five hours later, after dropping Hugh and Fern at New Paltz, the brothers continued south.

*"Don't cry because it's over. Smile because it happened." ~ Dr. Seuss*

## 26

# MIA'S STORY

> *"Wendy," Peter Pan continued in a voice that no woman has ever yet been able to resist,*
> *"Wendy, one girl is more use than twenty boys."*
> *~ J.M. Barrie, Peter Pan*

I volunteered to clean up while and Nick and Craig started splitting some of the wood we cut earlier. Mia sat on the porch watching them but came into the kitchen when she got bored. It was their first visit. She told me she was with Nick since he left the logging crew two years earlier. Her story was reminiscent of *Guys and Dolls*, a sweet innocent girl taming the heart of the tough bad guy.

While she talked, she went about scrubbing the kitchen sink. "Back in the day when Nick had big money coming in, he got used to wearing the handmade lumberjack shirts I made working as a seamstress in Lawrence, and I got to know him over a few years. I was a good girl and didn't like the guys from Nick's logging job. He always struck up a conversation and flirted with me. I resisted him for six months; but yah know, it made me feel special. I gave in and, well, here we are. Nick talked about the two years he spent logging in the White Mountains, telling me how they worked in three-man teams. He complained they would drive for hours sometimes and camp in the forest for five nights, cutting all day and into the night. The pay was great, but no life. It sounded very rough and scary to me. They made each team compete for the most trees felled. The company sent in different crews to skid them out to the waiting logging trucks. Nick bragged that his crew was the fastest and the toughest; most of the others did not mess with them. "I was a little nervous when he rolled his clenched fist in his left hand with a longing look in his eye and said, 'We did what we needed to when they did.' I thought I could never handle that way of life, then we built a log cabin in Sheffield. He got tamer and I got tougher." Mia was a free spirit trapped in the male expectation of a 1950's woman.

## Sheffield

"It was really hard there. We lived in a tent for the whole summer while they built the cabin. I couldn't take it after three weeks on the ground, so we put the tent on a platform. The outdoor kitchen was not bad under the tarp, but the outhouse, just a shielded area over a hole in the ground, was cold and smelly. The rainy days were boring and the mornings were cold and damp. Mosquitoes were bad after a rain. The winter was cold despite the state of the art wood stove the guys picked up. There was no electricity, and for months we carried buckets of water to the house every day until they dug a well higher on the hill. Even then, we needed a hand pump. The kerosene and oil lamps were sooty and dim. We had propane Coleman lamps which burned brighter and cleaner but cost more to run."

I interrupted, "Wow, Mia, that sounds so much like the cabin we planned to build on a homestead in Oregon. Your perspective makes me appreciate this farmhouse."

"It was much better when we could get to the cabin through the passage we made to the interstate. That made it so much easier to run into town for supplies or just to get away from the wilderness. Well, it worked well for a year, anyway. The entrance through the trees was hidden by a wooden frame covered with brush that could be moved in and out of place. In the winter, the brush was replaced by dead branches made to look like young trees. During the green months, we changed the brush every few weeks to keep it green. We could hide the tracks with brush but we had to be careful on wet days or the tires might sink in and leave tracks."

In retrospect, this sounded like the *Hole in the Wall Gang's* hideout. They went to a lot of trouble to keep this entrance secreted from the world. Hearing the story, I thought how cool it was that they built a log cabin.

"That sounded like a lot of trouble, Mia."

"It got worse after Trooper Neil pulled over a corvette."

Mia's tale was gripping, and as she talked, the Acorn stove was still hot, so I put up a pot of coffee. Both chainsaws were humming. The din from the two-cycle engines meant I had to speak up as I told Mia about our first winter here and how, when we got snowed in, sometimes we needed to run water through the same coffee grounds two or three times. The joke was it was done when the pot boiled over. Craig and Nick came in when they smelled the coffee.

It was amazing how much we accomplished that day. It would have taken us days to do what we had done in a matter of hours. The techniques we learned proved to be helpful. We sat around drinking coffee for another hour and then Mia said she was tired and they got ready to head back to Richford. Before they left, Nick said, "So you cutting tomorrow?"

I responded, "Yeah, I want to finish the logs we have left. The way you showed us it should take less than an hour."

"No I mean cutting down some trees. You know, logging for firewood. Tell you what. I'll be here at seven AM tomorrow morning. Let's go up the mountain, cut a few trees, and skid the logs down here." Craig and I looked at each other and said, "Sure! That sounds great."

"Mia, let's go. You ready?"

"Nick, you may have to postpone that plan. We're supposed to leave for Conway tomorrow. Don't you remember I have to get fitted for my cousin's wedding? We may not be back for a couple of weeks."

"Weeks," Nick replied, I forgot all about it. You sure you told me about this?"

"I won't even answer that. Hope to see you guys soon. I love it up here."

"Sorry, boys," Nick said, "How about we play it safe? Three weeks from tomorrow, say seven AM, weather permitting."

"Wow. Thanks, Nick. We'll do what we can until then. Say, Bob, why don't we mark some dead trees with paint until then?" Craig suggested.

### Somewhere near Kennebunkport, Maine

Two-hundred miles east, four men exited a dark blue Ford Econoline Van parked behind Janson's Wilderness Supply Warehouse. The youngest of the four men, a stocky "kid," snapped the chain with bolt cutters and opened the gate. A tall, thin guy deftly disabled the alarm. The little guy knew the company payroll was in the safe; but he was a gun nut and was more excited about rifles, handguns and ammunition. Once inside, the first guy worked his long fingers like a magician, cracking the lock on the Diebold's Special floor safe. His father was a locksmith who taught him on Diebold safes. Inside, a locked compartment yielded to his skill. The biggest guy with a bald head kicked open the weapons cabinets.

They loaded the van with the cash, weapons, ammo, hunting knives and assorted camping gear. The safecracker said, "Might's well grab this gear; we may need it if'n we gotta run." Just as they finished loading up the van and were getting ready to flee the scene. The big bald guy shouted with alarm, "Let's get outta here, a rent-a- cop just turned the corner." HP, the wheel man said, "We should've been out of here already." With that, they all jumped into the new dark blue van, painted with light from the security cop's spotlight.

## MOUNTAIN MAN MENTOR

*Mentorship happens organically, and you can't just force it. Many men don't even know HOW to mentor, and often mentor others by accident. It's not a mentor's responsibility to mentor, it's the responsibility of the mentee to seek mentorship and appropriate it."*
~ Josh Hatcher

The weeks flew by. We were ready for our new firewood advisor. The Land Cruiser rolled up at the stroke of seven. I cut down many trees and understood the logic and mechanics of felling a tree; or so I told myself. A tree sometimes fell where it wanted despite my intentions. Nick fired up his favorite Homelite, then standing at the first tree said, "Where do you want it to fall?" A precise request.

He sized up the tree, calculated the position of the branches and started cutting. The tree leaned into the notch as he pulled the saw free and pointed straight down the road. It leaned away from the road then turned; landing where requested, dead center of the road. I was impressed, it was great having a mentor. I looped a chain around the pieces then Nick connected the other end to the trailer hitch and skidded them down to the house.

By late afternoon, we cut over two cord of wood. Five more to go. Nick went back to Richford. Energized by having learned so much, Craig and I split and stacked the blocked wood. Splitting wood is great exercise and we were on a roll, each in our own Zen space lulled by the thwacking, cracking and thudding of the wood as it split and fell from the chopping block.

Nick returned as planned a few times for the next month or so. The wood shed was filling up. Climbing higher up the mountain, we were soon cutting large trees. The leaves were changing and the colors peaked early in the month, though short-lived. The first snowfall left the leaves sparse long before Halloween. We learned about a local custom known as "Cabbage" night; the day before Halloween was more like a hell night for many teens. Last year a group of wayward youths set fire to an old barn then blocked the road and hid in the woods as the barn burned to the ground before the fire department could get through their barrier. This year we heard that the cabbage night antics had become even more menacing. Constable Munkard arrested a group of teens for breaking storefront windows on Richford's Main Street. What started as simple pranks turned nasty.

The Constable was busy that week. Deer season was open and several wealthy Canadians were hunting in the area. When I saw him, the Constable was putting handcuffs on one of the hunters. The Canadian was indignant about being stopped. He proudly displayed his kill strapped to the hood of his car. He would have received a ticket for blocking his view anyway. Constable Munkard arrested him because he shot a farmer's cow, thinking it was a deer.

## Rollover

The next time we went up the logging road we took shovels, pickaxes and the rototiller. It was back-breaking work, but we cleared a path for the Land Cruiser to climb over the erosion mounds. For the first time, we made it to the power lines with a vehicle. The loggers left plenty of wood behind when they harvested the blowdown. We cut and skidded the logs to the logging road. Building up speed, struggling with the chained logs over first mounds, Nick powered through, moving fast down steep, sharply-canted mounds, changing the center of gravity and lifting the passenger side wheels off the ground. Riding on two wheels, the airborne vehicle lifted further, reaching beyond its apex, teetering on the edge of no return. An instant before we rolled over, I threw my body out the window to put as much weight as I could on the high side. Nick was almost in my lap. Like in slow motion, we hung at this precarious point for a long, frightening moment before the wheels settled down. "Yee Ha!"

During those woodcutting days of early fall, Mia drove up with Nick and, to our delight, she loved to cook—and cook she did. We were eating better than we had since arriving in Vermont. The kitchen always smelled wonderful. With each new adventure, we became more and more impressed by the skills that Nick and Mia had to share. Craig and I started thinking about how well they would fit in at the Phunee Farm. We thought they might be interested in the empty downstairs room.

## Housemates

Yes, Nick and Mia wanted to move in, they were about to ask the same thing. Thanksgiving, a week gone and three months after our first meeting, they moved in with two dogs. Things kept getting better, until they didn't.

In fact, things got much better. Nick was mellow around us and Mia appreciated the effect we had on him, but we didn't understand what he changed from. Our main speed was mellow. We continued to be blinded by the imagery of the macho mountain man. Ironically, machismo was never a good thing in our circle of the world. We believed in the gentler side of people, and abhorred sexism and racism, and were eclectic in our pursuit of spirituality and religion. Everyone was equal and we did not hold ourselves to any lofty standard. The best we could be was measured by our own rubric rather than on a comparison scale with others.

New routines were established and we became housemates. Meals were planned and chores assigned. It turned out that Nick didn't do dishes or clean up; he had a woman. Nick talked of the log cabin in Sheffield. Our minds raced with the fantasy we shared as youths of building a log cabin in the wilds of the Pacific Northwest. Here was someone who actually built one. He offered to take us down to the cabin the following week. We were like kids waiting to go to Disney World.

## Log Cabin

We drove south past Sheffield on the interstate. Nick pulled over to show us where they made the illegal entrance. All we could see was dense forest with the exception of four wooden bollards. Nick said, "You'll see why we wanted to use this soon." Exiting I91, we followed small roads for twenty minutes before we turned into a maze of progressively worse dirt roads little better than a logging road. The last ten miles took as long as the forty that preceded.

We stepped out of the Land Cruiser into a meadow studded with tree stumps. The cabin nestled among the tree trunks was dwarfed under the dark vaulted ceiling of white pine trees. It reminded me of a scene from the movie Sergeant York. Gary Cooper was clearing trees to open a field. The stumps spread to the horizon. A great movie. Cleared stumps were dumped along the perimeter of the Sheffield garden with entwined roots, creating an impenetrable barrier of sharp-edged roots washed clean of forest soil and bleached white by the sun. The cabin was reminiscent of the log cabin portrayed in the same movie, which typified the hard life in Appalachia before World War One. The four inch logs were chinked with a mortar mixture that appeared grayish white between the darkened hardwood logs.

Rough and rustic, it was beautiful in a primitive back-to-the-land sort of way, yet I was overtaken by an overshadowing dreary feeling.

## Psychometric Sense

There is evidence to support that intense emotional reactions can linger long after the event that caused them. Have you ever walked into a room and felt sad or agitated before being informed of what happened? Psychometry, a term coined by Joseph Rodes in the 1800's, means measuring the soul, but actually all things emit energy.

I learned about this first hand at a pagan group meeting. Items were passed around and we were supposed to feel an event associated with the item. Most had little impact until a small, odd-shaped piece of worn metal was passed to me. I had no idea what it was, but when I touched it I cringed. An overwhelming sense of panic, fear and pain washed over me and I dropped it. Discontent to let it rest, I picked it up again; and I felt at peace. My reaction was written on my face; I was puzzled, saying, "What was that?"

My friend Drake, wounded as a soldier in Vietnam, was smiling at me, sensing my reaction. The metal was a piece of Viet Cong shrapnel from a mortar barrage on the position where he and his fellow soldiers dug in. Most of the other soldiers, some good friends, died that day. Drake was at the brink of death when the medics arrived and, after hours of surgery at a Mobile Army Surgical Hospital, and years of follow up surgery, he survived. The piece of metal I was holding was pulled from his body. He kept it with him as a good luck piece, a reminder of living through the ordeal and of friends who did not. Between Drake telling the story of the horrible events and me holding the metal, I could feel the horror and peace that it represented. Intense! You can't always find this energy, most times it finds you.

The cabin got smaller as we approached. The ridge of the roof was less than two feet above my head and the eaves were about my height; I felt the need to duck. We entered into a vestibule. The primitive country kitchen was contrasted by a gorgeous, antique White Oak Bakers Cabinet up against the far wall. Two camelback sofas and a vintage overstuffed chair with a fleur de lis pattern filled the open space. Homemade quilts hung down from the rafters about two thirds of the way down the room partitioning the "bathroom." Chamber pot would be closer to true.

The wood stove in the center of the cabin was one of the fanciest stoves I had ever seen—five feet tall with ornate, chrome filigree everywhere sitting on cast iron lion's feet with a broad rounded door. It was rustic, primitive and reflected a hard life; but after all of the effort, I wasn't sure why they left, so I asked. Nick responded uneasily and was vague, saying something about trouble with the government involving a nebulous, nefarious fate that had befallen them. Mia, visibly uncomfortable, turned away, avoiding the conversation. I wondered why all of this cool stuff, including Mia's handmade quilts, was still here. We were still riding a mountain man high and we gave it no thought. Instead, we were 'empathic'. Damn government! Below the surface, my psychometric sense picked up the early feeling of dread. Something powerful happened here.

We moved closer to realizing the pragmatic side of our back-to-nature dream. We worked hard, got stronger, learned the way of the woods and moved from the idealistic, poetic mindset of spiritualism and peaceful commune with nature to a baser, more animalistic survival mode. Our bodies and endurance had toughened; we were eating meat. Damn, we were eating often! Transforming into woodsmen or something like them, hands calloused and skills honed, our peaceful commune with nature had turned into a willing assault. Fierce, toothed chainsaws ripped at the fabric of the trees. The roaring cacophony of the two-cycle engine screamed, disturbing the chorus of the forest we strove to be one with. Gray-black smoke poured into the pristine forest air and, with it, an olfactory intrusion—the lingering odor of burning petroleum.

All told, we stacked ten cords of seasoned dry wood plus another of slab wood and hockey stick scraps before the snow started. When it started, it hardly ever stopped. The cold came on the heels of the snow; we were into December and hoped we had enough wood. It was getting hard to move in the woods even with the four wheel drive, so we spent our time tightening up the house where we could. We were getting ready to hunker down and mole out for another fierce Vermont winter.

A few weeks after they moved in, the house was as tight as it would be for the imminent winter; the wood shed was filled, the water was running and the power was reliable. Snow covered the valley for weeks and as the holidays approached, Craig and I went south, giving Nick and Mia a chance to settle in. The way Nick treated Mia, "his woman," started a silent warning bell.

The philosophical, spiritual and poetic dialogue we shared the first winter waned. Since we hooked up with Nick and Mia, we began in earnest to embrace the survival plans we crafted while huddled near "Maggie" on those first cold winter nights. Our conversation became about manly logging adventures, fixing up the cars, tightening up the house and embracing pragmatic concerns. We were evolving and we thought it good.

## 28

# TWO STEPS FORWARD

*Sometimes, carrying on, just carrying on, is the superhuman achievement.*
*~ Albert Camus*

### On or About Day Eight Hundred

Nothing in life is free, and the cost is not always clear. The woodshed was full and my woodsman's knowledge grew exponentially; and I learned volumes from Mia about cooking, canning and sewing, yet all the while, the spiritual energy of the land had been supplanted in slow, silent co-occurrence. We returned in January to a warm, clean and homey house—neither of us anticipated how territorial they would become in our absence. In fairness, while Craig and I returned in January, he soon departed for a trip to Oregon. Midwinter we were out of dough and there was no work to be had. I was called home because my father was laid up after surgery. I found odd jobs and sent money up to the farm. Nick and Mia had a lot of time, with full control, in the long wait of winter. The real Nick began to emerge.

### Message from a Pickup-hood Sled

At the end of March, three months after Nick and Mia moved in, firewood was getting low. Craig, back from out west, Nick, Jake and I set out on foot, dragging the hood of an old pickup truck which we had converted into a firewood sled. The waning snow, dense from spring thawing and refreezing, receded, exposing the orange marks we made in the fall. Walking atop the crusted snow was like wearing snowshoes, but getting the wood to the sled was a challenge. Gathering up our tools we dragged the loaded sled back.

Nick said something dopey, stammering and stumbling over his words, so like friends do, with a playful smile, I mimicked him. In a flash, he threw down his tools and got right up into my face, his eyes like those of a wounded predator, glared inches from my face, his body and fists tightened for battle. "Wow," I said taking a step back. "Nick, I was just teasing, making a joke. Calm down, bro."

"Don't ever mimic me again, Buff!" Even a little thing like that could not go unchallenged in the violent world he was from. Calling me 'Buff' signaled it was over. He nicknamed me Buffalo Bob, which morphed to Buff, a term of endearment. I was learning but thought, what do we know about them, are these their real names? Mountain Man!

The contrived sled worked pretty well until we got to the ice-covered steep rise of the driveway. We off-loaded the wood and moved the empty sled to the top of the rise and each took a cut log and carried them one by one up the hill. On my third trip up the icy incline I took a log that was too heavy for me. I dropped it and went back for another I could manage. Craig had already crested the hill on the way back to the house and I figured Nick or Jake, much stronger than me, would take it up. They didn't! I guess it was a man thing. I was still taken aback by the confrontation moments earlier. I had little experience with that kind of aggression. No one in our group said a word, the silence was deafening. Screw that. I was the brains of the operation and I wasn't up for the challenge. The log got burned, but it took awhile for me to go back for it: when I could get my car to it.

Reeling from the nose-to-nose with Nick, I felt more threatened than by the bull snorting through the fence or the approaching black bear. With every step, missed signals, unnoticed over the prior months, became clear. Our first chance meeting hearing the story of Zeke intervening in a fight with two unknown guys, the mystery at Sheffield and increasing episodes of violence. Heretofore, I thought my personal changes were welcomed, constantly learning from our new housemates. We surrendered to survival. Like in a fantasy novel, the magic was fading while I remained mesmerized by life's sleight of hand.

The castle Craig and I built was breached, his time was ticking away; but I moved forward with my ideal of the Phunee Farm. Castle was the symbol we used to encapsulate our original dream. A castle in the sky, a fortress in the wild, wrapped in spirituality protected within the walls of the mountain. In the early days of the Phunee Farm, it was compelling to gather, discuss poetry, art and God; oh, how so little time can yield so much change. Changes come in many forms and they need not be mutually exclusive; but sometimes they become consuming, yet no one can take your dreams, steal your soul or change your course, unless you let them, or maybe if you're not paying enough attention.

## Inner Space

During the winter months, as the crush of winter squeezed the farm house with debilitating cold, I found a haven in a quest for inner space, a welcome solace amidst the growing violence. I emphasize quest because results were often illusory. Gazing out my window, meditating, and focusing on distant Pinnacle Mountain, I stared through the ferocious winds incessantly blowing the snow into a whiteout fog that obscured my view but aided my journey. The fog led to a momentary clarity of nothingness and completeness. Exposure to such a dearth of knowledge and awareness was beyond my ability to absorb but left me with an overwhelming feeling of contentment.

Meditative sojourns were pursued throughout the seasons as the journey and ultimate destination are within one's self. The energy in the early days of the Phunee Farm was spiritual, positive and motivated by a shared innate goodness. Beyond the oneness with my surroundings and reaching for cohesion within the universe, there was an overlap with what is defined as the occult. Many things once considered occult are now within the mainstream of modern science. I experienced things considered occult or paranormal to be intriguing and worthy of pursuit. To be clear, experience is far from an empirical absolute, more like an understanding of belief that may have crossed the borders of imagination.

## Extension

With the car-hood-sled incident a few weeks behind us, we slipped into a new normalcy with our housemates. The closeness of winter led to building an extension. I drew up concept plans for a twelve by twelve room. The next challenge was how we would pay for it. Nick and Mia got back their security which covered nails and insulation. There were tumbledown barns and sheds all over town. We set out scrounging for wood.

The first score was a hundred and fifty year old house, razed after a fire. We approached Zach, who spoke with us about Faught Mills and asked if he had plans for the joists and main beams. The floor joists were massive, rough hewn and twelve feet long, sitting on three one-foot square main beams. He said we could have the wood.

I re-drafted the plans to make best use of the new material. We gathered up our demolition gear, crow bars, breaker bars, sledge hammers, framing hammers, hand saws and two of the chain saws. The weather broke, chasing the clouds; and we descended on the house. Tom and Brice came by to give us a hand easing out the wood in an effort to preserve it. The wood was like steel, seasoned for over a century. It was a bitch pulling the old square nails holding the joists fast to the main beam. The main beams were more difficult; fit together with mortise and tenon joints connected with hardwood dowels. They were supported by huge Hornbeam posts, sometimes known as Ironwood.

One by one, the beams yielded to our efforts. When the main beams were free, it took four of us to get them to the trailer.

Zack was impressed and offered the ironwood posts and any wood that survived the fire. Before we left, Zach said he knew a guy looking to take down a big shed. We were exhausted when we returned from the second trip, but we had enough wood to get the building started if we could coordinate with Mother Nature's schedule. Next trip into town we would find that shed. We all slept well.

Winter returned with a fury, dumping a foot of snow overnight and burying the plastic covered lumber. The snow lingered, so I put my energy into converting the sketches to quasi-detailed building blueprints. While waiting, I got work at Brice and Summer's.

## Brice and Summer

A few months after I arrived in Vermont I answered a call to assist in a barn-raising-like project at Brice and Summer's tower, and found that I liked them. They were both native Vermonters. Brice was too much the capitalist to be described as a hippie, but he pursued a similar back-to-nature lifestyle as a consummate businessman. His narrow light blue eyes were shrewd, intelligent and wary. He was a seminal salesman, smart, ambitious and crafty. Summer was a beautiful, angelic woman with long, curly dark hair and a flawless light complexion. She was in great shape, thickened slightly from childbirth. She was the quintessential perfect mate. A cross between a soft-spoken, sophisticated lady and a rugged mountain woman. To me, they were the perfect couple. We became good friends after our first meeting and they came up to the Phunee Farm often.

Tower Berkshire Flat Circa '82

Like most of us who had land in northern Vermont, they kept a large, robust garden which Summer tended and pot crop that Brice managed. He found hybrid seeds that blended Hawaiian and Afghanistan plants. I came to realize later that these seeds had worked their way through many Vermont communes throughout the state. The Afghan properties allowed the plant to thrive in the soil, terrain and temperature of northern Vermont, while the Hawaiian properties encouraged the plants to grow to seven feet tall with purple-red-green buds wrapping around the main stem.

Brice was impressed with the cabinets I built at the Phunee Farm and hired me to build cabinets at his three-story, octagonal tower about twenty feet in diameter on a hill overlooking the Berkshire Flats and the Missisquoi River in the distance.

I worked with Summer designing the kitchen that seemed to grow out of the walls in harmony with the tower's ambiance. The cabinets became the envy of many who visited—or so I was told.

# 29

# SPRING FORTH

*"Behold, my friends, the spring is come; the earth has gladly received the embraces of the sun,*
*and we shall soon see the results of their love!"*
*~ Sitting Bull*

### Scrounging

"You must be one of those hippies Zach told me about from that funny farm. I've been on this good earth seventy-five years and never had no hippies come to my door," Bert Heckman said, stepping out of a side door. "Follow me, boys. The shed's out back. Here we are, just passed the barn, it's in none too good shape, but it's standing." The biggest prize from the old tractor shed were the twenty sections of tin roof. He said, "Why don't you boys come back after mud season."

Bert directed us to a neighbor who gave us a trailer full of storm windows—a great score. So I redid the plans for the fourth time. May was moving fast; we already celebrated Fae's fifth birthday and my twenty-second. Memorial Day was around the corner, when a real pearl emerged. Hidden in the thick forest along the Jay Road, above the Lucas Brook, we found an old sugar shack with at least twenty sheets of tin roof and hundreds of board feet lumber—and best of all, the cupola was salvageable. We tracked down the owner, who heard all sorts of stories about the farm and blushed when she recalled stories she heard about naked people up there. Betsy, in her fifties, had a plump, friendly face, with auburn hair worn like Doris Day. "Sure, boys. You can take that old sugar shack down. Just clean up when you are done."

Example of a sugar shack

We rallied friends for a "barn razing," so to speak. Summer and Brice came up with his large trailer; Tom came up with Bruce in his truck and combined with our host of Phunee farmers, everyone had a job. Tara joined the men with the demo work; Hugh and Tom were on ladders pulling the tin roof. Craig and I removed the rafters, while Brice and Bruce stacked them for triage; pulling nails and squaring the board ends. Mia and Summer pulled nails and sawed the board ends square. The kids scoured the worksite for nails which they sorted by size and then straightened. The cupola was the last to be transported, after we policed the area.

## Warren & Shane

Dairy Day arrived. It was mid-June and, like everyone else around, we were there to shake off the gloom of winter and welcome a verdant summer. The bluegrass music had everyone dancing a circling hoedown. I noticed a guy and a wild-haired boy, dancing crazier than we were. We danced over and struck up a conversation, talking about the Phunee Farm and the extension we were building. He said, "Dude, I'm a framing carpenter. Give me a place to park my camper and I'll help you out." I took one hit from his pipe, then wandered off to find Brooke, with a plan to meet him at the farm the following afternoon.

Warren was a scruffy looking guy, five foot six, long curly strawberry blond hair and a long mustache covering much of his ruddy Celtic complexion, reddened further from excessive drinking. His face was etched with laugh lines engraved by his perpetual smile. He was a wandering, happy-go-lucky hippie sort with his five-year-old son Shane in tow. They were traveling around the northeast, sleeping in the camper, since they left a communal group in southern Vermont. His wife, Siobhan, left in the middle of the night after a heated argument.

Warren and son arrived in a beat up 1962 GMC light gray pickup truck fitted with a homemade camper. He was raring to go and jumped into action; his carpentry skills proved true. With his help, we installed the sub-flooring and completed framing the walls by the following day. They fit in well and, although victims of the coming storm, they stayed for months.

A few weeks later Warren climbed up a large maple to remove an overhanging branch. He watched his dog, Roach scampering around the field's edge with Bon Ami, Craig's dog. A nanosecond after Warren said, "Stand clear—it's going," the dogs darted in our direction. Bon Ami raced under the tree ignoring our shouts, but Roach was not so lucky. The three-inch-thick branch fell squarely on the dog's back. His legs splayed. Gasping in unison, thinking the dog was dead or seriously hurt, we ran over to remove the branch. As we approached, a triumphant but shaken Roach squirmed out from under the branch and scurried off to finish his game with the older Bon Ami. Roach's supple puppy nature allowed him to mold himself to the ground, achieving about a half an inch of clearance. Cool dog!

## Mark

We arrived at the Richford luncheonette, and I ordered my usual vanilla milkshake  We sat at the counter on the ubiquitous round red vinyl chrome seats, spinning around like kids, enjoying the shakes, when a friendly guy came in and introduced himself as Mark and started up a conversion. His thick, dark mustache betrayed a childlike face that never stopped smiling. He was working at the Sweat-Comings Company, a short distance down Main Street. He moved to Richford earlier that year from Massachusetts with his wife, Marsha, and their two-year-old daughter, Melissa. Aside from his radiant personality, we were intrigued by his job. "I put the hardware on doors for the top-selling kitchen hutches," he said. "Let me tell you, they would not be for us. Can you believe they're getting upwards of two-thousand dollars? Here look!" He reached into his back pocket and pulled out a folded piece of paper that he opened to reveal a picture of the hutch with three-dimensional drawings along the borders. He said, "I wanted to show Marsha what I was working on, and then I found this picture this morning. You see these doors on the right? These are my doors. They took this picture right after I finished attaching the last door."

I told him about the cabinets I started at the Phunee Farm. "Say, Bob, do you have hinges yet?" Without waiting for an answer, he continued, "Good, I will bring you a bucket of hinges and some of those locks and pulls. Don't worry. It's on the square. They have buckets of seconds. I'm allowed to pick through them."

"That sounds great to me; I could use them. You know, Mark, you're our kind of people." We invited him and his family up to the Phunee Farm for a visit the following Saturday.

## Marsha and Melissa

Staying home with Melissa was more challenging for Marsha than most. She was tiny and thin and read lips well, overcoming the complication with Mark's heavy mustache. I knew the sign language alphabet, so that helped. Marsha had keen eyesight. She didn't miss a thing, and I believe she developed a sixth sense of knowing where Melissa was at all times. She was active like most toddlers, but she had also learned how to communicate with Marsha and also how to take advantage of her disability.

Mark, Marsha, and Melissa drove up in their light blue 1967 Ford Falcon station wagon. Nick yelled into the house. "We got company." Mia came out with the rest of us to meet our new friends. Mark said, "You weren't kidding. This place is amazing. Damn. Look at the mountain views." We walked through the barn and pointed out the garden when the kids said, "We're hungry!" As the summer progressed, Mark, Marsha, and Melissa were coming back a couple times a week. Our personalities meshed well.

Our scrounging efforts paid off. We had enough material for a building several times the size of our original plan. Then, the second floor apartment Mark was renting on Richford's main street was condemned when a car plowed through the first floor. Back to the drawing board. I drew new sketches based on our latest cache of materials. By the time my ad hoc blueprints were ready, we were into June. The extension had grown to include a second floor. The new two-story, twelve-by-thirty-foot extension would accommodate two families, four times bigger than the first draft—without buying a single board. Mark, Marsha and Melissa moved in.

## Bright Light

When the security guard's spotlight lit up the van's interior, the little guy said, "I got it" as he pulled one of the scoped hunting rifles out of their booty sack and, with the precision of an army sniper, loaded the weapon, took careful aim and shot out the spotlight. The car swerved hard to the right when the light exploded; the sparks blinding the guard. Trig fired twice more, and both front tires exploded, sending the car over an embankment. Wheels smoking, the driver, Byron, spun around and drove past the security guard climbing out of a ditch. "That was some shoot'n Trig," the kid said, amazed. "Shit, that was nothing. The credit goes to the driver. He kept the van going straight and smooth.

The big bald guy said, "Yeah, HP. Great drive'n." He was their wheel man; his real name was Byron, nicknamed Horse. Everyone thought this was funny because his last name was Power. Over time, his handle morphed down to HP. Big continued, "You stole the perfect van, brother; we were invisible on the road with all the others."

The van was the first part of an orchestrated heist. They pulled over in thicket they scoped out earlier and drove the van deep into the brush. Unloading their cache, they hiked up a trail over a low rise that led to another dirt road where they hid a different vehicle, one of their own. The waiting van, fitted out as a camper, was owned by Billy, the stocky kid. His van was complete with a hidden compartment where they stashed their ill-gotten gains.

## Gravity

It was great being young and fearless. I thought nothing of walking along the top plate with a beer in one hand and a circular saw in the other. One day, I was balanced on a board spanning the stair opening nailing the surrounding decking boards but failed to notice that my makeshift scaffold moved a skosh, with every new board nailed into place.

I felt like an animated cartoon character hanging in the air for an extended moment; and then gravity being what it is, I followed the board plummeting to the floor below. The pain in my side was sudden and consuming. The wind knocked out of me, I couldn't breathe. Slamming my ribs into the edge of an unforgiving floor joist, I found myself hanging in the opening. Instinctively, I used my arms to slow my fall, succeeding in scraping much of the skin from each forearm. I hung there, feet dangling, lodged into the corner of the opening. Signals raced from my flayed arms and crushed ribs, overwhelming my brain with pain, bringing me to the edge of consciousness. Jake, working down below, grabbed my legs and lowered me down to the floor. I took the rest of the day off.

Efforts to thwart the fall were successful—but at what cost? Maybe I should have taken my chances with the drop? Darn instincts. My arms hurt like hell and I probably broke and/or bruised a few ribs; never did find out for sure. I wrapped my ribs with duct tape and gooped and wrapped my arms with gauze, and was back to work framing the next morning. The ribs still hurt months later.

The project was slow going; we knew there would be timing issues. Sometimes visitors would come for awhile, which meant partying—but guests were often put to work on various tasks. We got good at demolition. Yet each new score meant that the extension would take on another element. The sugar shack's cupola inspired an observation tower.

Then came the summer, and the throngs of summer visitors would soon begin. Just not who we expected.

# 30

# THIRD SUMMER

*Summer will end soon enough, and childhood as well."*
*~ George R.R. Martin, Game of Thrones*

## Rabbits, Dogs & Husbandry

The flow of visitors from Long Island slowed, as did visits from our friends from Northern Vermont. Those who came were there to work,; but there were exceptions, and not all good. Growth toward true living on the land took on many forms. We learned rabbit meat was a delicacy in Montreal. A teacher of ours convinced us to be rabbit ranchers, but we delayed the project. If we weren't encouraged by Nick, I doubt I would have agreed to rabbit rearing. As on-again-off-again vegetarians, the idea of raising rabbits for the cultured pallet of wealthy Canadians was unsettling. I set out to be a farmer; but nonetheless, I tried to mute the imagined screams of rabbits going to slaughter.

The rabbit project was going strong. Starting with two bucks and ten does, what they say about rabbits is true. It took no effort to mate them; we soon had a warren of kits. The cages were set up, lights were in place, and we were getting comfortable handling the fattening rabbits. I knew come dead of winter, it would be a challenge. Throughout the process, Brooke's words kept playing over and over in my head, "Have you ever heard rabbits screaming in a slaughterhouse?"

The rabbits were secure in their cages, the doors latched with wire. We were concerned about any number of critters doing them harm. We had issues with weasels killing chickens, foxes killing guinea hens, even a bobcat killing goats. We felt comfortable knowing that Nick's German Shepherd, Zeke, was on the job with Bon Ami, the Collie, and Heidi, the Basset Hound, as backups.

Craig and I were driving into Enosburg to meet Jonas, who was helping us sell the bunnies. The rabbits were locked up and the canines were on patrol; no worries. En route, we were rehashing our progress, when Craig asked, "Did you latch the barn door when you closed it."

"Uh, I thought you closed it. The door was closed when I got in the car."

Craig said, "I guess the wind must have blown it closed. No big deal. The dogs will keep the varmints away. What do you think?"

"Well?" I said, "Let's go back; remember the fate of our chickens?" Maybe we should just hit the IGA in Richford and head back up to the farm and make certain. Let's call Jonas from there and tell him we'll be a little late."

The open barn door was a bad sign. The dogs were panting, lying ten feet from the barn, pellets of rabbit food evident on their muzzle. I stopped short and we jumped out of the car and rushed into the barn. Two of the cages were knocked over and the rabbit food was spilled all over the floor. None of the cages appeared opened, which gave an initial sense of relief until we looked closer. Half of the rabbits were dead in their locked cages. What the hell? It took a while to digest the subtle carnage. From the looks of it, the dogs got into the rabbit food and terrorized the rabbits, running around the cages and toppling some. We learned later, the threat of the dogs caused half of their little rabbit hearts to give out from sheer terror. The image of screaming rabbits was more prescient than I realized.

I sucked at animal husbandry. Nick didn't. I was happy to take my share of the chores, but I did not have an animal aptitude. Nick went on to get three pigs. I worked on the building the pigsty, for which I was more suited. It was well built and solid. Nonetheless, the pigs escaped, escape artists that they are. I was a fair swine wrangler.

We got more chickens and boarded Lady, the mare. Nick rode that horse all over the valley and up mountain trails. His prowess with mechanical, animal and logging continued to impress; but as the summer progressed, the scales of ambivalence toward our mountain man mentor tilted, as knowledge of missed signs accrued.

### Commotion in the Barn

We were sitting down to dinner, the kids had just come in from playing in the barn. Conversation was ripe with plans for finishing the extension and the day's hunting. Nick went out with his kids at dawn and jacked a doe up on the hill near the wild apple tree. Rory was excited as he recounted the story. "Dad lifted the rifle just as two bucks bolted. He fired at the six-pointer, but the big buck darted left. Ya shoulda seen it. The bullet ripped through a green apple hanging above the buck. The rest of the deer scattered. He fired again but the bucks were gone, so he took a bead on the last doe and downed it. One of the fawns lingered by its mother until instinct told it to flee. It was a lot of work dragging the deer down the hill and into the barn." Mia stopped him when he started to talk about bleeding and gutting. A bucket of the deer's blood and guts sat on the floor near the deer's head, saved to feed to the pigs.

Everyone was seated at the kitchen table when a loud banging interrupted the meal. The din was coming from the lower level of the barn where the kids were playing minutes earlier. We raced outside. Nick leading, opened the barn door expecting to chase a critter harassing the rabbits. Instead, a large black bear came charging out. Nick stumbled backward, ducking behind the door. The bucket of deer guts swung in the bear's mouth. We were queued behind Nick, standing in the driveway, unwittingly blocking the bear's egress. The beast dropped the bucket and rose up to its full six foot height while letting out a bloodcurdling roar. We were so close, we could feel the heat from the beast's breath. You never saw three people scatter so fast. Craig and Hugh made it onto the porch and I was able to slide away back behind the bear toward the barn, meeting up with Nick. The bear dropped down on all fours, took a less aggressive posture, grabbed the bucket splashed red with blood, entrails spilling; it sped up the same deer run the hunters had used in the morning. We surmised the bear picked up the blood trail and followed it into the barn.

Like something out of a western movie, Nick ran into the house and grabbed his Remington 788 bolt-action centerfire rifle and tossed Mark the Marlin 30-30 and ran up the hill after the bear. Warren grabbed a Remington shotgun from his truck, Jake following close behind, grabbed a bag of shells. I wasn't sure what Nick was more indignant about—that the bear was in the barn, the sanctity of human space violated, losing the bucket of guts or that it practically knocked him over running out of the barn.

Nick yelled back to house, "Rory, Cory—stay here and listen to Mia." It took everything that Mia and Marsha had in them to stop the kids from following. The difficulty was with Nick's kids from his first marriage. Shane, at five, and Melissa, at three, were easier to contain. Everyone's adrenaline was pumping. Mia, more like a big sister than a mom, was in a panic.

"Omigod, the kids were just there. What would have happened if they were still there?"

The avengers followed the bear tracks into the forest. The bear was moving slower now and could be seen sauntering along through the trees. Nick took aim, fired and missed, hitting the ground in front of the bear. At the same time, Mark leveled the Marlin and fired two quick rounds. One of them hitting the bucket, the other sheared a branch above the bear's head. Nick, frustrated, fired again before the resounding echoes of Mark's shots had drifted to silence. Once again,

Nick's bullets missed the mark. A new echo rang back from the mountain. Warren started to aim the shotgun but lowered it, realizing he was too far away.

Startled by the first shots hitting the ground, the behemoth, still trying to protect its prize, looked around. The bear dropped the bucket when the next bullet pierced the metal with a loud percussive clang. The bear ran off into the woods at full speed. When they reached the bucket, blood staining the forest floor red was spreading out around what was left of the deer's guts.

Back at the barn, the deer carcass ready to be butchered was on the ground, torn and imprinted from the bear's sharp teeth. I spent a lot of time as a vegetarian and couldn't imagine shooting a deer or bear. Our farming experience was getting real. Craig said, "Good thing the bear went in through the front door. It could have gotten ugly if it came upon the pigs out back or Lady, (a Palomino mare), in the makeshift corral."

"I'm surprised the rabbits are not more shaken," I said. We hung the deer back on the ceiling hook and tasked the boys with cleaning up the mess.

Craig and I went back inside to comfort Mia and Marsha, still shaken by the incident. The women jumped with every shot echoing through the valley. Mia commented about Nick's ex-wife, "The boy's mother, Darla, was seventeen when they got married; and he was eighteen when Rory was born. She ran away from the marriage two years later, six months after Cory was born, after Nick was sentenced to seven years in a maximum security penitentiary in New Hampshire. *This time we picked up on the sign.* Craig and I looked at each other with a look of "What have we gotten ourselves into?"

"Mia? Did you just say prison?" I asked.

"When he was twenty, he got busted for B and E's with a couple of his friends, you know, breaking and entering," she replied.

They didn't shoot the bear, but they returned with feigned victory. Their body language was that of a posse returning from an ill-fated effort to apprehend the bad guys, but mitigated by the retrieval of their ill gotten loot, in this case the mangled bucket. They were pumped up with adrenaline and fatigued from the race up the mountain. Mia and Marsha scurried around the kitchen, bringing the meal back to life from its dormant place in the warming oven of the Acorn.

The men were quipping about the near misses and patted Mark on the back as they showed us the bullet hole in the bucket. The boys were fascinated by the hole in the blood-stained bucket. Mia yelled, "Get that disgusting bucket out of the kitchen right this second." Craig and I listened as the story of the chase was told; but ringing in the forefront of our thoughts was the news we just heard from Mia, giving us a wary new perspective on our new housemate.

## Ford Falcon

Mark, driving his Ford Falcon station wagon, was leading, with Jake riding shotgun. Craig and I followed in his 1960 GMC pickup. We crested the hill, beginning the steep decline into the valley below. Craig and I were talking when we noticed something wrong with Mark's driver's side rear tire.

Beeping the horn, we frantically waved him to the side of the road. Too late! Before he could react to our warning, the entire driver's side rear wheel assembly—including half of the axle—worked its way out of the axle hub, dropping the car to the pavement with a loud shrieking, as a shower of orange red sparks shot out behind the car in an expanding cone of fireworks. We were transfixed by the shower of sparks and Mark's desperate attempt to keep control of the car. The car swayed, fish-tailed and yawed, riding along the shoulder, then back into the road. At one point, it looked like it would go over the cliff, down to Lucas Brook. An instant later, the wheelless rear end dug into the dirt along the shoulder. Mark brought the car to stop at the edge, two wheels balancing in the air. It happened so fast; seconds elapsed from first notice.

While we watched Mark's car, the wheel and axle became a wobbling projectile moving like a top spinning on its axis then bouncing erratically left and right. Craig couldn't tell which way to turn. Just as it appeared the missile would crash through the GMC's split panel windshield, Craig cut hard to the left, moving out across the double yellow line, fortunately bereft of oncoming traffic, just as the off balanced spin of the oncoming wheel propelled the tire to the right, grazing the truck bed on the passenger side just as the Ford stopped teetering on the precipice of the steep drop far down below. Once clear of the tire, Craig jerked the car back onto our lane and screeched to a stop a few feet behind the Ford. We jumped out to see if anyone was hurt. Mark and Jake, ashen, were getting out as we walked up. Mark just kept repeating, "What if Marsha and Melissa were in the car as they had planned. Thank God I was driving; it was all I could do to control the car. Marsha would have sailed over that cliff. Omigod!"

The windows would have to wait. We retrieved the wheel and axle, piled into the pickup and drove back to the farm. Returning to the scene with Nick and the Land Cruiser, three of us lifted the back of the car and walked it back as Nick winched the car to level ground. There, we jacked up the rear of the vehicle and put the wheel and axle assembly back into place. Most remarkable: a simple clip was all that held the axle to the axle hub. We jerry-rigged it with a cotter pin and the Ford was able to drive home where Marsha, in a panic, echoed the same mantra that Mark had. It sounded even more profound with Marsha's hearing-impaired speech.

## New Deal

It was different now. Nakedness became uncomfortable, the spiritual essence but a veiled memory surrendered to the pragmatic. Life changes and moves on, and I was beginning to dislike it. Dissent was building just below the sightline of my psyche.

# SIBLING SURPRISE

*"Rejoice with your family in the beautiful land of life."*
*~ Albert Einstein*

The extension was weather tight as we moved into August. The house, bigger and better than ever, was full of men, women and a baby; and yet, I never felt more alone. Hugh, Tara and Fae came and went; sometimes they were gone for months. Craig was spending far less time at the farm. Nick and Mia were anxious to move into the second floor bedroom, having claimed the prime space of the addition. He was getting ornery, short-tempered, and drinking more than ever. Some of our salvage found its way to East Franklin where some newcomers settled, but more on that later. Then came a reprieve, a different visitor surprise, putting on hold my growing concern.

## Brothers

My two youngest brothers, John, fourteen, and Ray, fifteen, came up to visit and asked to bring a friend. They arrived in St. Albans via Amtrak. My brothers exited the station with two friends, then two more, then two more— totaling ten teens, fourteen to seventeen. We had room for four. Packing some of them into the waiting vehicle, Craig drove back to the farm to get a trailer. Two and a half hours and ninety miles later, they returned with the trailer and two cars. On the trip home, I realized, there was little money between them. Ten more mouths to feed and we were low on dough. They pooled their money and we stopped at the IGA market in Richford. They were proud as could be when they got back to the car.

Most of them had never been off Long Island or away from home, for that matter, and were fascinated by the ride along the river; and they were in awe of the Phunee Farm. Once settled, I inventoried the supplies they bought. They planned to stay for two weeks but purchased six packs of hot dogs, some hot dog buns, a few cans of beans and dozen of boxes of Kraft macaroni and cheese. Oh, boy!

A few nights of roughing it in the woods, and two of the ten opted to head home, hitchhiking back to Amtrak from Richford; the others had money wired from home. Back to the IGA. This time, we supervised their purchases. That night we feasted; everyone helped. Next day we showed them how to get to the swimming hole. They took the Uncle Tom's soap so they could bathe; they were getting ripe.

## Woodshed

We took advantage of the free labor and put them to work building a bigger wood shed. There was a stand of tall straight poplar trees beyond the garden, perfect for the rails and posts, which were treated before being put in the ground. The petroleum odor from the creosote-coated posts hung in the air all afternoon. Maple slab wood was used as siding. It wasn't important to be air tight but we tried. It looked great and kept the snow out; the boys were proud of themselves.

One of the boys wandered off to pee and strolled into our reefer patch. Twenty five plants, five feet tall were growing, but far from budding. One by one, they snuck off to see this wonder. We got wise and admonished them to keep it quiet. But since they knew, we recruited them to be water bearers. Three days later, after a heavy rain collapsed the tent at Bronze Beach, the crowd came running up to the house, soaking wet, and opted to sleep in the barn. Two more of them could take no more and found their way home. While in the barn, they helped set up a workshop in the upper part of the barn. Mickey arrived with a cast on his forearm. He conspired with a few of his cohorts to remove his cast using a saw, leaving a small cut on his forearm. To the best of my knowledge, there were no negative ramifications.

## Bicycles Beyond Border

Clay and Brad borrowed the bicycles from the barn and were gone for hours. We became concerned and went to find them. When we did, they were coming over the Missisquoi River Bridge, struggling against their pedals. The dopey kids, oblivious to the border, rode over the bridge, ending up near cheese lady territory in Canada, passing the Canadian Border guard who waved them through. When they figured it out, the two young, unthreatening teens on bicycles with no ID pedaled back to the US Border crossing. The border guard approached them. They were scared, not a good look at customs. Asked for ID, they said they had none. They explained they were at the Phunee Farm with me and Craig and Hugh. The guard said, "You mean cheese Hugh? Nice guy, haven't seen him in a while. Tell him Reni said, "Hi." They were waved through. We loaded the bikes in the trunk and returned home.

## Hello And Goodbye

Taking full advantage of the vacation, my parents went the long way via Quebec, then dropped back down to northern Vermont. My mother claimed Craig as another son, and he saw her as a surrogate mother.

The remoteness of the farm raised a Brooklyn girl's concern. Shane, age five, was scurrying up a rickety homemade ladder to the top of the wood shed when my mother got out of the car. She gasped in alarm at the danger yet was impressed with the little long-haired boy. In her world, he would have been sheltered and kept away from such risk. This was less a hippie thing and more of a country farm thing. Boys his age could be seen bringing cows in from pasture.

Overcome by a debilitating hay fever attack, my mother's actual time at the farm was limited. She stayed at the hotel, but the next day I gave my father a better tour of the farm. He was impressed and proud of what I was doing, even if he didn't get the hippie thing. My parents loaded my two brothers and their one friend into the Buick and drove down to Long Island. Dad, whistling as usual, slipped me a few twenties as he climbed into the driver's seat. I know he felt the power of Lucas Brook Valley. I watched them drive off, wondering if they would ever return to see our dream blossom in the coming years. Although I applied to take the Civil Service test, I had no intention of leaving the farm. Little did I know how quickly things would devolve.

## 32

# HOOLIGANS

*Now, neighbor confines, purge you of your scum! Have you a ruffian that will swear, drink, dance, revel the night, rob, murder, and commit the oldest sins the newest kind of ways?*
*~ William Shakespeare*

### Hail Hail the Gang's All Here

Nick invited friends from his prior life who arrived with his kids, Rory and Cory, in tow. The ringleader of the bunch was a guy named Rickey, a muscular six foot four, two hundred and eighty pounds with a bald dome, thick mustache and menacing eyes. Covered in prison tattoos, he cut the figure of the top dog in the yard.

Nick introduced him along with the rest of his gang—meant in the most literal sense. Rickey said, "Nick, my man, you were right about this place. What a great hideout." In the yard, he was Big Rickey. The others came off far more pleasant than their intimidating visage portrayed. Billie, short and stocky with a face scarred from severe acne, was the youngest, known as "the kid." Snatch was tall, thin and wiry, and earned his nickname from his sticky fingers. He could pick any lock and would snatch anything not nailed down. Trig, who looked the meanest, was the smallest and slightest of the group. He was named for his quick trigger finger and deadeye reputation. Nick's friends were getting too comfortable, but with some coaxing, left after a week, with plans to return. The visit struck me as a prison reunion.

## New Hideout

A few weeks later the whole lot of them, plus one, returned in an overloaded old Ford pickup and a Chrysler van, towing a trailer with all of their stuff, planning to take up residence at the farm. I was adamant they should not. Five days later, the newcomers found a secluded place hidden in a cluster of pine trees, twenty-five minutes away along the East Berkshire Road, in East Franklin. The house was big. Peeling blue paint barely clung to the walls listing ten degrees off plumb. They were the advanced team. Another from their cadre was to accompany the women of the group after the house was set up—which coincided with the woman getting out of the local jail for "reckless endangerment."

## Hideout

The newcomers were preoccupied and didn't come back to the farm for weeks, a fortunate absence when my brothers and their friends arrived. Nick went to their East Franklin lair often with the pretense of helping them cut firewood or patching up the house. I went with him when they first arrived and was palling around, smoking and drinking beer like one of the gang. I felt cool at first, welcomed by these older seasoned men. They called me Buff, shortened from Buffalo Bob, after Nick used his nickname for me. Rickey was impressed with the new kitchen cabinets and asked me to build cabinets in their new farm house. As I think of it, I was more cajoled into the project than asked.

I found time between lags in the extension building and visitors at the farm. Each time I went back, there was new stuff somewhere in the house. A couple of TV's, a high-end stereo system, and a new refrigerator were evident on one visit. I returned a few days later and there was an assortment of boxes, a different stereo system, new chainsaws, tools and whatever cabinet hardware I needed. My "Spidey" senses were tingling. The house had an eerie aura about it and gave me an uneasy feeling. Maybe it was the residents. *Nice hideout you have here.*

## A Story Heard

While working at the East Franklin house, I often overheard them talking—more like bragging—about past crimes. One instance was about a burglary in Maine the previous fall. Rickey said, "Your fingers moved like a fifty dollar whore the way you cracked that safe, Snatch."

"Thanks, Big. You did alright kicking open those gun cabinets," Snatch replied.

"Yeah, but not with the same finesse," Rickey said, holding up a one of the Winchester rifles like a cat with a mouse. He patted Trig on the back, "You were on fire that night." You too, HP. Nobody would suspect those tags; great job counterfeiting the plates." A voice I had not heard before said, "I guess I learned something in jail." I noticed a red-haired guy standing by the window through which I saw the crime camper parked in the driveway.

It's bad enough to shoot at a car. It's quite another to take aim at a person. They seemed to forget I was there, working away on the cabinets, while they continued to drink and get more and more loose of tongue with stories of their exploits. Although none of the stories were directed at me, their stories became more and more violent. In the course of their conversations, I came to believe this was a common occurrence more than an isolated act of boredom or restlessness.

## Trig's Story

They retold the stories of how they were caught and sent to the New Hampshire Penitentiary. Nick was the most circumspect, while Trig's story was the most disconcerting. He was drinking and drugging one night in a New Hampshire bar, trying to hit on a young overweight woman with long, dark hair. She hung out of her low cut blouse, exposing two dart tattoos, one on each ample breast, which pointed to the bull's-eye tattoo circling each areola, peeking out when she moved.

She was accepting of his advances until he started getting obnoxious. She was a fixture at this road house bar; he was not. Four of the regulars got up from their bar stools and intervened. They surrounded him and helped him leave. He was a small guy, so he relented; they shoved him out of the door sprawling face first onto the dirt driveway. They turned and walked back inside, laughing. The four of them wore the same jean vests displaying their motorcycle gang name *Dover Sons of Satan*.

The rough handling sobered him up fast. He got up spitting dirt and gravel as he took a Colt .45 revolver from his car and fired four shots into the motors of each of the Harleys parked out front. This brought the men rushing out of the bar; exactly what Trig had planned. As soon as the first guy reached the parking lot, with the others close behind; he fired at the first guy's chest and hit him just below the right shoulder and above the heart. The second guy, who looked like a moving mountain, was exposed when the first guy fell to the ground. He fired one round into the big guys' knee; and before anyone could reach him, he had combat reloaded, using the speed loader he clipped to his belt. He fired again at the next guy, shooting off most of his ear. The rest of the group backed into the bar realizing every shot went where he aimed.

The bartender called the police, when the first shot was fired. Trig was getting into his car to leave when two police cruisers blocked his escape. The cops jumped out behind their doors with their assault shotguns aimed at him. He gave up without a fight; he was almost eighteen. The first week of his incarceration, he befriended Nick and came under the protection of the neo-communists. Trig got out of jail two years after Nick, he was twenty-eight.

## Kabal

It became clear that the stories of past exploits were firmly rooted in the present. I learned the supplies they brought with them on their first trip were all from snatch and grabs at small stores en route from Massachusetts. They were smart about their big jobs, which were always at least a hundred miles from their base, and then only after extensive research.

"Whatta ya think about an armored car, easier than a bank?" I heard Billy say.

Lowering his voice I barely heard Big say, "Nah. We're not ready for that, but I heard from Skeet; he lined up another factory payroll outside of Brattleboro."

Later that summer, I noticed a headline in the *The Newport Daily Express* newspaper. *Vermont State Police are working with their New Hampshire counterparts to solve a recent spate of interstate burglaries along the I-91 corridor.*

## 33

## MONKS AND THE FALL

*"This old world keeps spinnin' round; It's a wonder tall trees ain't layin' down."*
*~ Neil Young*

I told Nick about the monk's cache. A decision I will regret to my last breath.

We met the monks at their would-be cloister a few weeks into our first summer at the Phunee Farm. Driving back from Richford, on the hottest day of the year, we noticed a large man laboring up the hill, sweating profusely. He was wearing a heavy brown robe, tied at the waist with a rope belt. I slowed, pulled up next to him and offered him a ride. Struggling for breath, he leaned over, hands on thighs, took a few short breaths, expressed his gratitude and climbed into the back seat. He introduced himself as Brother Demetrius; his destination was a mile or so up the road.

A fellow monk clad in the same brown robe but tied with a dark purple sash came walking up to the car from their garden. Demetrius got out of the car and greeted his approaching brother, "Galinthias, praise be what a good, glorious day." Another brother stepped out of the front door and was introduced as Erasmus. Demetrius explained, "These charitable young men picked me up just as I thought I would collapse. I thought myself unworthy, they were like manna from heaven sent to aid me on my quest."

"Such deeds should be rewarded," Galinthias offered. "Come into the house for some ale."

When we entered, the ripe smell in the air made it clear personal hygiene was not a priority. A hallway led out of the kitchen to a small dark parlor where two monks were kneeling on the hard floor their faces about six inches from the wall. They remained motionless and silent for our entire visit. They were part of an Eastern European Christian Mystery Sect that held their existence and dogma close. Strict vows of poverty, chastity and celibacy guided their faith; but when it came to food and ale, they leaned toward Dionysius. All of them were portly, between two hundred fifty and three hundred fifty pounds, ranging in height from five eight to six two, like Friar Tuck without the tonsure. They could drink beer, apologizing for the familiar Genesee Cream Ale; their first batch of home-brewed ale was still a couple of months away. Noticing the bag of weed I pulled out of my pocket, Erasmus smiled and said, "Dionysius was fond of cannabis."

We talked and drank beer at the table for over an hour. The commitment to their order was genuine, but they could party. They liked to laugh, joke and kibitz about each other. They goofed about how they ended up in this mystery sect here in the cold of northern Vermont. They took their current names when they were inducted. At birth they were Thomas, Richard and Harold, from Chicago, Atlanta and Trenton or, literally, Tom, Dick and Harry.

Demetrius mentioned a stand of tall ancient trees deep into the forest. We followed a grassed-over road into the woods for about a mile, coming to a huge stately beech tree with branches spreading ten yards from its five foot thick trunk. A great treehouse tree. Two hundred yards beyond the beech, the tall trees were evident.

The canopy was so high it was impossible to make out the lower branches blurring with the foliage. Huge coniferous and deciduous trees spread out all around us. The smallest of them was a hundred feet tall with a circumference equal to three arm spans. The area was surreal, like an antediluvian primordial forest. The primeval essence of the place was like rocketing back in time, a time when these gargantuan guardians were seedlings. Closing my eyes, I could feel the passage of time transpiring over the eons. These trees stood tall when Ethan and Ira Allen and their cadre of Green Mountain Boys were the bane of the British soldiers. The history of Vermont emanated from their bark. I wondered how they survived the clear cutting of Colonial Vermont.

Returning to the house, we passed through an organized stand of smaller trees. Demetrius confirmed the woodlot was planted by the prior owner. He offered us half of the wood if we were up for the task. We confessed those trees would have taxed our skill level, but said we would be back when we felt more proficient.

## The Fall

That was more than a year ago. Leaving the monks and my Rambler American at the house, we drove into the wood. Nick was agog over these behemoths and was itching to take the saw to one. Craig and I cautioned him that the woodlot was further into the forest ahead. The Land Cruiser arrived at the woodlot, and we started cutting the thirty foot maples. The first load was for the monks. We dumped the trailer and Craig and I stayed back to help stack the wood. Nick and the others drove back to continue the cutting.

The first load stacked, Craig and I walked back toward the woodlot, expecting to meet the others—but they were nowhere to be found. The roar of the chainsaw caught our attention. I looked at Craig with some concern and said, "He wouldn't, would he?" Knowing time was against us, we set out at a run. Arriving out of breath, our worst fears were realized. Nick's twenty-four inch Stihl chainsaw was partway through the smallest of the giant Ents. Unlike Fangorn of Tolkien's Middle Earth, this tree could not defend itself much. I took slight solace knowing the oldest among them were spared from this assailant.

"What have you done!" I screamed. The tree under assault dwarfed the sixty foot white pine trees that surrounded it. The area was spongy from the ages of accumulated leaves and pine needles. He stopped cutting and said, "Calm down, Buff. What's the problem? It's just a tree. Besides there's enough wood in this tree to get us to spring." The tree he was cutting was close to two hundred inches in circumference. I stood there mouth agape, shocked that he offered no apology, and worse, felt no remorse. Aside from the horror of this moral violation, the tree was so big, the effort to convert it into firewood would be enormous. The damage was done, unable to stop now, Nick resumed cutting. The behemoth fought back, leaning into the first cut, trapping his saw. I wanted no part of this, but his Homelite was broken so he asked to use mine. My saw was sixteen inches long and had no business cutting a tree of this stature. I relented and handed him my saw. I was astonished when he completed cutting the notch, which he pushed to the ground, freeing his 24-inch saw; the long bar bent beyond use, so it was all about my little McCullough.

He labored for thirty minutes when the first signs of movement were expressed with a creaking noise, a forerunner to the audible screams of this magnificent soul. Leaving Nick to his dastardly deed, we moved about a hundred feet away, in the opposite direction the tree was directed to fall. A loud final crack heralded its demise as it started to fall. The tree listed as the upper branches threw off the center of gravity and the tree began to turn. It was imperceptible at first, then as the inertia broke, momentum prevailed, and the monstrous guardian of the wood, weighing more than house, turned toward where we stood. It arched over our heads blocking the light, leaving us in a momentary blackout, then, contorting with agonizing groans, it completed a one hundred and eighty degree turn and fell to the ground. The concussive force with which it hit sent a shock wave through the spongy ground, sufficient to lift our cowering bodies inches off the ground. The tree, to my continued horror, teetered on the edge of a cliff and fell into the canyon were it rested; irrecoverable. It was bad enough to take the life of this ancient one; but without the expected result, it was impalpable.

Gaining my composure, I could not look at Nick, I was so devastated. My soul was wounded. I felt an overwhelming surge of finality. I recognized our mountain-man mentor for the fraud he was. He was numb to the essence of that ancient tree who spoke so fluently to my soul.

Grateful I brought my own car, I left and took the scenic route through Montgomery, over Jay Peak, and returned home from the east. I did not want anything to do with Nick, for a while. I needed time to clear my head. While on the other side of the mountains I picked up a radio station from New Hampshire. *"A body was found several miles from the interstate north of Hinsdale. Preliminary identification points to an inmate released from the New Hampshire Penitentiary two years ago. Police are looking into a possible connection between recent burglaries along the interstate. Detective Berett from the NHSP said, 'We sent an officer to Kennebunkport, Maine to meet with detectives investigating similar crimes.'"*

Slowly, the impact of the news story grabbed me, taking my thoughts and distracting me for a short time from the day's dire events. What have we gotten into? I was done. Decades later, I still feel that sorrow and regret for my little part in the annihilation of that centuries-old denizen of the pristine and ancient wood. Dead dream walking.

# 34

# ASTRAL & OTHER TRIPS

*"How many things have been denied one day, only to become realities the next!"*
*~ Jules Verne*

### Sugar Cube Autumn

It was the first of October; I returned with Hugh after Jim's wedding. Alone at the farm, finishing up checklist items for the extension, we were ahead of schedule for the day but behind for the season. The valley was awash with brilliant reds, yellows and oranges cast in a spectrum of hues. Distracted by the spectacular display of colors and the crispness of the cloudless deep blue sky framing the mountain pallet, we took a break.

Hugh walked down to the mailbox, about a quarter of a mile from the house. He got there as our rural mail carrier was arriving.

"Hey, RFD Fred, beautiful day today, 'smiling trees.'" Fred always got a chuckle when he read the PHUNEE FARM lettered mailbox, and even more so, when the letters he delivered were so addressed.

"Howdy, Phunee farmer. Got some mail for you and a package. You know my wife is friends with Darla Lareau's mother Greta—a real busybody, that one. She said she picked up Darla here a few weeks back and told my wife about the prune hippies and how she wasn't sure about her daughter going there. Mary stopped her and said, 'Fred told me all about them and he said they were good hard-working folk. And oh, Greta, it's not prune it's pronounced like funny'."

"Good story, Fred," Hugh said, anxious to get back and check out the package without a return address. It was clear from the writing and postmark that it was from Andy. The rest of the mail was mundane by comparison. Impatient, he opened the mysterious package and, reading the note on his way back, he started running. He was out of breath when he reached me. I looked down to see a brown paper opened to reveal two sugar cubes with a note that read, "Yes, they are."

Time to take a ride on the sugarcube express. Acid tends to be a bit 'speedy' so in a short time we had the roof opened and the tower walls framed. Sitting on the extension roof with our feet dangling in the tower well, the acid kicked in. The foliage began to move in swirls around the mountain. The mountains were undulating to the Grateful Dead blasting from the speakers in the window. The rungs on the ladder were moving like an escalator as I was transported to the top of the barn roof looking down at myself and Hugh sitting on the extension's roof.

Maybe it was the vantage point that gave us the wherewithal to work through our altered state, leading to an "aha" moment wherein we hauled the cupola up the ladder onto the roof and mounted it on the top plate of the turret walls we finished along with three quarts of home brew and a handful of flash dried homegrown joints. Laying on the roof, the essence of the house and barn had fused into the fabric of the valley where everything seen and unseen merged into lava like flows of foliage colors spinning into a white stream of pure quantum energy. For a brief moment it was as if I had reached the control center of my supra consciousness.

## The Church Trip

Six months before I moved to the farm I split a tab of paper acid with Mario. We were hanging out at Byron's House in Huntington, and after a while there was little reaction. Mario said, "Let's drive over to Jack and Millie's church; it's only twenty miles away." Before leaving, we each took another half, figuring it would take an hour or so to kick in, if at all. I was wrong! Driving on the Long Island Expressway just past dusk, the white lights of the approaching headlights and the red tail lights of the cars ahead started to waver and merge; all of a sudden the white lights turned into a single stream of light followed by an explosion of red as all ten lanes as of the expressway transformed into a white and red liquid light stream flowing in opposite directions. No fear or concern for loss of control; in fact I had a clear understanding of how and where my stream of color fit with the rest of the contra-flowing red and white light streams. We arrived unharmed at the church and Tom was thankful to be there. My ramblings about the flowing lights merging into a psychedelic highway of colored light made him nervous.

I had been to the old church several times, helping with renovations. It was a small church, but the interior felt vast with a high, airy vaulted ceiling and huge stained glass windows at the gable ends. We went down to the common room in the basement and fell into acid land. Sitting in a captain's chair at one end of the basement room I meditated; maximizing the acid's effect to lift the veil of reality and transcend the unexplored levels of my own inner consciousness. I was guided by John C. Lily's books, *The Human Biocomputer and Center of the Cyclone*. Lily did extensive research using LSD 25 and sensory deprivation chambers to explore deep into the human mind and reach levels theretofore unimaginable. Being in a chamber without physical senses was intense enough, but adding the psychedelic was awesome and terrifying at the same time but making it possible to delve deeper into one's self.

Eyes open, I focused on a spot on the basement wall across the room. I was aware of the institutional, color-flecked painted cinder block walls and the other people present— then I wasn't. I drifted away. The wall became supercharged with light and shape. Each individual block presented in all shades of the color spectrum. The cinder blocks began to undulate and morph in size and shape. I was absorbed by an explosion of transforming color as each row of cinder blocks started to move in opposite directions. The old rounded refrigerator in my periphery burst into color and melted into the phantasmagoric movement of the breathing wall moving in cadence with my heart beat.

I entered the transition phase into my inner self, the realm of the physical now hidden behind the veil, a world opening to me and, by extension, the entire universe. The colors were beyond description, oscillating and flowing like a journey to the center of the mind. I was infused with a colorful liquid careening through my psyche, emerging into what Lily described as the supra human programming phase. I was free of the liquid transporter as I was floating in a limitless space without top or bottom, like a cylindrical expression of the universe reaching through my soul and essence. It was like a control center of the universe, to some it might have been God. All around me were an incalculable number of places, windows, portals and openings of every imaginable size and shape—indefinable sensations and lights beyond what my mind could imagine. Colored geometric shapes morphed into and out of the light-filled gateways. Here were the thresholds to all that is and all that ever was and the means to achieve all that will ever be. I moved through like an observer, unable to understand the magnitude of the simplest expressions but gifted with the opportunity to simply observe. I had no thoughts of changing anything; everything was as it will be in those sparse moments I was granted, conceived or imagined. This was a life-changing event.

I drifted back to the world and could hear voices. Piercing the veil, the real world returned and the colors abated. I can remember saying as I came back, "Where's Rick? The colors—tell Rick I found the colors." Rick had tripped many times but he complained of never seeing the colors. The voices were of concern. They thought they had lost me; gone, yes, but far from lost. I had no words to express what I experienced but spoke to them to assure them I was fine. I wandered upstairs, still tripping, and went into the bathroom. As I looked into the mirror, my face was foreign. A resurgence of the acid urged me back to my inner self. My features all became exaggerated; my eyes popped like a cartoon character and spun clockwise and then up then down. My ears folded into themselves, as my nose inhaled my mouth, soon to return as my whole face melted into the sink. As I moved deeper into myself, voices called me back.

I never fully returned to that omnipresent place again; but that day on the roof of the extension, looking up at mountains with a natural explosion of color in the surrounding foliage, I came close.

## Now Boarding

The sole plane trip I took while living at the farm was on the astral plane. The path to the astral is through imagination. After my experience in the church's basement, I became more convinced than ever that hidden possibilities existed. There is no guarantee, via substance or mindfulness, that the veil separating conscious reality from our own limitless inner space will ever be lifted. Transcendence with or without psychedelics opens your awareness to infinite possibilities.

Reading tales of Carlos Castaneda and accounts of Edgar Casey, I was inspired to seek the astral plane. In some ways, this pursuit was in conflict with other beliefs. Be here now, living in the moment, was at odds with the "be somewhere else" nature of astral projection. If you believed, meditated, and focused your energy, you could send your consciousness elsewhere—an exercise of extreme imagination. The astral plane is the acme of imagination. Imagination realized! I spent hours, especially before going to sleep, believing with all my being that I could send my consciousness out from my body. On a few occasions, through the uncertainty of sleep, dream, imagination or just desire, I looked down and saw myself sleeping in my bed. I wanted to believe, but who knows?

The closest I ever came to believing, happened while riding shotgun in my car. Craig was driving, Tara was in the back seat. Laying back in my seat ,I closed my eyes and pulled the brim of my hat down over my face. I felt the car move along through turn after turn on a lazy county road. Suddenly, I was soaring above the car, watching it move through the turns. I saw the red roof of my car, the tree tops, and the lay of the road approaching in the distance. A peculiar old turquoise blue truck, paint worn down to rusted metal, loaded haphazardly with chicken crates, approached from the oncoming direction. After the truck passed my car, a woman driving a silver Corvette convertible, top down, with long red hair blowing in the wind, passed my car from behind. I sat up, opened my eyes, pushed my hat up and asked if a crazy truck went by and if they got a look at the redhead in the Corvette.

They were both puzzled; my head was down, my hat covering my eyes. I felt like I did it. I was as high as a kite with exhilaration. Was it absolute? It sure felt like it. Could I have somehow caught a glimpse under the brim of my hat or is it possible someone in the car said something that let my imagination fill in the blanks? Perhaps, but for those few minutes, I had my greatest reason to believe I was soaring above my body, as it traveled below me in the car, with witnesses, tacit as they may have been.

# 35

# UNRAVELLED

*Life is divided into three terms—that which was, which is, and which will be. Let us learn from the past to profit by the present, and from the present, to live better in the future.*
*~ William Wordsworth*

### Constructive Eviction

Something unsettling was hanging in the air when I returned from Bread and Puppet. Nick spent most of his time at Ricky's place getting wasted with his old gang. Warren and Shane went off in his pickup, to parts unknown. My psychometric sense was tingling. Neither Nick nor Mia offered any detail; but I found out later that Warren had an altercation with Nick, who returned home drunk and nasty and tripped over Shane's toys. He lashed out and pushed the five-year-old flying across the room. Answering Shane's cries, Warren came running and was challenged by Nick, who started swinging. Warren, happy-go-lucky but formidable in his own right, had the momentary advantage of sobriety and bested the wasted Nick, who in his rantings, threatened to get his posse on him. Neither Warren nor

Shane ever returned to the Phunee Farm; a shame—they were good people.

Nick was mean-spirited when he awoke with a hangover and most other times after that. Over the din of his bitching, we continued to button up the extension. I sensed my time at the farm would be coming to an end, yet I advanced the open projects with my usual vigor. Within the early days of September, the building was tight to the weather. Nick and Mia left for Massachusetts to bring his kids back home. I savored the time without them there.

## Growing Awareness

We learned about Nick's time in prison from Mia, but knowledge grew while I was working on the gang's kitchen. Every prison has its cliques and affiliations. Nick and his cohorts found camaraderie as communists. They were anarchists, not content to accept any governmental rule. This was more about breaking the law and self-indulgence than making a political point. They preferred to live outside of the mores and taboos of the greater society. This included a "survival of the fittest" mentality. A "take what you want" attitude. Craig and I were peaceful, non-violent activists. We retreated to the mountains not to overthrow the government and hide out, but to retire from it, disillusioned after spending years trying to do good things that seemed under-appreciated.

On one visit to the farm, Nick's gang was partying, getting drunk and rowdy. One minute drinking and kibitzing, the next pistols were drawn and rifles pointed and all were firing. I was glad it was not at each other but the weather vane on the barn roof didn't stand a chance.

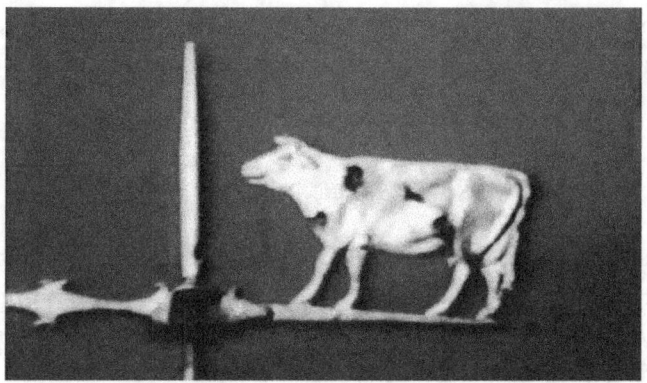

I became wary but embraced this crowd of ruffians, seeing myself as part of the crowd although my "fly on the wall" presence building the cabinets continued to render me invisible. I heard many tales, criminal in nature, and lots of braggadocio which made it hard to separate truth from hyperbole. I became increasingly concerned as evidence of truth emerged. Then the occurrence of the stories overheard merged with the present. It was one thing to hear "war stories" from the past, quite another in the here and now. The Phunee Farm, while distant from the crime scene, suffered from the wayward culture of Nick's criminal-minded friends and the lure drawing Nick back to that way of life.

Tales continued about their violent past, with stories about Nick rampant in his absence. Their voices dropped to a whisper as they discussed the problem in Sheffield. I strained to hear. Trig said, "Did you hear that Skeet and Murf got out last summer. They wouldn't let that beef with Nick go and followed him to Vermont. They wanted the skinny on Sheffield and jumped him in his driveway. He would be dead if Zeke didn't save him. I hear they ran off broken and bloodied."

Snatch followed with, "He better watch his back. I'm surprised they got out already. They were lucky they were only charged with conspiracy with the Sheffield land. Not sure how Nick avoided that."

Their voices lowered further, but I could make out a few words: killed . . . accident . . . signed over, deed, buried . . . construction site . . . near the interstate. Someone said, "Fucking asshole. We agreed not to bring that up again."

Then I heard Willie clearly, "Whatever you do, don't tell Nick." Not believing my ears, I could not unring the bell. Nick and Mia returned two days later.

## Altercation

Like most homes, the kitchen was a gathering place. On a lazy day in late September, Nick and some of his friends were standing by the Acorn stove, I was tinkering with the new cabinets, and Marsha and Mia were sitting at the kitchen table. Marsha was enjoying her free time because Mark took Melissa into town to show her off to some of his work mates. Jake came up from his yurt and walked into the kitchen, opening the door, which smashed into Nick's back causing him to spill his beer all over himself and his friend, Ned. Nick snapped. He turned into violence personified. Jake, realizing that he bumped someone, was quick to apologize. Before he could finish his apology, Nick charged him and pushed him hard—sending him backward onto his ass. Jake was a passive guy who was strong and muscled, but who took no shit.

He jumped up and what followed was like a scene from a movie. He charged Nick, who started swinging. Punches were flying and blood splattered around the room with each new hit. Nick's arms moved like hydraulic pistons. His forearms appeared to move three hundred and sixty degrees like a Popeye cartoon, making constant contact with Jake's face and abdomen. Jake, a blacksmith, had his own huge forearms and returned every blow. I didn't know what to do. Marsha was hysterical, moving away from the table and tucking herself behind the stove, terrified. Mia was screaming at Nick. Nick's two friends were getting ready to join the fray. I yelled, "What the hell are you doing? Stop!" No response. I took the pots and pans from the counter and threw them to the floor making the loudest racket I could conjure. My strategy worked. They both stopped and turned toward the noise, and for the first time saw me and the women. With a final push, they each stepped back, their faces bloodied and swelling.

I was shocked, but in the fore, the sanctity of the Phunee Farm had been breached. I hadn't been this close to such abject violence or in a fight since I was a kid—and then there were just two encounters. The first was when I was thirteen with my brother Thom, who was one of the tougher kids in school, and while I was older, I was skinny, non-violent and ignored his taunting abuse. Then one day I fought back. We knocked over the kitchen table; my mother squeezed herself into the corner by the sink. He swung and I ducked. The momentum of his swing hit and dented the refrigerator and tore skin from his knuckles. We rolled out the back door and onto the back lawn and when we stopped, bloodied, we started laughing. I barely spoke to him for two years after that but the episode formed a new bond. He had a new opinion about me.

My next encounter came two years later, although I never took a swing. Craig and I were walking across a school yard adjacent to our high school, following a school play. Eight guys from the football team came running up behind us and tackled us. They claimed that we insulted one of their sisters, a made up situation providing a warped justification to attack whomever they chose. A claim we vigorously denied. We were two skinny kids facing down huge defensive linemen. We remained stoic and one of them took a few shots until they got bored and left. These were guys who, for sport, would drive around town looking for kids riding bicycles. They would drive up close to the cyclist and then, with all of the force they commanded, punch the kid off the bike as they drove by.

## Polar Shift

Conflicted and trapped within the gates of my castle of spiritual solitude, the growing awareness that those walls were breached loomed large. The strength of the dream that brought me to this wonderful place loosened its grip on my longevity on this cherished land. I noticed, perhaps for the first time, a new force drawing me, pulling in the direction of my roots. We facilitated change because we were by nature all about trust and finding the good in people. But being one with the world didn't mean the world was one with us.

I was blinded no more by the woodsman, the chameleon who changed to feign assimilation into our spiritual world. Or was it an invasion? My soul merged with the land along the banks of Lucas Brook, and I tried to endure the violent changes; and I might have, but ambivalence weighed heavy, and the place I came to know as home, my oasis in the world, was coming to an end. Craig was more astute about the severity of the change in the "force" at the Phunee Farm, as he was with opting out of joining the Air Force. He reacted to the veiled signals about our new housemate months ago when he made arrangements to attend Johnson College. How had we been so gullible to have allowed this blissful valley to fall into the hands of such a bad person. An important distinction: my dream was not taken, it was surrendered.

# 36

# AND THEN WE WERE NONE

*"What we call the beginning is often the end.
And to make an end is to make a beginning.
The end is where we start from."*
~ T. S. Eliot

The halcyon days on my side of the mountain succumbed to the greatest of all antagonists: time, through which growth, maturity, reality, conflict and the world at large all played their part. I am not sure if we ever had a clear idea of what "back to the land" meant, perhaps just what we wanted it to be. Could we truly live the romanticized fantasy of our youth? We brought suburban values to this remote farmhouse such that art on the walls competed with firewood in the shed. At first we were determined to use bow saws, but quickly found the value of a chain saw. We fancied the idea of a horse-drawn plow, but made good friends with a rototiller and never graduated to a tractor. Becoming farmers was a goal, but we never got further than a big garden.

Once our dream included a hand-hewn log cabin, but our rustic old farmhouse was shelter from suburbia. We had a huge barn left over from its working days as a dairy farm, yet never considered getting cows, instead managing goats, pigs, a bunch of chickens, a rooster and a Guinea hen or two; we tried our hand at raising rabbits, and even earthworms. Essentially, we sucked at animal husbandry—at least I did. We got very good at cutting, hauling and splitting firewood; and I learned that the work of surviving on the land took more than knowledge.

Sometimes the price you pay for a dream is manifested in the loss of the very dream pursued. I think back about the events that brought my thousand-day tenure at the Phunee Farm to a sudden conclusion. Twenty-two years old, cloistered away in a valley far from my roots, remembering my belief the world was too screwed up to be part of, and realized that I had changed. Who the hell was I to hide out in the mountains as the world moved on? I was nineteen when I arrived; I knew everything, right? Wrong! Maybe I should find my place in the world. Were my feelings organic? Did my dream follow a natural expiration and evolution or was I already wet from the coming storm—soon to wash out a once shared spiritual dream. Just as life's current pulled me here, another was pulling me south to the home of my youth. There was a big world out there and I wanted to make a difference. I wanted to be part of it. I wanted to make a mark. I wanted a piece.

### Sole Survivor Escape Plan

I was the sole survivor of the original Phunee Farm triumvirate. I hedged my bet when I gave in to my uncle and filed for a civil service job in New York. I had zero plans of taking the test—let alone the job—when I filed earlier that spring. As I neared the test date, my thinking changed. Yes, I would take the test in December. What's a Court Officer, anyway? Reeling from the growing violence, criminal awareness and the fall of the sentinel of time, I began to think I would take the job if I could. Culture shock.

Painful as it was, I was ready to leave, believing my mark on the house, barn, land and brook was indelible. I would come to discover just how profoundly wrong I was. I hoped, when Mark and I met with the landlord, and I formally turned the tenancy over to him, the legacy of the Phunee Farm would endure in his hands. I helped to build the ideal of the collective Phunee Farm concept and worked, paid for and purchased most of the tools needed to do so. When it came time to leave, I intended to return home with some of those tools to continue my life; especially those that I brought with me upon my arrival.

Nick tried to claim all the stuff. I was met with profound resistance. "That stuff belongs to the Phunee Farm. You can't take that." The discussion got heated, bordering on violence; but I powered through my fear and claimed what was mine by right. His menacing physical strength was formidable but the battle of wits lent me an advantage. I took all of my artwork, hand and woodcarving tools and my chainsaw. In my mind at the time, he hijacked the land and my dreams that went with it. In retrospect, Nick was but a catalyst in the progression of the childhood fantasy I shared with Craig.

## Aura of Despair

Everyone emits an energy field, a product of our electrical nervous system, the light of the soul—or both. The field of subtle, luminous energy that surrounds a person is called an aura. It is known as a halo in western religions. To most, this energy field is unseen. Yet each person has an aura that changes color throughout life, like a long-term mood ring. I think anyone can see the color of auras, and sense the surrounding electromagnetic energy of others if they are focused and fortunate.

I have been fortunate to see an aura several times. Specific colors represent certain moods, health states, or personality. I have seen a dark red aura surrounding mean or angry people and a shimmery dark blue from spiritual folks. On two occasions, both before I knew much about auras beyond knowing they existed. I saw a black aura. Within a day or two each of those people died; this scared the hell out of me.

Emotions heightened and sensitivity piqued, I was not surprised on the day I left that Nick emanated a menacing dark red aura; but I was overcome with dread believing the greater demise of the farm was imminent, when Mark, Marsha and Jake presented auras dark gray and black.

I drove down the driveway empowered by the past and uncertain of the future. I never looked back.

# Epilogue

*It is good to have an end to journey towards; but it is the journey that matters, in the end.*
*~ Ursula K. Le Guin*

Two years after leaving the farm I was interviewed for the Court Officer job. My interviewer was a large, socially conservative woman who cringed when she saw my ponytail and hippie beads. I sent in my UC-5 job application where, under work history, I wrote: Three years on a communal farm in Northern Vermont, duties include farming, logging and construction. It was 1979 and the mystique and romance of the back-to-nature pursuit intrigued the interviewer, allowing her to see through the hippiness and see who I was. I wanted to be hired for who I was, but I said I would conform to whatever the job required. She hired me. Ironically, it was the Union President who made me take off the beads.

Two things happened in my first week that eased my apprehension. My first courtroom assignment was to observe a non-jury trial. A shrewish woman was testifying. I watched the judge copiously writing. He handed it to the court clerk. It read: *This woman could stand in for the Wicked Witch of the West.* She handed me the note and ran out of the courtroom, laughing. A day later, a couple of Court Officers were talking outside a crowded courtroom. One said, "This is nothing. Last summer we had a trial with a shitload of media—standing room only. The Braunze trial was arguing that marijuana shouldn't be illegal. This guy, Gregg Braunze, was a hippie from a Vermont commune. I couldn't believe all of the witnesses, even that psycho, Timothy Leary." I held my tongue, but took it as an omen crossing **Gregg the Guru's** path after all. Hey, Gregg, if you read this, I have your manuscript.

## Tragedy and Carnage

Some months after I left the farm, fleeing the unchecked violence accruing at the farm, and fearing for her safety, **Mark** and **Marsha** took **Melissa** back to their hometown. Six months after that Mark was killed in a car accident. Two weeks later Marsha died in an unrelated accident. I never heard whatever became of Melissa.

**Jake** left the Phunee Farm and moved to a neighboring town with Philomena, a woman I met through Tara. Less than a year later he was murdered, hitching home to Louisiana.

**Mia** fled from an enraged Nick and moved to the other side of the mountain, finding a safe house and employment as a live-in domestic, under an assumed name.

**Nick** allegedly moved to New York and became involved with the Free United Communists, a group involved in the shooting and killing of a police officer in a neighboring state. I believed this rumor was true. The facts aligned with the same birth area, age, prison history and communist affiliation. If true, after several years of being on the run, he died in prison.

The Phunee Farm underwent its own demise.

Ten years after I left, I returned with my wife and daughters to find the upper barn had been removed and sold to a New York City interior decorator.

Burnt Mount was visible from house without barn

In time, the land was sold and the house was razed. There is nothing left of what I knew. In its place, a modern house was built near the path to Bronze Beach. Another house was built down by the old bus and two more up by the Bell house. The pasture and fields that lined Lucas Valley have yielded to the reclaiming forest, now dense and thirty feet high.

**Trig** and **Snatch** were arrested attempting to rob an armored car in Rhode Island. Trig was implicated in a cold case. His fingerprints were found on flask under a body buried fifty miles south of Sheffield. It wasn't him, but he never squealed.

**Bread and Puppet**. Once bitten, I was hooked and returned for many a year after the Phunee Farm demise. By the nineties, the pageant was drawing crowds of tens of thousands and became unmanageable. The horde was less and less concerned with the performance as its energy turned into an unruly free-for-all in the surrounding campgrounds. When someone died in the mêlée, the pageant was discontinued. It resumed years later with smaller shows lasting less than a day—which continue today.

While finishing this writing, I visited Bread and Puppet and had the personal honor to meet Peter Schuman. We spoke of my book and later he handed me a B & P 2020 calendar and said, "Here's another 365 days."

**Brice** and **Summer** split up.

**Sweat-Comings**—Three years after I left Vermont, the last heir of the Comings family got into a tax dispute with the town and shut down the place in protest, which was bad luck for the Richfordians. Several decades later I was given a maple dresser, and centered on the back panel was the indelible "Sweat-Comings Co." logo.

**Craig** completed school, stayed in Vermont, married, had a son and excelled as a teacher and principal; **Hugh** became politically active, getting involved with notable radicals and aggressive but peaceful political organizations, but that's another story; **Tara** got wilder and bounced between Long Island, Albany and Vermont and worked with Byron in several businesses, drifted apart from Byron, suffered a life-threatening brain injury, and re-settled with **Byron**, who nursed her back to health. **Fae** attended free schools her whole life, graduated, moved to the west coast, and grew into a modern day hippie, poet, artist and meticulous craftsperson. As an adolescent before that, she was a bridesmaid at my wedding. I lost track of them for a decade—but what's ten years?

While attending a Renaissance Fair in upstate New York with my wife and Tara, we watched a knife throwing exhibition. Tara said, "He's using my uncle's knives." After the show, the knife thrower confirmed the story of the knives and treated Tara as a hero, having worked with her famous uncle.

**Leigh** stayed in Vermont, married a Vermonter and raised new Vermonters, and took over the restaurant **Mitch** and **Ginny** started in the Burlington area. **Mitch's** friend **John** was convicted of murdering his wife. **Bruce** stayed in Vermont, bought a team of horses, and pulled things out of the forest. **Ronnie**, I learned years later, married, had kids and moved out of state. **Jim** married **Layla,** moved to the southwest, they split, and he married someone else. He didn't divorce first.

**Walking staff**—Years after leaving the farm, I let someone borrow my trusted staff to augment a Halloween costume. A bouncer at a local bar stopped him from bringing it in. He went in, my staff stayed out—never to be seen again. Should've followed my instinct and said no; I love Halloween.

As for me, I met my beautiful wife, raised two wonderful daughters, continue to spoil four amazing grandkids, and spent thirty years in the New York State Court System, comprising many tales for another time.

## In Case You're Interested . . .

### HARP

While writing this story, I validated everything Kendal told us in part from *A Brief History of the HARP Project,* written by Richard K. Graf. He wrote, "It is said that Jules Verne chose a supergun for his story, *The Earth to the Moon*, because he didn't think that anyone would believe that a rocket could actually take people to the Moon. This reference led to the gun's nickname as the "Jules Verne Gun."

*The Chronicle,* Vermont's Northeast Kingdom past and present online magazine, reported on June 4, 2014 in an article by Chris Braithwaite about a museum exhibition that opened in Sutton, Quebec, heralding the positive side of Gerard Bull's contributions.

An entry in *The Vermont Encyclopedia* by John J. Duffy, Samuel B. Hand and Ralph H. Orth, on page 71, on November 24, 2008, spoke of a darker side of Gerard Bull. It discussed the property straddling the border that allowed him to secretly move the weapons he made in the United States to the Canadian side and ship them to places like Iraq and South Africa. The Israelis were thought to be complicit in his ultimate assassination in 1990 because of his "Babylon Project" for

Saddam Hussein, a gigantic cannon capable of launching huge ballistic shells into Israel.

**HARP and the Jules Verne Gun**

Gerald Bull's Project Babylon Supergun - Vermonter.com

https://vermonter.com › gerald-bull-project-babylon-supergun

## Gravity Hill

The East Richford Slide road climbed up the steep hill past the East Richford Cemetery which straddled the Canadian border. The road drifted into and out of Canada. I learned decades later that this stretch of the road is purported to be a gravitational anomaly. This phenomenon, first documented the year after my leaving the Phunee Farm, is known as "Richford's Mystery Spot," according to Joseph E. Ocumented and Diane E. Foulds in their 2004 book *Curious New England: The Unconventional Traveler's Guide to Eccentric Destinations*. The "mystery" is that gravity in this spot behaves unorthodoxly. Cars are said to roll uphill. This phenomenon was detailed further in 2016 by Chad Abramovich's article "WTF Is Richford's 'Mystery Spot?'" for Vermont's Independent Voice. Abramovich quotes, "These oddities aren't unique to the Green Mountain State. Various places around the U.S. manifest the same puzzling phenomenon. Nearest to Vermont, there are two "mystery spots" in the Massachusetts towns of Greenfield and Harvard, and one in Middlesex, N.Y." There is another in New York State.

The occurrence in New York State is one that I learned of as a child in the early 1960's. My mother went to visit Father Dick at St. Bonaventure University. She told me parking at the bottom of Dugan's Hill, imperceptibly at first, the car moved up the hill a short distance, increasing speed.

Proponents argue that is a paranormal event, where for reasons unknown, Newton's Law doesn't apply. The late Dolph Dewing of Franklin was the first person to report experiencing the mystery spot's effects in 1978. According to Joseph E. Citro, *Weird New England:*

*Your Travel Guide to New England's Local Legends and Best Kept Secrets,* Dewing shared the discovery with his friends, and then brought a busload from the Franklin Senior Center to witness the phenomenon. In October 1985 *County Courier* reporter Nat Worman accompanied Dewing to the spot and watched as he stopped his 1979 Dodge there and revved it to prove it was in neutral. After about 60 seconds passed, the car began rolling uphill, accelerating gradually to 10 to 15 mph.

To the contrary, skeptics argue that there is no actual upward elevation change just optical illusions that are manifested by visual terrain changes. Abramovich indicates there are a bunch of "mystery spots" around the globe, some with evocative names such as "gravity hills" and "gravity roads." So, do the laws of physics stop applying there? Nope. What baffles tons of spectators is in fact an optical illusion. The gravity anomaly has been debunked by physicists. Or, at least, that's the prevailing theory. "Gravity hills" and the like are places where the geography of the surrounding land produces an illusion, making a downhill slope appear to go uphill.

Brock Weiss, a physics professor at Penn State, concluded that isn't that odd. "You are, indeed, going downhill even though your brain gives you the impression that you're going uphill." Using GPS, the investigators demonstrated that the hill's starting point had a greater elevation than its ending point, despite appearances to the contrary. And, if these mystery spots were gravitational anomalies, wouldn't your sense of balance and the objects around you be affected, instead of just your vehicle?

Challenging this contrary position, Linda Collins of the Richford Historical Society was quoted as saying "I know about the hill. I think it's called a 'gravity hill'. I learned about it when I was researching the UFO sightings in town," said an amused Collins. Back in the 1970's, she related, a few Richford residents reported seeing strange moving lights over town. Wanting to chronicle the frenzy for the *Burlington Free Press*, Collins made phone calls, which led her to a government facility in Boulder, Colorado. She refers to it as "the strange things facility," because "I don't remember what they were called—it's been so long since I've talked about this!" According to Collins, the feds told her that a singular magnetic pull or gravitational force in the Richford area had the potential to "attract things." They didn't specify what things, and she surmised there was probably more they weren't telling her. "You know government secrecy? They were likely doing testing or something and didn't want that getting out to the public," Collins said.

## Weird Richford

Reading this article so long after my days at the Phunee Farm brought some memories soaring back. Collins had been investigating lights in the sky around Richford. On several occasions, we had experienced these same lights at the farm. Remember we were in an extremely remote area about eight miles from Richford. The first time we saw the lights, we thought it was a plane or jet flying low in the sky. Then the lights continued with some frequency over the course of our first summer, following an erratic staccato-like flight pattern. Sitting out in the field or watching from the barn we would see mysterious lights travel across the valley then cut a zig zag pattern south, travel low along the North Jay slope, moving with deliberation, sometimes darting up or back or down, or bolt forward to the peak returning, following another travel pattern. Despite the fact that we had witnessed these lights many times and joked that we were watching UFOs, we kind of chalked it up to drug or alcohol induced illusions. Now I wonder.

Linda Collins went on to say, "Richford is a weird town. If all this business about the UFOs and gravitational pulls is true, then who knows?" Abramovich added to the quasi-credibility of our encounters saying, "Border towns are weird in general, in both their local lore and political complications and the infrastructure meant to delineate a sense of placement. Richford's mythology resume is a bulky one of giant birds that have swooped down and snatched babies, UFOs, giant wolves that may live around the border, a possible "window area" near Jay Peak, and a former rendezvous for rumrunners and smugglers. If the Richford, VT/Sutton, QC area does have some sort of unique magnetic force, that would set Vermont's mystery spot apart from the scores of others around the globe that can be debunked by aesthetic tomfoolery."

https://vermontdeadline.blogspot.com/2014/11/awful-and-naughty-richford.html

## ADDITIONAL LINKS

**Kilgores and Them Fargo Brothers**

https://madisonmusicblog.wordpress.com/2015/05/29/the-archives-of-a-country-rock-band-kilgores-trout-saloon/

**Bread and Puppet**

Bread and Puppet Theater | Puppeteers and Sourdough ...

https://breadandpuppet.org

# About the Author

Raised on Long Island, in New York State, Bob Verneuille moved to the wilds of Northern Vermont as a teenager, in search of a back-to-nature alternative lifestyle. Eventually Bob joined the New York State Court System as a Uniformed Court Officer,  and later opened a thriving woodworking business that piqued his interest in art, antiques—and writing.

Bob lives on Long Island with his wife, with two daughters and four grandchildren nearby. His stories to his grandchildren about his Vermont adventures coalesced into this first book. With a newfound passion for writing, Bob hopes to relate many more tales of his courtroom experiences, including a few "chambers of horrors."

His second book, Tempus Treasure, set for release in 2020, weaves a tale of two physicists experimenting with time travel. Vikings, Templar Knights, Pirates, and the Mid Knight Killer all intersect—on opposite sides of an ancient prophecy.

www.ingramcontent.com/pod-product-compliance
Lightning Source LLC
Chambersburg PA
CBHW052133070526
44585CB00017B/1805